The

Privileged Poor

The
Privileged Poor

HOW ELITE COLLEGES ARE FAILING

DISADVANTAGED STUDENTS

Anthony Abraham Jack

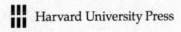 Harvard University Press

CAMBRIDGE, MASSACHUSETTS

LONDON, ENGLAND

First Harvard University Press paperback edition, 2020
First printing

Names: Jack, Anthony Abraham, author.
Title: The privileged poor : how elite colleges are failing
disadvantaged students / Anthony Abraham Jack.
Description: Cambridge, Massachusetts : Harvard University Press, 2019. |
Includes bibliographical references and index.
Identifiers: LCCN 2018037298 | ISBN 9780674976894 (cloth : alk. paper) |
ISBN 9780674248243 (pbk.)
Subjects: LCSH: College students—United States—Attitudes. |
Minority college students—United States—Attitudes. |
Cultural pluralism—United States. | Multicultural education—
United States. | Minorities—Education (Higher) —United States.
Classification: LCC LC210.5 .J33 2019 | DDC 378.1/9826942—dc23
LC record available at https://lccn.loc.gov/2018037298

To Marilyn Butler Jack,

   for teaching me from whence I come

To Gregory Glenn Jr.,

   for showing me how far I can go

I am what time, circumstance, history, have made of me, certainly, but I am, also, much more than that. So are we all.

JAMES BALDWIN, *Notes of a Native Son*

Contents

Abbreviations

Social Classification

DD   Doubly Disadvantaged

PP   Privileged Poor

UI   Upper Income

Racial / Ethnic Classification

A   Asian American

B   Black

L   Latino

W   White

Introduction

CAN POOR STUDENTS BE PRIVILEGED?

"Toto, I've a feeling we're not in Kansas anymore."

—DOROTHY, *The Wizard of Oz*

"Where are the *other* poor black kids?" This is the first question I remember asking myself, a chubby freshman with my hair in cornrows, while walking across the Amherst College campus. I was in the center of the main quad, standing outside Johnson Chapel. The lawn was freshly mowed. It looked pristine, a shimmering deep green. The evening, slightly chilly for a Miami transplant such as myself, was filled with excitement as the incoming freshmen meandered around, nervously greeting one another. Conversations bubbled all around me. Wasting little time, my new peers enlisted me in a rite of passage that, fifteen years later, I now call "convocation conversations"—those quick, casual introductory chats that happen en route to meals and classes, where students conveniently work in verbal versions of their resumes and narrate their summer itineraries for any and all to hear.

These strangers—my new classmates—swapped stories of summer fun. Multiweek trips abroad. Fancy parties at summer homes. Courtside

I

seats at professional basketball games. Invitations to private premieres of movies that, as far as I knew, had not yet hit theaters. Many of these kids were white, but the black students were chiming in too, going tit-for-tat recounting the elaborate stories behind their passport stamps. One black classmate casually mentioned that she had flown on a private jet. I thought back to my first time on a plane, which had been just a few months ago: me struggling to chew five pieces of Wrigley's Doublemint gum, because everyone had made me afraid that my ears would pop, as I boarded a Delta Airlines flight from Fort Lauderdale to Hartford, Connecticut, for my Amherst football recruiting trip. I tried to think of a story that I could add. The only family vacations I had known were drives up I-95 from Miami to a cousin's house in Georgia. These rich kids had their own version of summer. In my family, summer was just a season, a hundred days of heat, humidity, and hurricanes. And mosquitoes.

I was surrounded by affluence; some of my Amherst classmates were flat-out rich. The Amherst brochure boasted that roughly 40 percent of students received financial aid, but I knew what that really meant: more than half of my classmates came from families that made too much money to qualify for any financial aid. I was not surprised by the wealth. After all, I already knew what it meant to go to school with rich people. I had just finished my senior year at Gulliver Preparatory, a wealthy private high school in Miami. Although I was only there for a year, it gave me a taste of what was to come, both socially and academically. My best friend at Gulliver, whose father convinced me to start eating burgers medium instead of well done, which was the rule in my house, received a car his senior year, and an all-expenses-paid backpacking trip through Europe as a graduation gift. The first time I heard the word "hostel" was while sitting in the larger of the two family rooms in their sprawling, Spanish-style home.

But there was a difference between what I had experienced at Gulliver and what I found at Amherst. While I was not shocked by the wealth, I was surprised by its color. The rich kids at Gulliver, those who drove Range Rovers and boasted of extravagant vacations, were not black. But at Amherst, many of my new wealthy classmates were.

❧✦❧

What I discovered that afternoon was the same thing I would read about years later, as a sociology graduate student, in William Bowen and Derek Bok's groundbreaking study of American higher education, *The Shape of the River.* Bowen and Bok found that the majority of black students at the twenty-eight elite colleges and universities they studied (from Ivy League institutions, like Columbia University, to flagship public universities, like the University of Michigan at Ann Arbor) came from upper-income families. My Amherst classmates were no exception. Some were the sons of Bain Capital and McKinsey & Company. Others were the daughters of the Mayo Clinic and Massachusetts General Hospital. I was not. I was a Head Start kid from Coconut Grove, a distressed community that, in 2013, the *Miami Herald* called a "neighborhood that time forgot." My mother patrolled the hallways of Ponce de Leon Middle School for over thirty years, wearing a green polo shirt with SECURITY in white block letters emblazoned across its back. By day, my older brother, his pale blue uniform peppered with bleach spots, cleaned the classrooms of my old elementary school; by night, he cleaned the emergency rooms at South Miami Hospital.[1]

Before I transferred to Gulliver, the closest I got to rich was through the stories my grandmother told me. For her entire adult life she cleaned the homes of wealthy white families, mainly doctors and lawyers. When my cousin was arrested for possession of a controlled substance, one of my grandmother's employers, a lawyer, represented him as a favor for her twenty-plus years of service. She did not gossip about what went on inside her employers' homes. Now and then, however, she would let slip a detail about an expensive purchase or a lavish family trip. The father of one of the families, a commercial pilot, invited my grandmother to travel on one of his flights so that she could hear his voice come across the intercom greeting passengers as they took their seats. (She never did go.) But second-hand accounts and unanswered invitations were the extent of my exposure—wealth was always just a story to me. Hearing my classmates at Amherst recount their adventures, just as distant as those my grandmother shared when we sat at her knee, I resigned myself to be, yet again, one of the few poor black people in a rich (mostly) white place, just as I had been at Gulliver.

My hasty conclusion that afternoon was reasonable. Higher education in America is highly unequal and disturbingly stratified. Youth from poor families of all races, but especially those from black and Latino families, are less likely to go to college than their wealthy peers. When they do go to college, they rarely attend schools like Amherst. Although half of all undergraduates in the United States are the first in their family to go to college—with most of those coming from poor backgrounds—first-generation college students are disproportionately relegated to community colleges, for-profit colleges, and less-selective four-year colleges. Those institutions share some troubling traits: resources are few, aid for students is scarce, and retention is low.[2]

That same disproportion, of course, works in reverse. The more selective the college, the fewer the number of students from disadvantaged backgrounds, in terms of both class and race. In their examination of college demographics between 1982 and 2006, Anthony Carnevale and Jeff Strohl of the Georgetown University Center on Education and the Workforce clearly documented this phenomenon. At the most competitive tier of colleges—think Columbia, Princeton, Stanford—

just 14 percent of undergraduates came from the bottom half of the country's income distribution. At the second-most competitive tier—the likes of Dickinson, Furman, and Skidmore—just 16 percent did. This paucity of lower-income students at the most selective colleges and universities, which comprised 193 institutions at the time of their study, stands in stark contrast to the fact that in these same two tiers, 63 and 70 percent of students, respectively, came from the top quartile of the income distribution. Put another way, children from well-to-do families, as measured in terms of earnings, took up two-thirds of the seats at the best schools.[3]

New data provide a more detailed, and even more discouraging, snapshot of where Americans from families of different income levels go to college. In 2017, the economist Raj Chetty and his colleagues found that students from families in the top 1 percent—those with incomes of more than $630,000 a year—are 77 times more likely to attend an Ivy League college than are students from families that make $30,000 or less a year. The study showed that a startling number of elite colleges—38, by their count, including places like Colby College and Bucknell University—have more students from families in the top 1 percent than from families in the bottom 60 percent (the growing group of families that make less than $65,000). At Colorado College, the ratio is greater than 2 to 1. At Washington University in St. Louis, it is just over 3.5 to 1.[4]

Another comparison, this time looking at the college destinations of the super-rich, puts this inequality into even sharper perspective. Chetty's report showed that the percentage of students from families in the top 0.1 percent who attended elite universities (40 percent) was the same as the percentage of students from poor families who attended any college at all, either two-year or four-year.

We might have better data now, but the situation itself is not new. Indeed, for more than two decades, colleges have faced significant pressure to do more to combat inequality, and in particular, to use their considerable wealth to address the affordability problem of higher education. In 2008, just before the financial crisis, the Senate Finance Committee admonished colleges for not spending more of their growing endowments on financial aid and access. The public has chimed in as well, lamenting the rising tuition costs that have priced out a growing segment of the American population. Colleges were (and still are) missing out on students from humble means who have a powerful drive to succeed. To address this inequality in access, which was keeping poor youth from reaping the benefits of an elite education—as well as to respond to public outcries against skyrocketing costs—a few colleges introduced no-loan financial aid policies in the late 1990s. Rather than the usual combination of scholarships and loans, which was still prohibitively expensive for many poor families, schools began to create financial aid packages that replaced loans with grants and other forms of aid intended to help recruit and then support academically gifted applicants from disadvantaged backgrounds.[5]

Princeton University began this movement in 1998. Then president Harold T. Shapiro noted of the policy, "Our aim is to do as much as we can to be sure that no student decides not to apply to Princeton solely for financial reasons." A number of colleges followed Princeton's lead. Amherst did so in 1999, which helped pave the way for my admission a few years later. By 2008, all the Ivies were on board. Stanford University, MIT, and Duke University adopted similar policies. Although enacted mostly by private colleges, no-loan financial aid was taken up by some flagship public universities as well. The University of North Carolina at Chapel Hill was the first public university to do so, in 2003. The University of Virginia and the University of Michigan followed suit soon thereafter. Donald Saleh, former dean of admissions and financial aid at Cornell University, expressed the general sentiment about this new approach to aid: "There's an importance in having socio-economic diversity, so that campuses reflect the country in general rather than a campus that is upper income."[6]

These revolutionary policies increased access to many universities, especially elite ones. The effects were felt right away: student bodies began to look different. Vassar College, which in 2015 won the inaugural Cooke Prize for Equity in Educational Excellence, nearly doubled the percentage of Pell Grant–eligible students—students from families in the bottom quarter of the income distribution—from 12 percent in 2008 to 23 percent in 2015. The University of North Carolina and Amherst reported that at least 20 percent of the students who enrolled between 2012 and 2014 were from lower-income families.[7]

Elite colleges may be few in number, but their influence—on the lives of individual students and on American society as a whole—is outsize. For students from disadvantaged backgrounds, attending an elite college or university serves as a mobility springboard. Graduating from any college provides benefits, especially to students belonging to groups that are the recipients of policy initiatives aimed to diversify universities along class and racial lines. But this difference is even more pronounced for elite colleges, where graduation rates are higher. The nation's most selective colleges boast graduation rates of 90 percent or more, while the average for community colleges is 57 percent. While some of this gap is due to differences in the preparation of the students who attend each type of institution, there is no doubt that more resources and support are available at elite colleges and universities. The economic payoff of attendance is also larger. A 1999 study found that graduates of elite private schools had incomes 39 percent higher than those of their peers who attended low-ranked public universities. Whether looking at Supreme Court justices or leaders of different industries, alumni from elite colleges and universities are the norm rather than the exception. The sociologist Lauren Rivera has shown that students from elite institutions have an advantage when trying to enter lucrative fields like management consulting, law, and investment banking; as a result, alumni of elite colleges dominate the ranks in those companies.[8]

The shift in the makeup of the undergraduate population at elite schools is remarkable. More and more colleges are enacting policies to promote the social mobility of those from humble means. They are being celebrated and rewarded for their efforts to diversify their campuses, and by extension, to expand the ranks of the future leaders of America. The doors to elite colleges are increasingly open to lower-income students. But just how wide open are they? Let us not forget that Princeton, despite introducing this change in financial aid policy, remains one of the thirty-eight universities that have more students from the top 1 percent than the bottom 60 percent. Lower-income students may be entering elite colleges in greater numbers now than they were fifty years ago, but these campuses are still bastions of wealth, built on the customs, traditions, and policies that reflect the tastes and habits of the rich.

I believe we should congratulate these colleges and universities on their willingness to innovate. Yet we cannot stop there. We must inquire further. Who are the students admitted to college under these new financial aid regimes? And what happens to them when they arrive on campus? Now that they have gained access to an elite institution, how do they make a home in its hallowed halls?

⊰⊱

That afternoon on the Amherst quad, after milling around and making small talk, I marched along with my classmates into Valentine dining hall. Imagine my surprise when I learned that the young black woman sitting next to me, who had just graduated from a snooty day school and had studied abroad in Spain the previous year, also came from a single-parent home and was the first in her family to attend college. After discovering our common past, we felt the flush of comfort that comes with shared impoverishment but also shared freedoms. We immediately started telling stories of life before Amherst. We both grew up in segregated neighborhoods where just about everybody was black. The white people we did see fell into three easily identifiable categories: police officers, crackheads, and people who had lost their way. Her family, too, struggled to make ends meet from time to time. Both of us had done homework by candlelight, not for atmosphere, but because the power was out.

She and I laughed and commiserated over that desperate search for end-of-the-month money. Soon, a few other students at our table joined in. We were not the only ones, it turned out, who had experienced poverty in our youth but had been exposed to a different world when we went to a prep school. The vacation homes I heard about from some of my new friends during those convocation conversations, I discovered, were not always their own. They often belonged to the families of their wealthy high school classmates, the ones that we all made nice with for a few glimpses at the good life. I was not alone. I was not the only poor black kid on campus. And I was not the only one who had already been granted access to experiences and places beyond what my family could afford or even knew about. My classmate and I were not as different as I had thought. We were both poor. And privileged.

❧

College "viewbooks"—magazine-style recruiting tools that colleges put together to advertise themselves—contain glossy snapshots of campus life. These days, such snapshots almost always highlight diversity: the black and brown faces are placed front and center, as are the statistics documenting the cosmopolitan nature of the student body. But appearances, as we know, can be deceiving. And statistics can lie or, at least, hide deeper truths. While it is doubtless true that colleges are more diverse now than they were a generation ago, this does not mean that these institutions reflect the full variety of American society.

Essentially, colleges hedge their admissions bets: they diversify their student bodies by drawing from old sources. We know that poor youth make up only a small fraction of the students who attend private high schools in the United States; we also know that poor black students are only a fraction of that small population. But it is this tiny slice of a slice, I discovered, who are primarily admitted to selective colleges. Over 50 percent of the lower-income black undergraduates who attend elite colleges get there from boarding, day, and preparatory high schools— well-endowed, highly selective schools that pride themselves on fostering independent thought and extending learning beyond the classroom through close contact with faculty. Chances are, at least half of the poor black kids I met that first day at Amherst had graduated from elite private high schools, like Phillips Academy Andover in Massachusetts and St. Paul's School in New Hampshire.

When you envision a wealthy private high school—with its top-flight facilities and abundant resources—that image likely has a color attached to it: white. Thus, when most people see poor black students at an elite college, they simply don't think that those students might have come from an exclusive high school. These prep schools are full of students from affluent families—mostly white but not exclusively so—and offer academic and social opportunities usually reserved for the rich, from study abroad opportunities to language immersion programs to contact with faculty who have advanced degrees. Lower-income graduates from these high schools enter college already accustomed to navigating elite academic arenas, already familiar with the ways and customs of the rich. True, they are poor, but they have the privilege of an early introduction to the world they will enter in college. I call this group of students the *Privileged Poor*.[9]

Then there is the other half of lower-income black students at elite colleges. This group of students enters college from exactly where most people would expect: local, neighborhood schools that are often distressed, overcrowded, and under-resourced. The teachers are likely to be younger and have less experience in the profession (and less support) than their counterparts in more affluent communities. Maintaining order often takes precedence over teaching, as neighborhood problems penetrate school boundaries. These schools are also likely to be segregated, both racially and socioeconomically. Undergraduates who enter college from these schools traverse troubled hallways and endure disordered classrooms before college. When they first set foot on an elite college campus, it looks, feels, and functions like nothing they have experienced before. I call these students, who are both poor and unfamiliar with this new world, the *Doubly Disadvantaged*.[10]

This situation of two distinct tracks to college is not limited to black students. Many lower-income white and Asian American students also travel an alternative route through private high schools, albeit at lower rates. Latinos, too. One-third of lower-income Latino students at elite colleges and universities hail from private high schools like the Brearley School in New York and the Thacher School in California. The other two-thirds stayed close to home for high school.[11]

Before I arrived at Amherst all those years ago, like most eighteen-year-olds, I was blissfully ignorant of the complexity all around me.

I knew that I had studied hard, and now I got to go to a great school and do something that no one in my family had ever done. But I had no idea that my detour through Gulliver was a well-established on-ramp that a great many students across the country traveled en route to college. Until I learned the stories of some of my classmates at Amherst, I thought I was the only one. It was only years later that I started to fully grasp these truths. It was also years later, as a graduate student in sociology, that I realized that I was far from the only one who was ignorant here. The very social scientists I was now eagerly reading, analyzing, and learning from had also ignored this distinction within disadvantaged youth, its origins, and how it manifests itself in college.

So I set out to add a missing—overlooked but nevertheless crucial—piece of the puzzle. For two years I lived and made observations at a prestigious undergraduate institution that I call Renowned University. (For a full discussion of my data and methods, including my use of pseudonyms, see the Appendix.) Some readers may wonder why, if I hoped to learn about inequality, I chose to examine life at an elite university. But studying inequality cannot, and should not, always be about studying poor people in poor places. Doing so assumes that the inequality that stifles the development and undercuts the well-being of the poor only occurs in the places where they live. The reality is that while our neighborhoods may be segregated, our fates are intertwined. And what happens at colleges and universities like Renowned has a significance beyond their small number. So it is crucial that we understand the experiences of lower-income students and investigate whether these institutions are ready for the increasingly diverse students bodies they are now trying to recruit.[12]

During my first weeks at Renowned, when I was just beginning my research, I met two students, Patrice and Alice, who were both Latina and from New York City. We talked. We got to know one another.

When they told me their stories, I learned that they shared similar beginnings but had traveled along divergent paths to college. Both had grown up poor, but one went to a prep school and the other didn't.

Driven and determined, Patrice and Alice made their academic dreams come true when they earned admission to college. They were both short, both curly haired, both golden brown—as if they'd just been kissed by the sun. But the similarities went far deeper than appearance. Patrice and Alice were social twins, too. They saw and experienced many of the same things at home, in their neighborhoods, and in school. They traversed the same streets. They shopped at the same bodegas. From time to time, they even worshipped in the same parish. "We went to the same church. Patrice's mom lives around where my grandma lives," Alice said eagerly, while sitting in my office. The path to college was not easy for either of them. Both of their mothers had immigrated to New York in search of a better life, but immigrant dreams quickly became American nightmares. Limited by language barriers and lack of support from Patrice's and Alice's fathers, their mothers each worked two jobs until health problems from strenuous work and long hours forced them to quit.

Patrice and Alice grew up on government assistance, but evictions and the constant strain of moving made uncertainty a constant reality. Moreover, their moves were not always to better neighborhoods. "It's not really projects 'cause we do pay for electricity, but it's subsidized. Everyone there is poor," Alice said about her current neighborhood. Although they both cringed when outsiders called their communities "ghetto" or "sketchy," they knew that a rose by any other name still has its characteristic thorns. They saw beauty in the struggle they faced, even though neither felt safe walking around the neighborhood, even during the day. Patrice was particularly torn; her anxiety about how to talk about home was palpable as she fidgeted with the cuff of her sleeve. "There's so much Hispanic culture; I love that. People know each other. It's kind of chill," she began. In the same breath, however, she noted, "I don't like the violence; that's a big thing. There's a lot of violence. A lot of shootouts. I witnessed one this summer." Seeing so many of her friends fall victim to the street, Alice questioned why she made it to college and her neighborhood friends did not. "John was so smart; he used to do so well. Now he's in and out of jail," she said. Slapping her leg sharply with an open palm, she asked, "What happened? Why did I get out? How did this happen to me but not everyone else? It's sad."

Elementary and middle school provided no refuge from neighborhood woes. Alice, becoming stony faced the longer she spoke, revealed that a fellow student who lived three blocks away had brought a gun to school and accidently shot her younger brother's grade-school crush. The student's rationale for bringing the weapon to school was simple, she explained: he wanted to feel safe. Patrice, looking downcast, discussed how constant fighting left students bloodied, teachers scared, and the school on high alert.

Patrice's and Alice's paths diverged after middle school. Both applied to Prep for Prep, a New York–based program that places lower-income, minority youth in boarding, day, and preparatory high schools. The program's intent is explicit: to transform the nation's leadership pool. Patrice was accepted. Alice was waitlisted.

Alice was not offered a spot, so she ended up attending her local public high school, where the people and problems from middle school followed her. Ninety-five percent of the students were black and Latino; equal numbers were poor. Roughly 40 percent of the students dropped out. Her high school was underfunded, under-resourced, understaffed, and underperforming. Disrespecting the teacher was part of the daily routine. Antagonistic rather than cooperative relationships developed between students and teachers, prompting Alice to keep her distance from all but one or two of them. It took years of seeing those same teachers day in and day out before enough trust was built to enlist them as mentors. Threats to person and property were frequent. "Teachers didn't know how to control their classrooms. There would be fights, people setting garbage cans on fire, people smoked weed in school, cut school," she said somberly. "All these things became more commonplace as the years went by." Alice was not innocent, she admitted. She, too, skipped class with her friends. She, too, was not always respectful to her teachers. Still, gifted and naturally inquisitive, with an uncommon ease in expressing herself through writing, she maintained high marks even as she played hooky.

Toward the end of her sophomore year, Alice decided to invest her energies into making sure she graduated and went to college. With its lack of resources and unpredictable funding, the school did not always make it easy to do so. Alice loathed having to travel to other schools for science labs because her school didn't have the appropriate equipment. She applied to Renowned on something of a whim. When she received her acceptance letter, she was a ball of emotions: happy, surprised, terrified. People from her school often did not graduate, let alone go to college; and if college was in their plans, they did not attend places like Renowned.[13]

Patrice, by contrast, was accepted to Prep for Prep. She went through the grueling fourteen-month academic boot camp, a prerequisite to prepare urban middle schoolers for the expectations of private high schools. She eventually left New York City and the ten-block radius in which she had spent most of her life for a boarding school three states away. The school buildings sat on three hundred sprawling acres of manicured lawns and fields peppered with red brick buildings. "My mom never had to pay for tuition: I got full financial aid, it paid for books and trips," Patrice explained. Someone else's dime paid her $50,000 tuition and fees, which covered not only snow tubing adventures and European exchange programs, but also health insurance and winter clothes. Her boarding school, rich and mostly white, boasted a $200 million endowment. Nearly three-quarters of the faculty had advanced degrees, and the student-to-teacher ratio was six to one. With a jovial look spreading across her face, Patrice noted, "My school was smaller than some of my lectures now" at Renowned, allowing her to get "very close to the teachers; there was a lot of overlap with who was your coach, who was in your club, who was in your organizations, and then who was in your classes and dorms."

In fact, one of Patrice's fondest memories of boarding school was that she was given the resources to pursue her own independent study project. She chose to investigate the social meaning of hair for women of color. It is true, she said with a wry smile, that the research project was spawned by ignorant—or perhaps racist—questions by some of her white classmates about the cleanliness of "black hair." Nevertheless, she laughed the comment off and emphasized her appreciation of her teachers' encouragement to explore a project that sparked her nascent interest in identity and culture. The school also helped her family at home when unexpected trouble hit. "We've always had to struggle; we got a lot of help from the school," she said. "When my grandfather passed away, the school sent a check to help with funeral expenses."

As senior year approached, Patrice benefited from two additional perks that her boarding school provided. Along with the college counselor supplied by Prep for Prep, she worked closely with a school counselor, who had a caseload of fewer than fifteen students, to coach her through all her college applications. (In 2014, the national average caseload for guidance counselors was five hundred students, and at schools like the one Alice attended, the number was nearly double that.) And second, by virtue of the long history of students from Patrice's boarding school enrolling in Renowned and other elite colleges, her college admissions interview took place on the campus of the boarding school. In other words, Renowned came to her, rather than the other way around.[14]

As fate would have it, Alice and Patrice never met while sitting in the neighborhood church. They met in college. Calling Renowned the "polar opposite" of her life at home, Alice worried whether she would be able to fit in. "I didn't know whether I could be myself and still make friends." Alice completely withdrew from campus life for the first couple of weeks of the semester. One day, when she was feeling isolated in her room, she stepped out of the dorm for a short walk. Coming out of another dorm on the opposite side of the freshman quad at almost the same time was Patrice, a brown face in a sea of white ones. They crossed paths. They started talking. They quickly discovered their shared past. They eventually discussed their divergent trajectories.

As they compared notes, Alice and Patrice realized that they had markedly different feelings about being at Renowned. Alice, who felt out of sorts and unsure of her place at Renowned, noticed that Patrice and her other classmates who had gone to boarding school "have very different experiences because they've already been through it, have thought about it, and know how to work the system or make it work." She elaborated:

> My friends who did go through prep school—because their
> high schools were way smaller—became friends with white
> people. For them the transition was finding themselves again
> in a different way. For me, it was, I don't know . . . prep

school to here is way easier than from my high school to
Renowned. . . . Prep school changed Patrice, not in a bad
way, but she's changed.

Although she admitted that "it is a struggle nonetheless for each of us,"
Alice saw herself at a distinct disadvantage. Everything was new and,
more significantly for Alice, unfamiliar. Alice saw that for poor students with prep school backgrounds, Renowned was an extension of
high school. In her eyes, they were ready for Renowned. But she wasn't.
    Patrice had also thought about the differences between her experi-
ence and Alice's. In our many conversations, she reflected on already
knowing what it meant to move between two different worlds, and especially to gain citizenship in a rich, white place. At the same time,
she felt an aching sting as she became a visitor in a place that she used
to call home:

> I associated my life in Brooklyn with pain and suffering.
> When I got to boarding school, I really appreciated every-
> thing that was there because people were actually nice. I got
> everything I needed, things I didn't even have before. . . .
> Talking to Alice, and kids who didn't go to boarding school,
> who came from Harlem, who came from the Bronx, they're
> going through things in college that I went through in high
> school: "Oh shoot no one gets my hair. No one gets this." My
> high school was white; I understood that earlier. Alice is
> going through that now because she didn't go away.

Patrice made her transition long before coming to college. At the age
of thirteen, she immersed herself in a world that looked, felt, and operated like a college. She brought those life lessons with her to Re-

nowned, along with a keen understanding that her experiences were far from universal for people who came from homes and communities like hers.

What does it mean to be a poor student on a rich campus? Who is at ease navigating the social side of academic life, both with their peers and their professors, and who feels lost? I went looking for answers to these questions in the scholarly literature. More often than not, I came up empty-handed. The existing research did not reflect my own experiences at Amherst over a decade ago or those of the students like Alice and Patrice whom I came to know at Renowned.

Most social scientists do not acknowledge students like Patrice in their narratives about the poor youth who make it to college. Focusing on the role the family plays in shaping students' trajectories, they assess undergraduates based on their level of "cultural capital." Cultural capital, a term first developed by the French sociologist Pierre Bourdieu, refers to the collection of taken-for-granted ways of being that are valued in a particular context. The children of middle- and upper-class parents are seen as having an advantage when they get to college because the norms they learned at home are the same ones that govern campus life—norms such as looking someone in the eye while giving a firm handshake, feeling entitled to adults' time, and being proactive in forging relationships with authority figures. Children from lower-income families, in contrast, are regarded as having been scarred by poverty with all of its familiar ills, including a lack of social and academic preparation for college life. These students show up on campus, the narrative goes, and, unfamiliar with the new codes and customs of college, they struggle to adjust and adapt. The struggle is especially acute for those attending elite institutions. The sociologists Elizabeth

Armstrong and Laura Hamilton, for example, contend that "students from similar class backgrounds share financial, cultural, and social resources, as well as lived experiences, that shape their orientations to college and the agendas they can readily pursue." Basing their policy decisions on this research, deans and administrators often adopt a monolithic approach to lower-income students, and thus—with all good intentions—create programming for an undifferentiated group of "students at risk." But the story, as I learned my very first day at Amherst, is much more complex than this.[15]

To understand the full complexity of life for lower-income students at an elite college, in 2013 I initiated the project that culminated in this book—taking a close look at undergraduate life at Renowned University. The heart of this project involved talking with students about their day-to-day experiences with their peers, their professors and other college administrators, and the policies that govern university life. I formally interviewed seventy-six lower-income black, Latino, and white students at Renowned. Twenty-one of these students fit into the category I call Privileged Poor, and fifty-five into the category Doubly Disadvantaged. In order to compare the experiences of the Privileged Poor and the Doubly Disadvantaged with those of wealthier students, I also interviewed twenty-seven middle- and upper-middle-class black students at Renowned. These upper-income students, although from an underrepresented racial group, would be expected to successfully navigate college, both socially and academically, by virtue of their class background.

In addition to formal, in-depth conversations with students, I spent two years observing campus life. I got a sense of how students see the campus and their place in it by engaging in a variety of activities, from attending meetings of student groups, to eating in the cafeteria, to hosting open discussions about social class on college campuses. Beyond formal interviews, I also spoke with many students from all backgrounds as well as deans, advisers, faculty, and other staff over the course of my two-year study. (See the Appendix for a detailed discussion of how I carried out this research.)

I recognize that race and gender play key roles in students' college experiences, and I highlight these factors in cases where they were brought up by the students I talked with at Renowned. But class constitutes the primary focus of this project. All too often, university communities do not have as robust conversations about social class as they do about gender and race, and this book is an attempt to help remedy that shortcoming.

One of my primary goals in this book is to introduce readers to the Privileged Poor, a group of students that has been largely overlooked, and to compare their experiences with those of the Doubly Disadvantaged. The Privileged Poor know what life is like below the poverty line. They also know how the 1 percent learn and live. The Doubly Disadvantaged only know the former. Ignoring the divergent experiences of the Privileged Poor and the Doubly Disadvantaged has been a mistake, and continuing to do so limits our understanding of the ways in which poverty and inequality shape the lives of today's undergraduates. The contrast between the Doubly Disadvantaged and the Privileged Poor can tell us a great deal about how experiences later in adolescence and outside the home can influence students' ability to move between cultural worlds. In particular, high schools play a powerful role in shaping students' cultural competencies, serving not only as judges of academic success, but also as crafters of students' strategies for achieving it. We do poor students as a whole a disservice if we assume that their stories are all the same.

Moreover, exploring campus life from the perspective of these two groups provides a unique vantage point for examining how university policies exacerbate class differences among students, often in ways that connect to historical legacies of race and exclusion. The conversation about why some students thrive in college and others don't often centers on the question of which students possess the social and cultural resources that the Privileged Poor access in their elite high schools. But we know that a person's success in college is not just about symbolic resources, powerful as they are. We also know that students do not learn and live in a vacuum. Their experiences are also shaped by their access to material resources—money—or lack thereof. Money remains a requirement for full citizenship in college, despite institutional declarations to the contrary. It is essential to explore the ways in which the cultural skills each student brings to college collide with the very blunt reality of how much money they have. Examining cash at the same time as cultural capital reveals the complexities of the lives of disadvantaged students. Comparing and contrasting the Privileged Poor with the Doubly Disadvantaged makes this possible.

Access alone is not enough for fostering inclusion and generating mobility. What you will find in the students' stories that follow is that university policies are failing disadvantaged students in a number of ways. The experiences of the Privileged Poor and the Doubly Disadvantaged differ most clearly in their disparate institutional knowledge of and familiarity with elite spaces, and these differences affect both their well-being and their strategies for navigating college. The Doubly Disadvantaged are not adequately integrated into the norms that govern student life at an elite institution—practices like connecting with professors during office hours—that the Privileged Poor learned in high school. As the stories in Chapters 1 and 2 will make clear, the Privileged Poor have the kind of cultural capital that enables them to be at ease when engaging with their peers and professors. Yet when it comes to money, the distinction between these two groups disappears.

Students in both groups are burdened by a lack of financial resources, as we will see especially in Chapter 3. Both the Privileged Poor and the Doubly Disadvantaged are harmed by policies, such as the closing of cafeterias during spring break, that exacerbate class differences and are profoundly disorienting for lower-income students. When formal university policies push poor students to the margins, a process I call structural exclusion, even the most savvy of lower-income students will hit a wall that no amount of cultural capital can overcome. Scholars and university officials alike must recognize and account for these influences on the undergraduate experience to fully understand how inequality is reproduced in college and to prepare themselves better for welcoming and supporting all students.

Elite universities are now a bundle of confusing contradictions: they bend over backward to admit disadvantaged students into their hallowed halls, but then, once the students are there, they maintain policies that not only remind those students of their disadvantage, but even serve to highlight it. Hiring poor students to clean the toilets in rich students' dorm rooms is not a way to break down class boundaries.

The best way to understand what disadvantaged students experience at an elite university is to hear about it in their own words. The students at Renowned whom I got to know while I was conducting my study invited me into their hearts and minds. They permitted me access to their personal narratives so that I could address crucial questions about equity and equality. Some might say, "These students have it made now that they've gotten into a school like Renowned; what do they have to complain about?" But this is not a story of spoiled kids lamenting that they have not been given everything they want. Quite the contrary: these are students who have been given very little and yet have earned admission into one the most selective colleges in the world, only to face additional obstacles as they work toward achieving the American dream. The experiences of both the Privileged Poor and the Doubly Disadvantaged remind us that access is not inclusion. Their words deserve a response. We should encourage colleges and universities to create more inclusive communities and urge the government to address the even more entrenched inequities that exist in primary and secondary education.

This book gives voice to those students who have not yet told their stories, or even worse, who have had inaccurate stories told about them. It corrects the dominant narrative—and, consequently, our too simplistic notions—of what it means to be a poor student on a rich campus. It challenges college officials and policymakers alike to better serve the next generation of students. It stands as a testament to those students who have overcome the odds to enter through the college gates.

I

"Come with Me to Italy!"

THE WEATHER IS REFRESHING after our endless winter, bright and sunny with a crisp breeze. I decide to walk to my meeting on campus instead of taking the bus. Mad at myself for leaving my headphones behind in the pocket of my heavy coat, I am reduced to listening to blaring car horns and to bikers yelling profanities at the drivers who veer too close. As I approach one of the dorms just off the freshman quad, four students, all young white women, cross my path. They each wear some combination of what I call the Renowned uniform: a Longchamp bag, black Lululemon yoga pants, Hunter boots or tan Sperry Top-Siders, and a North Face jacket. We enter the dorm and proceed to the elevator. Ignoring me, they continue boasting about how much work they have to do, how little of it they have done, how little sleep they got and are going to get, and how much coffee they will consume to make it through the day. Nicole must have needed a pick-me-up even before meeting her friends; the Starbucks drink she holds is still hot enough that puffs of steam waft up between sips. Molly confesses, "I've only had an espresso shot once in my life." Her friends look shocked. Rebecca, twisting her long blond hair behind her ear, responds, *"Oooooh. You should come with me to Italy!"* Without skipping a beat, Stephanie announces that she has Argentinean coffee beans in her room that are rumored to contain more caffeine than Colombian beans. At this moment, the elevator dings, the doors open, and we go our separate ways.

A conversation between friends—that is all I overheard in the elevator. Only one thing interrupted the banality of it all: when the young women discovered an imposter in their midst. How could Molly not be an espresso aficionado? But for these four friends, the response to this revelation was as routine as the ignorance about espresso was shocking: invitations for overseas travel and offers of luxury goods are utterly ordinary here.

In common rooms, cafeterias, and courtyards at Renowned, you can no more escape these kinds of conversations than you can escape the cold in the dead of a Northeast winter. This should not be surprising. Renowned is rich. And it has been for more than a century. Even with its adoption of no-loan financial aid policies in the early 2000s, one among many efforts to recruit a more diverse student body, the majority of its students are still affluent. Very affluent. During the time I spent at Renowned, roughly one out of every three undergraduates hailed from a family with an income of more than $250,000 annually. Many families who sent their children to Renowned made much more than that. One in eight came from the top 1 percent, meaning their families brought home at least $630,000 a year. These figures, like all matters of money, are more than demographic statistics: daily life at Renowned is shaped by the wealth of its students.[1]

Being enrolled at Renowned is a very different thing from feeling like you belong at Renowned. Yes, all students have some trouble adjusting when they go off to college. Yet many students, it seems, are unfazed by the social undercurrents of everyday life at a rich school. Indeed, scores of students at Renowned—whether middle class or upper middle class or just plain rich, whether white, black, Latino, or Asian—have grown up having some variant of the conversation like the one I overheard in the dorm elevator. They sail through their time at Renowned relatively unperturbed by their peers' wealth and the many manifestations of privilege. They feel connected to the community. They relax in the dorm lounges and feel ownership of the school's common spaces.

But for a smaller (yet growing) group of students, mainly those from poor families, those social undercurrents are shocking, painful, maddening, or some combination of all three. When peers in the dorm swap tales of excursions to Bali and extravagant purchases at Hermès, these students become instantly aware not only of differences in past experiences and present tastes, but also of the vast contrast between lives of privilege and lives of constraint. These new experiences— principally displays of wealth and privilege—are unsettling and exacerbate the feeling of not belonging. The common response, as we'll see, is for these students to distance themselves from their peers and withdraw from the college community, resulting in a circumscribed life on campus.

Feeling like you are part of the college community is a crucial component of undergraduate life. But a sense of belonging—as amorphous as it is essential—is an aspect of the college experience that scholars who study higher education tend to downplay. Our efforts at understanding college tend to focus more on differences in quantifiable outcomes, like grades and graduation rates, than on students' day-to-day reality. And there is one particular facet of this reality that remains especially underexplored: the relationship between disadvantaged students and their wealthier peers.[2]

Yet these daily interactions are closely connected with a student's ultimate success at school. Students who do not feel welcome at a college do not avail themselves of the many opportunities and resources that are available. Campus life is often more stressful for these students than for their peers, hampering their ability to focus on various tasks. They tend to underperform and to give up more easily. Students who delay integrating into the larger college community also have less access to social support from their peers and from the college as a whole—support that proves crucial to success both in college and in the labor market upon graduation.[3]

How comfortable students are at moving through an elite college campus populated mostly by affluent peers—often the first people they meet when they arrive—sets the tone for whether they feel at home or find themselves at a loss. Imagine if a fellow student had been in the elevator with the four friends that day, instead of me. Overhearing these friends, one student might brush off their words as par for the course. She might even chime in with a caffeine-related travel story of her own. A different student might view the exchange as yet another reminder of how unfamiliar and isolating life at Renowned can be. He might even become more resolute in actively avoiding "people like that" and the places where "those people" hang out.

It is easy to assume that we already know who feels comfortable at a place like Renowned and who doesn't. It seems pretty obvious: the wealthier you are, the more likely you are to feel like you belong at an elite college. The inverse would seem to be equally true: the poorer you are, the more out of place you're going to feel at a wealthy institution. Several decades of research have come to the same general conclusion: scholars report that students from affluent families experience easier transitions to college life than do their poorer peers. Wealthy students typically find social life in college to be largely unsurprising. The campus feels like a place that has been designed with their experiences and tastes in mind, as if anticipating their arrival. These students have little or no trouble recognizing that Renowned was made for people like them; it feels like home.[4]

But when it comes to students from poor families, our assumptions and prior research, it turns out, need a reality check. Although they may live in the same dorms, eat in the same cafeterias, and attend the same classes as their affluent peers, not all poor students experience these places in the same way. Despite increased diversity recruitment, Renowned remains a predominantly wealthy (and mostly white) campus. How much this demographic reality plays into lower-income students' sense of belonging is a matter of experience and exposure. The Doubly Disadvantaged and the Privileged Poor offer contrasting views on whether a school like Renowned is made for people like them. The Doubly Disadvantaged, poor kids from segregated communities and schools, experience intense culture shock—what sociologist Kimberly Torres describes as a sense of "strangeness and discomfort." That is not the case with the Privileged Poor.[5]

The path to college for the Privileged Poor is one of extreme opposites: poverty set against plenty, scarcity at home standing in stark contrast to abundance at their prep schools. After years of learning, socializing, and (for some) living with wealthy, mostly white students in elite, private high schools, the Privileged Poor are not shocked by what and who they encounter in college. Their high schools were a preview, a four-year trailer to the main feature. This is not to say that the Privileged Poor are inoculated from adversity. Problems at home with their families and friends—typically some combination of evictions, convictions, and violence—are disruptive, especially for lower-income black and Latino undergraduates who hail from segregated, distressed communities. Both the Privileged Poor and the Doubly Disadvantaged still live in poverty's long shadow. And yet, even amid the endless reminders of class (not to mention race) difference, students who have navigated elite academic environments before college—and who are familiar with the social norms that dominate those locales—are more at ease at Renowned regardless of their families' income.[6]

In what follows, we first look at what different groups of students at Renowned have to say about making the transition from their high schools to this renowned college campus, and how well they are able to fit in. Then in the second part of the chapter, we'll investigate how they deal with the displays of wealth—expensive clothing, luxury vacations—that surround them from day one.

A Sense of Belonging (or Not)

Students' sense of belonging and experiences with culture shock—or lack thereof—affect all aspects of their college experience, and we will see them emerge in various ways throughout the book. In this section, we'll focus on one particular manifestation: how disadvantaged students engage—or don't engage—with their peers. In setting out to do my research, I wanted to know how students perceived and related to the general culture of Renowned—from the people they found walking alongside them on campus to the experiences they heard and saw their new peers having. When I met with students, I asked how much of a culture shock, if any, they experienced when coming to Renowned. I left the question open-ended so as to let them reflect without any a priori assumptions about which aspects of college life made them feel either at home or like they didn't belong.

Gathering this information not only opens a window onto the lives of disadvantaged students at an elite college; it can also help generate ideas for what colleges could do to remove obstacles that sideline some students and handicap others. What I found was not a simple story of different trajectories through Renowned based on social class. It was more complicated than that.

Culture Shock? What Culture Shock?

Students from upper-income families (UI) surely face challenges in college, but culture shock is not one of them. When I asked affluent, black students what they found startlingly unfamiliar or unsettling about social life at Renowned, many struggled to understand the premise of the question. Long pauses and confused looks preceded their answers. When Renowned presented them with something new, that novelty did not make them feel like outsiders. Instead, they usually framed it as enhancing their college experience and, more generally, as helping them grow up. Such is the benefit of privilege—even the new can be seen as an advantage.

Shaking a light dusting of snow from her hoodie, Antoinette (UI,B) entered my office and reminded me, with a smile and a light chuckle, that we had met before. When she was choosing between majors, she attended an academic fair that I also happened to attend. Antoinette reported that she had chosen political science as her major. We then started talking about her transition to Renowned, and I learned that Antoinette had always attended private schools that catered almost exclusively to affluent families like hers. In elementary and middle school, she recalled, black cars with chauffeurs lined the Manhattan streets surrounding the school to drop off and pick up her classmates. Before I could ask if she too arrived at school in a hired car, she informed me that she and her brother preferred to walk, once their parents decided they could get to school on their own. For high school, she left home to attend the same prestigious New England boarding school that her mother had attended. In addition to being wealthy, her peers at boarding school were mostly white. Clearly loyal to her school, and eager to defend it against any misconceptions that I might have from this characterization, she made sure to let me know that she encountered a diverse group of students in high school. Sounding like an admissions officer, she said, "We have people from forty-seven states and twenty-nine countries. There's only nine hundred kids, but we have people from everywhere."

Her transition to Renowned was, in her description, "seamless." Laughing, she added that "not much at all" was new or alien about life at Renowned. She took it for granted that she would fit in. When I asked why, she responded, "Just because." After an extended pause, she noted, "I don't have many instances where I don't feel like I fit in." Antoinette listed some of the things that had prepared her for Renowned. Being away from home, for example, was not a problem. Her boarding school, which she called "the jam," was like "a mini college." Dorm life was old news by the time she graduated. She had long been used to going to school—and living in dormitories—with wealthy students of all races and nationalities. When it came to engaging her college peers, Antoinette reported that things were "pretty good" and that building rapport was "kind of easy." "I'm pretty friendly; that's why I like most people. It's been nice. It didn't take too long for me to walk around the freshman quad and say, 'Hi' and recognize people around campus." On this latter point, it helped, she admitted, that her high school sent roughly a dozen students to Renowned each year. Beyond seeing her old classmates, she also ran into students she had competed against in field hockey, who attended schools that were also feeders to Renowned. Even during her first days on campus, Antoinette saw many familiar faces in her new home.

Jessica (UI,B), a junior from the northern suburbs of Detroit who entered Renowned keenly interested in politics, was similarly flummoxed when asked about culture shock. After restarting her answer several times, she said, "Um, I don't know if I really felt all that shocked. I mean, just because, like, I don't know." Taking another twenty seconds or so to ponder the question, Jessica finally organized her thoughts: "I'm a pretty flexible person. It's part of how you value things. How you view life. For me, I'm just kind of go with the flow. That's how I operate. You know, nothing really shocked me." It showed. Jessica was quite a social butterfly. Even though she was rarely the first to speak in a social gathering, from her first semester to her last, she could always be found at a political event or rally, comfortably mingling with other students as well as with esteemed guests like senators and governors.

Carol (UI,B), a junior with a voice that was soft but still commanded attention, came to Renowned from a rich private school that sat on the edge of her upper-middle-class neighborhood. She enjoyed high school because administrators were "very big on making sure that we had a lot of help and a lot of support." With a nervous laugh, she explained that one example of her school's curated support was its construction of "three different computer labs and a full library for 250 students. We had the Mac lab and a PC lab." In addition to investing resources in computer labs—divided by operating system, no less—her school exposed students to different cultures both by recruiting students from various Asian and European countries and by hosting study abroad programs. Although from a small city where residents are either black or white, Carol developed close ties with friends "from Taiwan, from Russia, from Germany" in high school. She pointed to the continuities between high school and college as the reason why she felt at home when she came to Renowned. For Carol, even the new reminded her of the old. On the question of culture shock in college, she said she experienced none: "Yeah; I don't think it was shocking." Leaning back on my old, beat-up office couch with a contemplative look on her face, she continued,

> I guess living with other students was new. Being around them 24 / 7, that was something I have never experienced other than at camp. It was pretty new. The people just seemed very familiar to me. I feel like I could relate people I met at Renowned to someone I knew in high school. That connection was very familiar for me.

Carol's freshman-year roommates at Renowned presented her with a paradox: "new familiarity." She let me in on an inside joke—she and her roommates, who had all grown up in different countries, had teasingly nicknamed themselves "The United Nations of the Freshman Class." But this racial and geographic diversity did not unsettle Carol. In fact, it was quite the opposite. Her cosmopolitan corner of the freshman dorm made her feel quite at home. She and her roommates all spoke multiple languages. They all spent time traveling around the world, first with their families and then alone. And, Carol admitted, they all came from affluent backgrounds.

Now, even for affluent students, Renowned was not always wholly familiar. Kramer (UI,B), a Michigan native with a competitive streak, found himself interacting with a more diverse group of students at

Renowned than he had in high school. Describing what did and did not surprise him, Kramer said,

> The only thing that was really a culture shock was meeting a kid who won national science competitions or a kid whose parents were stakeholders in a major sports team. Meeting the ridiculously rich or ridiculously talented, I was really surprised. I experienced diversity in high school but not kids like, "My dad is a part owner of a sports team." In high school, kids are like, "My parents make $250,000 a year." Here, there are those kids who might as well be . . . have you heard of Rich Kids of Instagram?[7] Rich Kids of Instagram are kids who take pictures of themselves on their yachts with bottles of Dom Pérignon and Rolexes. I see that here. There are kids who have things that exude affluence. Kids in my high school are upper middle class, but it's not the range that's here. I wasn't exposed to that. And then kids that went to nationals, junior Ping-Pong team for Japan, or the national chess champion.

On the most basic level, Renowned, like all private, wealthy colleges, offers its students exposure to extreme wealth and talent—both to students from families at the top end of the economic spectrum, and to those with "ridiculously" impressive accomplishments. Kramer spoke of the economic, academic, and extracurricular elite with the same level of awe. He accorded the same status to the classmate whose family owned part of a sports team as to the one who was the national chess champion.

Beyoncé (UI,B), sporting a gray sweater with the name of her high school stitched on it, was on her way to a community service trip in

New Orleans when we first spoke. This was not surprising. She invested much of her time at Renowned volunteering in different communities. That was one of the things she liked most about the school—the opportunity it provided her to give back. Framing her college transition as "relatively smooth," Beyoncé said she experienced "no culture shock. I was prepared." Focusing specifically on relations with her new peers, she said that being around affluent and white students was nothing new. More novel for Beyoncé was encountering ethnic diversity in the black community. She recalled a conversation she had with some new students when she was a junior:

> Freshmen are like, "How do you deal with being around so many whites?" I am just like, "That was my high school." It's not surprising. A slight culture shock was international students. We didn't have an international program at my school so I didn't really know anybody who lived in Kenya. I was very ignorant about Africans. At home, there are not that many Africans. I knew about Haitian culture, Jamaican culture. I didn't know about African culture. That was different.

Unlike the freshmen who sought her out for guidance, Beyoncé joked about how "wealthy" and "white" were simply two apt descriptors of the students in both her middle school and her high school. But coming to Renowned permitted Beyoncé to meet more diverse groups of students of color. She ultimately befriended three African women, each one from a different country. Beyoncé welcomed the new topics of conversation she shared with them. Their late night talks, where they pushed each other about different understandings of their common heritage and discussed whether they should let their hair go natural or not, expanded her horizons beyond what her communities in high school and at home could provide.[8]

A few affluent students did identify differences in social norms as surprising and a little unsettling. But rather than describing confusion or discomfort related to social class, they framed culture shock differently. Some students mentioned regional or cultural differences that they contended with during their first semesters on campus. Those from California and the South, in particular, often struggled to adapt to life in the Northeast. Brittany (UI,B), a proud Texan with Caribbean roots, quipped, "To me, it was more of the Northern culture shock. People who live here aren't friendly. And the weather sucks!" Joe (UI,B), leaning back lazily in his chair, first said that when it came to culture shock he experienced "none at all." But then he quickly corrected himself, saying, "No; it was." He continued,

> People who didn't visit Renowned expected Renowned to be full of pretentious white kids. I didn't expect Renowned to be so laid-back and down to earth. When I came to visit, I got chill students. Maybe they were trying to put on a front. For the most part, students here are approachable. Some of them are weird. You have a conversation and then, if you see someone the next day or week later, they'll just pass by you. This is weird. Some people will have a conversation with you and then act like they don't know you, which leads to awkward situations. I don't know if anyone else brought that up. Maybe it's me being from the South. If I see someone, I'll say hi even if I don't really know them that well.

Joe connected his experiences with culture shock to being from the South. Differences in everyday etiquette, while surprising and sometimes unwelcome, were odd but not alienating. Renowned still felt like home to Joe.

When I asked the black students from upper-income backgrounds about culture shock and getting used to life at Renowned, they generally did not speak about their own racial background or the demographic makeup of the student body as factors or even as concerns. One reason for this could be, as many of them acknowledged, that more than three-quarters of them came from predominantly white, well-to-do communities, and more than half attended private schools that were also populated by wealthy, mostly white students. In the public schools that the others attended, white students from similar backgrounds were the majority group. This is not to say that race was not salient in their lives. Like Beyoncé, many students welcomed the chance to interact with more students of color. When speaking about the dominant culture of Renowned and the students they saw daily, however, they described Renowned as more of what they had already come to expect from elite institutions. They focused on how they, as individuals, had the right temperament for Renowned. They spoke about possessing the appropriate personality traits even as they connected their comfort at Renowned with their privileged structural positions. The makeup of the student body and the culture of elites that pervades the campus did not undercut their sense of belonging at Renowned.

Colliding Worlds

While their affluent peers stumbled over their words as they tried to articulate the absence of culture shock in their lives at Renowned, the Doubly Disadvantaged choked down tears. They felt like outsiders at Renowned, isolated from both their new peers and the larger college community. This sense of alienation and difference often started before they first arrived on campus. And even after they had unpacked their suitcases, found shortcuts to different buildings, and gotten to know their classmates, it did not always go away, or even diminish. For many, it grew. In my conversations with them, they highlighted the differences—cultural, racial, and socioeconomic—between themselves and their fellow students. Renowned may provide a ticket to economic mobility, but in the case of the Doubly Disadvantaged, there is a price for that ticket. For many, that price is steep.

Sometimes the Doubly Disadvantaged begin to experience painful alienation before they even set foot on campus. Joshua (DD,B) learned this firsthand when he and his family piled into the not-always-reliable family car to head to a reception for admitted students, a few miles away from where they were staying. An omen of things to come, their old GPS took them down streets that were unfamiliar, despite the fact that Joshua and his family had been living in the area for fifteen years. He quickly realized that "the reception was in the nice part of the city I'd never been to." As soon as they walked through the ornate doors of the host's home, Joshua realized that Renowned "would be culture shock on every level." Events at the reception amplified his fear. He described the scene:

> It was funny; that's the first time I had culture shock. I show up. Everybody is in nice polos, dressed up. I come in wearing jeans, Converses, big American Eagle shirt, and a cap on backwards that I snatched off of my head when I got there. I'll never forget that for the rest of my life. It represents so much. It was cool meeting people who had done well, but it was the first time I saw a system. None of them went to a school like mine. Private schools, good public schools, charter schools . . . schools I've heard very good things about. I don't see any scholars from my county there. Just me.

Joshua saw his two worlds—the one he came from and the one he was about to enter—collide. An hour before the reception, he had been getting dressed in temporary housing that he and his family were forced to call home after they lost the mortgage on their own house. Now he stood in a lavishly decorated house large enough to hold fifty talkative, excited people. The contrast reminded Joshua of his disadvantage as much as it highlighted his new peers' wealth. And as if the space itself was not enough of a reminder of how different Renowned would be, some of the other admitted students noted their surprise that he "spoke so well." One student explained why: people from Joshua's community were known for their "lazy English."

When hosted in wealthy homes or university clubs, such welcome receptions, as well as admission interviews, can work against their intended purpose of welcoming all students. Manuel (DD,L) ventured into unfamiliar territory for his interview. He traveled forty-five minutes on the highway from his house to "this really white, affluent, gated community. I was like, 'Damn, I never knew there was a place like this!' It was one of those places like I saw on TV." The discomfort goes beyond the physical location of the events themselves. Once inside, many lower-income students—and their parents—feel as if the only people they can relate to are the caterers who whisk in and out with trays of food, or the cleaning staff that shows up as the guests are leaving. This is most acute for black and Latino students, since those serving hors d'oeuvres are often the only other people of color in the room besides them and their families. The Doubly Disadvantaged students I talked with said they felt acutely uncomfortable being served. Not only were they being waited on by a person of color in a room full of rich white people, but they weren't sure they knew the appropriate customs. One student said that her entire family drove excitedly across town to a welcome reception at the house of two alumni, but as soon as they saw the house and the people who were walking in, her parents refused to leave the car. Her father told her to call when she was ready to leave, so he could come back to pick her up. The feeling of difference that results from these events can linger for a long time. It did for Joshua.

Jose (DD,L), a chatty senior who resembled a soccer player gone slightly to seed, hailed from a poor, predominately Latino neighborhood in Los Angeles where the threat of falling victim to a stray bullet or to a gang's initiation ritual was ever present. Even on your way to the local food truck for pupusas and plantains, he remarked, "you see prostitution, gang activity, poverty. You see people with no other option, people with no other opportunity. You see refugees trying to make it." Sometimes he could not complete the errands his mother gave him without encountering trouble. "I've never been in an actual fight one on one; I've been jumped a number of times." Still, it was home. He knew it well. He was comfortable. At the same time, Jose was ecstatic to get into Renowned and embark on new adventures.

Reflecting on life at Renowned, however, Jose lamented that nothing at home could have prepared him for life on campus. "My transition to college was a rough one," he said. Unlike Carol (UI,B), who rejoiced at the similarities between the people she knew at home and those she met at Renowned, Jose discovered that the shock of not finding "my people" left him feeling even more isolated than he expected:

> Renowned was a huge culture shock. I started realizing race and class didn't always go hand in hand. There were minorities I thought I could relate to, but when they talk about money, I feel the distance. . . . Moving in, my floor posted our hometowns on the doors. I see Mexico City. I was like "Another Mexican? We're about to be homies!" I was so

excited. But he was an aristocrat from Mexico. He says, "Dallas Cowboys; they're my favorite team. I have my dad fly me out to every home game." Excuse me! Plane ticket, game tickets, hotel: Are you joking? That was shocking; my first introduction to the huge disparities at Renowned. Same kid—at the end of freshman year—he has this Ralph Lauren velvet, beautiful bathrobe. He's like, "I don't want to pack this." He's going to throw it away. I took it. Thinking about it, his balls and dick were all over the thing but I was like, "It's Ralph Lauren." I didn't know Ralph Lauren was good, but I knew it was fancy. It felt hella good.

Jose learned an old truth: "All skin folk ain't kinfolk." He struggled to come to terms with the huge gap between himself and other people who looked like him. Coming to Renowned turned his world on its head.

Jose shared another one of his hard-learned lessons: the necessity of "developing a thick skin for microaggressions," those "small" slights that cut deep. And as he did so, it was frightening to hear his voice change. Pride gave way to anger. Anger quickly turned to shame:

> We had to overcome a lot to get here. We are warriors. We are invincible. Or so we think. Being in this toxic environment without resources changes us. When I got here, I was invincible. Over time, I started breaking down. If I went to another school where I was comfortable, I would be more of a leader. Since coming to Renowned, I've become quiet, more conscious, especially in the classroom. In a social setting, I'll talk to you. In class, I shut up. In a

class with more people of color, people that I can relate to, I feel comfortable. The thing is, at Renowned,
[being in class with students of color] doesn't really
happen.

TONY: Why do you call Renowned a toxic environment?

JOSE: Quick anecdote. One of my friends, he had to take
time off. I didn't know what that meant, like the
stigma associated with it. I was like, "What made you
take time off?" I'll never forget his answer. He said,
"I couldn't breathe here. This place totally destroyed
me." I was like, "Oh my God!" Seeing it happen with
me, I began to understand. We come here, we're so
alive and full of hope. This place puts you in a depression. He was saying he died here. I don't think I had
the same reaction to the same extent but we have
similar reactions. So, as to your question about the
toxic environment, it's isolation. You feel like you
don't fit in. You feel like you're alone, like there's no
one that can relate.

The term "microaggression" is one that Jose picked up in college.
He used it to capture moments when his peers assumed he could afford food from local restaurants, or when they questioned why Renowned invests in scholarships for "less-deserving" students when
their own parents have to pay full price. Over time, such disheartening
encounters deflated the very sense of invincibility that had gotten him
through the challenges at home to make it to college in the first place.
And despite Renowned's greater push for diversity, most of Jose's
classes were filled with wealthy students who were most often the
ones who made such comments.[9]

For the Doubly Disadvantaged, college is less about embracing new opportunities than it is about discovering new constraints. It is not that these students find out when they go to college that they are poor. They already know they don't come from money. Arriving on campus, especially a wealthy one, highlights the contrast between the privileges of their wealthy peers and the economic and social restraints that dictate not only what they can and cannot do, but also what they feel comfortable doing. Take Elise (DD,W), for example. Her family had endured at least six evictions. As a result, she never felt settled as she moved around different poor, white communities in Kentucky and Virginia. Looking on with tired eyes and picking over a barely eaten muffin that sat precariously on her lap, Elise described her constricted reality at Renowned. This awareness of her disadvantaged position only reaffirmed her outsider status. She explained,

> When you come to a place like this and you're low income, you know that being here is not a right. It's a privilege. Being in a place like this can easily be taken away. Everything you do here is at someone else's mercy. You're allowed to be here, allowed to take classes here because someone else is allowing that versus someone who can afford this. It is their prerogative. If they can't go here, they'll go somewhere else. For low-income students, there aren't other options. It feels that way. You're at the mercy of someone who took pity on the fact that you have no money. I know someone who's fourth-generation Renowned; it's insane. This is just another part of their life. This is such a defining moment . . . the fact that

I go here, is huge. For some people, it's just expected. That's crazy.

TONY: You still feel that now after almost four semesters?

ELISE: Yeah. I always feel lucky to be here. I always feel that I don't belong. Maybe it should be the other way. I should feel like I belong because I got in without any connections, without any family help, without any legacy status. Maybe I should feel like Renowned is more mine than it is theirs. I got in on my own merit. But it's hard to feel like I deserve it the way other people do. My choice is within the realms of other people's graciousness. My choice is within what I'm allowed to choose from. They don't have these limits.

Elise's classmates did nothing to allay her suspicions about the freedom (and protection) that money brings. During freshman orientation, Suzanne, a rich international student who lived next door to Elise, began drinking in her dorm room. By 2 AM she couldn't walk and had begun vomiting. Fearing that she would asphyxiate, two students in the dorm called an ambulance. Elise forgave Suzanne's blatant disregard for the fact that alcohol was prohibited in the freshman dorms, a policy that Elise appreciated since she did not drink. Elise lost her cool, however, when Suzanne returned the next day and joked about how much more expensive emergency transports were in the United States than in her home country. Unconcerned about the price tag, Suzanne bragged that her parents could easily afford the bill. Further angering Elise, Suzanne served up a repeat performance the following week and was again transported to the hospital by ambulance, sirens blaring and lights blazing.

"These people's lives are not real," Elise yelled as she thrust her hands in the air. Her peers' privilege and blind spots left Elise "frustrated because they just have no concept of money. . . . They don't understand that I have to work all these jobs to register for this semester and pay $92 for incidentals. That's a huge deal! They don't understand how something so little can be so big, how $20 can mean so much to someone when it's change to them. 'Let's not eat in the cafeteria; let's go out to dinner.' Sigh. The biggest, most frustrating thing is that it's never going to change."

William (DD,W), who hailed from a small farming town in the nation's breadbasket, echoed Elise's frustrations. He did not mince words. "People have a lot of money here. I don't." William was not ignorant of his family's poverty. "I never really felt like I was poor, but we always were." He had realized what a precarious position his family was in a long time ago, when his parents started to take on second and third jobs in order to make ends meet. But being poor had never made him feel like an outsider until he came to Renowned. Since he had arrived on campus, he said,

> I haven't eaten out or gone shopping. That seems to be a weekly activity. Daily. They say, "I hate going to the cafeteria for lunch. I went to town and got a lobster; cannot believe it's only $30. Home it was like $80 to get lobsters. It is so cheap here." I cannot eat anywhere else because my meal plan is paid for and that is amazing. To not eat basically free food is ridiculous-sounding to me. All you have to do is walk there. Why would I pay for food?

To cope with these alienating moments, William tried "laughing it off" because "being offended is a useless emotion." He was not always able to do so, however. William struggled to keep his emotions bottled up as he sat in front of me. Anger flashed across his face at the memory of his classmates' classification of a $30 lobster as "cheap," along with their clueless invitation for him to join them. William believed that being around "these people" perverted the moral and ethical development of their peers because it encouraged students, especially those from lower-income backgrounds, to pursue selfish goals. "The biggest challenge" of being at Renowned, he argued, "is the pressure to become one of them." He noted,

> When you come here, you become one of the elite. Like, "Oh yes, Renowned education, you're going to have so much money when you grow up." They just expect the goal of all this is to have money and be part of the upper class. People forget where they come from. They live here for four months and they're not living at home and they forget what it means. Then, after four years, they don't go back home. They go to New York. They're just consumed! Forty percent of people go into consulting after graduation. Forty percent of people don't come into Renowned thinking of consulting. People are transformed. It is just expected that one social class is inherently better than the other, more desirable.

William is right. Students from elite colleges do flock to high-status, high-paying professions like investment banking. His classmates will join companies like Bain Capital, Bank of America, and Goldman Sachs after graduation. His estimate of how many of his peers go the corporate route is high, but only a little: roughly one-third of seniors at Renowned, and colleges like it, enter the financial sector and management consulting upon graduation, greatly outpacing the flow of graduates into other sectors. William wanted nothing to do with the moneyed life at Renowned or the income-obsessed industries his peers would enter upon graduation.[10]

The experience of Valeria (DD,L) highlights the complexity of college transition for the Doubly Disadvantaged. On one hand, this was the first time she felt academically challenged and able to explore new subjects and ways of expressing herself. On the other, she found Renowned to be socially constraining and lacking in diversity, in that so many of her classmates were wealthy. She admitted wishing she could love Renowned. Though usually full of energy, she seemed downcast when she talked about the differences between high school and college.

VALERIA: Renowned's academically more rigorous. Even picking a course here, it's different. I learned how to think. In high school, everything was worksheets. Here, my professor read my essay and was like, "You're summarizing. Make an argument." By the end of freshman year, I understood what that meant. It was hard but really rewarding. Socially, it's a lot less diverse here. Forty percent of students are not on financial aid at all. That's crazy! They always say, "Sixty percent of students on financial aid. Let's celebrate!" That's insane! I've never been around that much wealth. Even if I don't think about it, I'm surrounded by wealthy people.

TONY: Renowned is more or less diverse than your high school?

VALERIA: Less; but that's not true. It has diversity that I haven't thought about. Renowned is diverse; it's just not the same. I don't know, I felt more comfortable in my high school. I associate diversity with being comfortable.

TONY: Why do you think you feel more comfortable in high school compared to Renowned?

VALERIA: Because more people can relate to my experience. I don't have to explain myself. Some things are a given. If I say, "Oh my god, it's expensive!" everyone agreed. No one ever suggested going to an expensive place, because we were all in the same income bracket. For dances, nothing was more than seven dollars. People will say, "No one is going to pay ten dollars. That's expensive." Here, I have to explain myself like, "That is too much to pay for this dance." And other people think, "No, it's a fair price." It's shocking. We're actually very different, and I haven't had to deal with that. I don't know if that's human nature, but it's nice to not have to explain yourself all the time. Here, less people get me.

Valeria characterized her academic journey as hard but rewarding, which she appreciated. Her social life at Renowned, however, proved to be rockier. Valeria, like Jose, equated diversity, which she defined as being around people from a similar class background, with comfort or even safety, something that she found hard to come by at Renowned.

One could argue that exposure to different people, customs, and ways of life is as important as the lessons students learn in their classes—that college is about expanding your worldview. But this learning too often comes in the form of poor students having to justify their decisions about what activities they do or do not want to partake in.

Not everyone is asked to explain themselves: poor students are often asked why they won't go out for dinner or to a dance club, but no one is asking rich students to justify spending $30 for a lobster. This lopsidedness is what unsettles the Doubly Disadvantaged. Valeria was astounded at what her new classmates took for granted. And when they questioned her sense of what was affordable, it seemed as though they were questioning her very way of life. More than being defensive about where she came from, Valeria became protective of it. She grew weary of having to explain herself.

Not all Doubly Disadvantaged students withdraw from campus life, though. Some try to integrate into the community. Ryan (DD,W), a lover of languages and history, came to Renowned from the hollows of rural Appalachia. Before college, all he knew was mining country. He lived with his widowed mother and two sisters. The men in his life had all died young from black lung disease, a common ailment caused by long exposure to coal dust. His mother worked two and sometimes three jobs to make sure Ryan and his sisters had what they needed. When Ryan got to campus he sought out new adventures. He found himself pledging one of the most exclusive fraternities. But his experience shows the social cost to joining up, especially for those who do not know the customs and rules that govern elite spaces:

> They took us to this big eating club. An eating club: I didn't know them things existed. A club for eating. I said, "What?" People there, you could tell they were old money. They were real high-class, fancy people. We sat down for dinner; it was a multicourse dinner. Back home, a multicourse dinner is going back to the fridge and getting some leftovers. They're bringing different sets of food, the final course, the dessert. They brought out this bowl of warm water. It had, I don't

know, herbs or something in it. I didn't know what that was. I thought it was some fancy, high-class dessert I'd never seen before, some kind of sugar water you're supposed to drink. I start to pick it up to drink. A real good friend of mine was like, "Don't! Don't do it!" Luckily I didn't. Yeah, I can speak about the big things that have been a difference coming to Renowned. But it's all the little things people have taken for granted. Bowl of water to wash your hands. Didn't know that. No idea. Yep.

Ryan and I shared a laugh. The hilarity mounted as we struggled to come up with the proper term for the water dish. Google eventually supplied the answer: finger bowl. I had never encountered one either; and, to be fair, I am sure most people have not. For Ryan, talking about, let alone joking about, this dinner was not always possible. At the time, he was mortified and embarrassed. Not knowing the rules of social life at this eating club seemed like another marker of his difference, along with his accent and his desire to smoke tobacco from a pipe once in a blue moon. After all, as Ryan joked, not many of his classmates could trace their roots to the Hatfields or the McCoys. He could. The "little things," in this case a finger bowl before the dessert course, truly tripped him up. Ryan never returned to the club. Moments like these turn students like Ryan away from these communities on campus, many of which have an even higher concentration of wealthy students than the general student body.[11]

For the Doubly Disadvantaged, Renowned is a whole new world. Frustrated at not being able to come up with a way to describe this experience, Joshua said, "I don't think I could name a similarity" between his home and Renowned. "I really don't know if I can. Culture shock!" he continued. Coming to Renowned underscored old realities of being poor, but it also highlighted new social constraints that only deepened students' sense of not belonging. Engaging with their peers made them feel like strangers in a place they could not fully call home. These encounters, which many of the Doubly Disadvantaged saw as assaults on their way of life, left them feeling socially isolated, emotionally drained, and, sometimes, angry. Their social and emotional well-being suffered. They encountered tacit social codes that they had never learned and that they struggled to decipher. They abhorred the fact that once they figured these codes out, even if they had wanted to abide by them (which many didn't), they were constantly reminded that they couldn't afford to, anyway. All these small reminders of difference added up to a large dose of alienation.

It's Just like High School

"Fifth year." "Next step." "Same old, same old." These are just some of the ways that the Privileged Poor described their transition from high school to Renowned. In contrast to the Doubly Disadvantaged, the Privileged Poor are not fazed by the campus culture or by their wealthier peers. Bolstered by years of socializing in prep schools, these students find that their experiences in high school—especially their interactions with well-to-do students—have prepared them for life at college. They navigate through Renowned much like their more affluent peers do. But this does not mean that life at Renowned is easy. Because of having grown up in troubled, disadvantaged communities, the problems they face disrupt campus life in ways that are wholly different from what their more affluent peers have to deal with. The constant fear of a call from home—whether a request for money to help pay a bill, or an announcement that someone has fallen victim to an attack by a local gang—keeps them on edge.

For the Privileged Poor, it is not a matter of whether they experience culture shock, but when. Culture shock occurred when they entered their private school, usually as high school freshmen, not when they entered Renowned as first-year undergraduates. Feelings of isolation and difference hit them when they left their distressed, often segregated public middle school for a posh, white private high school. Many of the students I interviewed described experiencing what has been called "assimilation blues"—the feeling of alienation that poor people feel in places that are supposed to provide them with a way out of poverty.[12] Michelle (PP,L), energetic and bouncy, participated in the New York City program Prep for Prep and entered an all-girls private school the summer before eighth grade. "It was terrible. It was so bad," she exclaimed. "Going to prep school was the biggest culture shock I've ever had in my life." Up until eighth grade, she said, "I had a lot of friends, all minorities." In high school, things changed:

> I went from having mostly guy friends, minorities coming from the same background, to all of a sudden being placed into this new world where you don't know the culture. It's a lot more proper and very sophisticated. You got to be this little perfect woman, budding woman. You need to be, I don't know, composed. And I think that's partially the reason why I used to just block anyone from going into my world.

Michelle was not used to being composed, at least not in the way that her private school wanted her to be. Socializing only with girls her own age was new. Having classes with wealthy people, and white people, was new. Watching crew teams practice on the river that ran along the edge of campus was new. The transition was unsettling. In fact, she hated it. She felt alone and had trouble connecting with her new classmates. Everyone had friends already, and she was the new kid who lived on the other side of the tracks. "No one would accept me for who I am," she said, so her strategy was "to reject everyone." "I'm not talking to anyone," she decided. Ninth grade, which came with a change of campus, was a welcome restart for Michelle. People got shuffled around and new students arrived. Michelle eventually found friends—first other scholarship students, and then teammates, and ultimately other students as well. Michelle got used to life in a ritzy place; it helped that she had to play sports as part of her scholarship and that she saw the same people day after day for three years. She slowly integrated herself into the community. "By the end of high school I was more accustomed to it, clearly. It was five years of my life." The biggest difference between high school and Renowned for Michelle was boys.

Michelle's story highlights another difference between students who have attended prep schools and those who haven't. Whereas the Doubly Disadvantaged experience the transition to a new environment during early adulthood, the Privileged Poor make their transition during adolescence, a time when young people can more easily adapt to change and are more willing to try new things.[13]

Like Michelle, Piper (PP,A) also found it unsettling to enter a private high school. The daughter of Asian refugees who had found their way to Washington State, Piper grew up relying on the charity of others. In eighth grade, her older brother found out about scholarships for students from poor families to attend boarding school and, going behind their parents' back, convinced Piper to apply. The transition to her private school in ninth grade was a painful one even if, four years later, it ultimately eased her move to Renowned. She noted of her two transitions, "They're different in different ways." Piper continued,

I think it was six or seven of us out of seventy in senior class that were from lower socioeconomic backgrounds. Diversity was not that great. Boarding school was a huge culture shock to me because I've never been exposed to that type of culture. The people at my boarding school didn't flaunt their privilege or wealth but obviously, as someone who comes from a lower socioeconomic background, you can tell, you know. That was difficult or just awkward because people would be like, "Hey, let's go to this place and eat out." It will be crazy expensive, and you don't really have the funds. Having that conversation is really awkward. Some of my classmates were white and I always felt there was a barrier because they couldn't truly understand some of the issues or just challenges that I face as an Asian kid from a poor neighborhood. . . . Boarding school was the first time I felt like I was a minority. The other piece of it was money. I just felt so indecent, not indecent, but I felt really poor at my boarding school. A lot of the times, just seeing what my classmates had and could afford, could easily afford, made me very self-conscious about my class background. My transition here has been less focused on my class and my race and more so about community.

Piper sounds here like a Doubly Disadvantaged student. Her new peers' wealth—and the privileges it afforded them—made her uneasy. She became hyperaware of her own background. Like Michelle, and the Privileged Poor more generally, however, Piper endured this shock several years before going to college. For her very expensive boarding school, it was a point of pride that nearly 10 percent of students had full scholarships. But Piper was looking from the other side of the statistic.

Being one of the few minorities in her school brought race to the forefront of her mind for the first time in her life. Yet, while her race and class were salient to her understanding of self in high school, she downplayed both as factors influencing her sense of belonging at Renowned. Instead, she focused on the difference in size between her small boarding school community and the larger one she discovered at Renowned.

The private schools that the Privileged Poor went to are significantly more affluent than the local neighborhood schools they would have attended. They were keen to speak about how their prep schools mirrored Renowned, especially in terms of their fellow students. "The backgrounds of the people I've met at Renowned virtually reflect the backgrounds of people I knew in high school," said Nick (PP,L). With the exception of Emma (PP,B), who attended a predominantly black private school in Maryland, their schools were much whiter, too. Javier (PP,L) called Renowned "really, just a huge amplification of prep."

Continuity fostered comfort. Stephanie (PP,B), wearing her signature white, collared shirt and pastel pants, said that Renowned was "literally déjà vu." Of all the students I spoke with, she had entered private school earliest, in sixth grade. Her parents, after moving out of a housing project that was continually raided because some of the apartments served as trap houses, let her accept a scholarship to go to boarding school. After such a long stint as a boarder, she felt well prepared for Renowned. In some ways, too well prepared. While her peers marveled at the newness of Renowned, she called college "banal." Stephanie explained why:

> I've been boarding since I was ten. I've been in this environment longer than most, being away, living out of a suit-

case, living around students. Y'all are excited. I don't really care. Freshmen are like, "Oh my god. There are guys in the bathroom." The things that are exciting for people coming to college were very banal to me and not even in a snooty, "I've already done this" kind of way. Yes, it smells like Renowned; that's what my high school smells like. I wish I were excited. This experience is kind of blah 'cause I was used to it.

In a thoughtfully blasé manner, Stephanie described how eight years of boarding in one of New England's most storied private schools left her, in some respects, jaded. In addition to being "prepared to socialize around white people," Stephanie was even accustomed to less discussed aspects of college life like running into boys in the bathroom.

Not everyone was so unmoved by what they found inside the college gates. Marina (PP,L) found life at Renowned to be exciting. She filled her social calendar with lectures, town hall discussions, and movie viewings that matched her diverse interests. Her relationship with her girlfriend was going well. She enjoyed her classes and relished exploring the communities that neighbored the campus. For her, Renowned was a "good fit" on a number of levels. When I asked how much of a match there was between herself and Renowned, she said, "Definitely 10 out of 10." She elaborated on the high score:

Coming from a small school, it's big enough. You find your niche. You find your group. I have. I'm very happy and fortunate. You run with those people. You meet your people. You expand your network. There's great people here. I haven't really met anybody like, "Stay away from me." Definitely not on such a level that I would say that I don't feel like I fit in.

In contrast to Jose (DD,L), who lamented not finding people he could relate to, Marina not only found her people, but also branched out from her initial group of friends and expanded her social network. She didn't feel isolated or out of place.

The Privileged Poor often described Renowned as more racially and socioeconomically diverse than their high schools. "I didn't know what to do having students of color; I was so excited I didn't know what to do," Patrice (PP,L) said earnestly. "That was new, having students of color here." Although she came from one of her city's most segregated neighborhoods, the last time she had black and Latino classmates was in middle school. Similarly, Ogun (PP,L), who was fascinated with social justice and history, remembered catching herself saying out loud as she walked around the freshman quad, "Wow, there's so many black people here!" She continued, "Sometimes, I feel like I go to an HBCU [historically black college or university] except when I'm in class. My social scene is an HBCU scene. I go to black events. We go to parties playing hip-hop, reggae. We go to LatinX meetings."[14]

Going deeper, Ogun discussed many parallels between her private boarding school and Renowned that extended beyond racial diversity but that also bolstered her sense of belonging. From classes to dorm life, she said that college is "the same thing, the same thing":

> Buildings are named the same. Glenn Hall [a lecture hall at Renowned] is where I had history class in high school. Wade, that's the library where I had my Renowned interview. Here, we have Wade the dorm. Convocation, I had that. Same holidays. I had an adviser in high school like the adviser I have here. The unwritten rules are the same too. It's ok to do some things but not others. For instance, in class, it is ok to

question authority but it depends on how you do it. . . . It's like a fifth year. I wouldn't say it's completely that, but it can feel like that. I live here now so that's different. I feel secure; my school prepared me for this. I know people here. A lot of people who've graduated from my high school said Renowned was easy. I don't think Renowned is easy but I don't think Renowned has been inexplicably hard when my outside life isn't influencing me. My whole life has been struggling with health care issues, things like that. When outside forces aren't influencing me, using the skillset I used throughout high school, Renowned's definitely doable.

With its familiar building names and institutional customs, Renowned did not shake Ogun. It also helped that there were familiar faces on campus, since her boarding school sent many students to Renowned every year. Even the unwritten rules, she intimated, were the same.[15]

Nevertheless, Ogun's familiarity with and knowledge of elite spaces did not completely buffer her from problems back home. As she noted, she could handle—and even enjoyed—Renowned "when my outside life isn't influencing me." Problems at home, like losing friends and family members to gang activity—something that disproportionally affects black, Latino, and poor students—often puncture the security bubble that surrounds students at a place like Renowned. Ogun knew this first hand. Speaking generally about home, she noted, "A lot of people got shot. The first hot day of the summer, you always know someone's going to get shot or stabbed. I lost a lot of people to violence." One drug-related incident stood out more than others. "I lost a friend, he was stabbed to death. . . . His buddy killed him. I'm not really over his death. He lived in the place that was the crack house. He lived on the first floor. The second floor was where they made it, sold it." She struggled to come to terms with losing a dear friend. She also worried about how to help her mother, who lived not too far from where her friend was killed, get the medical care she needed. Concern about rising rent due to gentrification kept her up at night. She did not know how long her family would be able to afford their apartment. Ogun also had to serve as the intermediary and interpreter for her mother at various state welfare agencies. These things— in addition to her twenty-page history paper and physics midterm— weighed on her, taxed her bandwidth, and interrupted life on campus in ways they typically did not for her affluent peers.[16]

Just because the Privileged Poor are accustomed to being around wealthy white people does not mean that they experience no unwelcome surprises. Some exchanges with their new peers at Renowned highlighted their classmates' blind spots. Others highlighted their ignorance. Like Ryan (DD,W), Jessie (PP,B) investigated joining different clubs. She understood that these clubs "might be useful for people that want to have connections and networks" that could help them after graduation. When she interned on Wall Street during high school, her bosses told her that being a member of clubs and organizations in college would help her in the long run. Jessie took their advice to heart and joined the most exclusive sorority on campus, where she enjoyed intimate contact with rich, mostly white peers in private spaces. But, unlike for Ryan, this was nothing new for Jessie. She went to a boarding school with a long history of educating the children of wealthy families from all over New England (and the world, for that matter). Still, one experience in the sorority hit too close to home. As part of the hazing ritual to initiate new members, the leaders of the sorority commanded new recruits to take selfies with the homeless people who occupy the benches and stoops around the campus. She hated seeing her peers secure these photos. Although she refused to participate, the memory of the incident was painful. For Jessie, life before Renowned was marked by instability and insecurity. "I just didn't want to hear sirens anymore," she said. "I've seen my dad get arrested. I've just had multiple incidents with the police in my life. I'm just tired of being around them." Disruptions and dislocations were frequent. From a friend's house in Arizona to transition homes in New Mexico, "I really don't know how many times we moved. Let's start like this, elementary school, I moved all five years. Middle school, I moved twice." The first time Jessie stayed in one place for longer than two years was in boarding school. As someone whose family had struggled to maintain a roof over their heads, Jessie resented her sorority sisters' insensitivity. Their wealth did not bother her; their callous disregard for others did.

Sometimes differences in trajectories to college caused tension between lower-income students. Conversations about being poor at Renowned could prove rocky, highlighting the hybrid reality that the Privileged Poor experienced. Patrice (PP,L), lounging on the couch in my office, discussed this duality. She claimed that, other than early (albeit short-lived) jitters, fitting in socially at Renowned was no big deal:

No matter how much people say the culture is upper-class, white male, I don't believe that. Those can be the most awkward people here. I definitely fit in here. At first, I didn't feel that way not because I was a Latina, not because I was poor, but because I felt I wasn't as bright as everyone else. But that's stupid. I definitely fit in here. I like places on campus that are my own. I have my own study space; it has a nice view. I like visiting places. I enjoy knowing the campus because I feel at home here. When people don't know where to go, I love telling them where things are. I share random facts with them like, "Did you know there's this store that has this thing or a museum here that you can get in for free with an ID?"

For Patrice, Renowned was home. She did not reject generalizations about the school being rich and white. Rather, she questioned the social primacy of those who fit that description. Her family background might not match that of the traditional Renowned student, but her academic pedigree did: she graduated from one of the oldest boarding schools in the country, which had long sent students to Renowned. In no uncertain terms, Patrice brushed aside her racial and class background as a barrier to fitting in. Patrice was so comfortable at Renowned that she served as an unofficial campus ambassador to visitors and new students trying to find their way around campus.

When her friends mentioned how different and difficult Renowned was for them, Patrice would proclaim her love for it and remark that it was "the same as high school." Her answer did not always sit well with them. And her friends' responses cut deep. During one late night conversation in the dorm common room, Alice (DD,L) scolded Patrice for her uncritical stance: "You're elite. Shut up. You don't understand. You're Latina, but you're elite. You think you're from there but you're not . . . look at the way you dress and speak." Patrice explained how her peers' dismissive remarks made her "feel less of a Latina":

> They tell me I haven't been home to suffer and struggle when teachers just don't show up, you're the only one in the classroom that actually cares, or when you have to do a lab report but don't have a lab at your school. "You had people help you through the college process. Of course your essay was

extra polished, you had twenty people read it. We didn't have all that in public school. Your school takes you on trips and pays for you?" It hurts. Getting here was a long road for me. I told you my story about my family and fighting to go away and to stay there. I understand; I had a lot of help. But that's why I went to boarding school. I wanted help. I'm really grateful for it. That's why I really admire people who didn't have help and still got here but I don't think that means I worked less hard to get into here.

Patrice had never discussed with anyone else how much Alice's words disturbed her. She sat on the couch, uncomfortably still, with her head bowed and eyes watery. The jibes from her peers hurt because they devalued the sacrifices she had made to get to college.

Patrice was not alone. Anne (PP,W), a round-faced senior, had a passion for creative writing that showed through in the quotes she had scribbled all over her sweater with colored markers. Before Renowned, she had lived an itinerant life. The Great Recession depleted her family's already limited resources, forcing Anne and her mother to live with different friends around the country—from Oakland to San Jose to Tucson—until her mother finally secured a job at a high-end retail store in the Midwest. When they finally settled down, she earned a scholarship from a local private school. She spent time studying abroad and visited her friends' vacation homes. Most of her classmates were white, but she also befriended a number of international students from Asia. "Because my high school friends were wealthy," Anne began, as she reflected on her new life at Renowned, being around people with money "wasn't shocking to me." She knew that not everyone could say the same, especially the lower-income roommates she had freshman year. "I didn't feel it so strongly as friends who are also low-income or first-gen." This difference in perspective on class issues—especially around wealth and privilege—caused problems within their dorm room. They fought often. Anne felt like her roommates ganged up on her. They only roomed together their first year. What was "weird" about Renowned, said Anne, echoing Kramer (UI,B), was being "around people who were more academically prepared in small details than I was. That was shocking."

The Privileged Poor who attend selective colleges might encounter some exceptional peers, but the culture as a whole feels familiar. Unlike the Doubly Disadvantaged, they have practice navigating elite spaces, and the similarities between high school and college bolster their sense of belonging. But they are not inoculated from poverty's influence. Family troubles and neighborhood woes, and even their classmates' responses to their divergent experiences, complicate their otherwise smooth transitions. These experiences of tension underscore how larger social inequalities limit the extent to which early exposure and cultural knowledge can mute the effects of culture shock and promote a sense of belonging in college.

Broadcasting Privilege

Students from more economically secure families have access to items and experiences that those from poor families generally do not. This difference manifests itself in many ways, from the clothes students bring with them to college to the off-campus activities they discuss while walking to class. At Renowned, students talked about clothes—a lot. In my conversations with them, they did not focus on style choices, like chic versus urban, or hipster versus WASPy. Rather, they discussed how certain clothing brands sent a signal about the wearer's background. The same went for vacations. Looking at other students' clothing, or talking with them about their vacation plans, often underscores the gaps that divide students from each other.

(Parents') Purchasing Power

At Renowned, clothes quickly become a proxy for class. This method of assessing wealth is imperfect; so many students wear sweats and hoodies that one would think the college was a four-year pajama party with classes sprinkled in. But if one student sports a $895 Burberry raincoat while another wears a $69.99 coat from H&M, or one has on $75 Vineyard Vines breaker shorts that stop well above the knee and the other has on $29.99 Levi's cargo shorts that extend below it, you get a pretty good idea of what each student spends on clothes.

Similarly, when a freshman walks into his dorm room, looks around, and, unimpressed with what he sees, calls an interior decorator to do a complete makeover, private wealth becomes public knowledge. And when, in another dorm across campus, a student offers one of her roommates $500 to let her have the single room of the two-room triple so that she does not have to share, she is broadcasting her privilege. The first scene is not out of the cable TV series *Property Brothers*. The second is not from *Gossip Girl*. Both occurred at Renowned. While some undergraduates settle for cheap decor and tight quarters, others wish for more luxurious surroundings, and they are not afraid to make that known to their peers.

In other words, demonstrating membership in the upper class is not cheap. But some students do not think twice about the price. In my conversations with students from affluent backgrounds at Renowned, they spoke openly about the privileges they enjoyed. "I love to decorate. I went harder with decorating than my roommates. . . . Fashion plays a big deal in what I think about," Marie (UI,B) began. Looking excited, she continued,

I brought a lot of clothes. My mom was very concerned about that; she didn't want me to appear to be too spoiled or too privileged. A lot of what I have would fit into what a typical Renowned student wears. There's pressure to conform. I think it's a stereotype; it's not true, because you see a diverse range but having a North Face . . . I did not mean to buy a North Face jacket but I did. It's not necessary, but labels make a difference. I grew up in an environment that has similar label pressure. I fell into that.

Marie had casually put down, next to her black North Face jacket, a jade Le Pliage tote from Longchamp, another of the most popular brands at Renowned. Since she had opened the door to talking about labels and the pressure to buy certain brands, I walked through it and asked her about her choice of purse. With a Cheshire cat grin, she said, "It's a Longchamp." She rolled on:

I get it. It was hot in high school. I bought one in ninth grade. Everybody had one. I bought it when I was studying abroad in France. When I bought these "marker items," I was definitely in a phase when material things meant more than they do now. I wanted to conform to an image. In Jack and Jill, these markers were signs of a black person having made it.[17] My Hunter boots weren't a fashion statement; it was saying I am now competing in this assimilated culture that I know I fit into. I think so. That's the way I saw it and saw it manifested in my friends, but it's a total stereotypical marker look. You can look around campus and count who's wearing the same boots, carrying the same bag, has the same Ray-Bans? It's all very calculated.

Marie's connection with Longchamp, which makes purses that range in price from $150 up to several thousand dollars, started long before Renowned. Fittingly, she purchased her purse in France, where the company was founded. Marie spoke about her other trips abroad—both alone and with her family—in the same way she did about her clothes: as a sign of progress for her family, specifically, and for black families, more generally. She shared these adventures with many people who crossed her path. She was very proud to be the daughter of two black doctors, and she did not want it to be overlooked by anyone, especially her white peers. And she knew how to make sure that did not happen. Marie knew the rules. As she noted, "It's all very calculated." Those careful calculations resulted in a curated style. In her closet were the same brands that the other wealthy students had—whether white, black, or otherwise. Even though she complained about her Longchamp purse lacking the functionality of other brands, she valued what it signaled about her family as it rested on her arm while she walked around campus.

Marie was right that Hunter was the brand of choice for rain boots at Renowned. As soon as it began to sprinkle, students would put on their Hunter boots as they trekked to class. Students' love for these boots did not go unnoticed by local businesses. One night, about halfway through collecting data for this book, I passed the university store en route to dinner. Something shiny and black caught my eye. A circular table laden with Hunter boots stood sentinel just within the door, instead of the usual T-shirts and sweaters emblazoned with the college name and logo. The cheapest pair on display cost $169. The store also sold Hunter socks, at $50 a pair. This prime location suggested to patrons—visitors, students, and parents alike—how central this brand was to undergraduate life at Renowned.

Out of My Price Range, Out of My Comfort Zone

Not everyone has the same purchasing power; the brands popular on campus and the excursions that are the topics of discussion in the common rooms are out of reach for students from poor backgrounds. The Doubly Disadvantaged distance themselves from peers who live the high life, those who spend excessive amounts on clothes and trips. The fact that their peers are free to do such things stands in stark contrast to their worries about how to afford basic necessities. To the Doubly Disadvantaged, anyone who spends money in what they consider an extravagant way does not know the value of either hard work or an honest dollar.

Dripping with pride, Miranda (DD,L) told me that her parents worked "freaking hard" to support their family. Both of them often took on second jobs as janitors to make ends meet. "My dad worked nights and through the day; he would also clean a couple of buildings. My mom would work, clean buildings." Miranda admitted being nervous when she learned that her freshman year roommate's parents were both surgeons and alumni of Renowned. Meeting them did not help. When she arrived on campus, her parents could only afford to stay that morning because they couldn't take any more time off from work. They drove through the night, dropped her off with her things in the morning, and headed back after a hearty breakfast and an emotional goodbye. It did not take long for Miranda to unpack. She mainly brought clothes from home and a few pictures of her family. By the time her roommate came in with her parents, sister, aunt, and grandparents, along with six suitcases, several boxes, and furniture, she had already shuffled her few things into place. After a quick hello, the questions started. Miranda spent most of the conversation uncomfortably deflecting questions about her family. "They assumed my siblings are in school. 'Where did they go to college? Did they come here too?' I told them, 'No; they didn't go to college. They're working.' They're like, 'Where do they work?' I'm trying to cover up the fact that my sister is in prison." Once the family left, Miranda began noticing differences between her and her roommate that undermined their relationship further. She explained,

> I feel very insecure about my clothes. I was like "Oh, snap," because with my roommate, everything is designer. She had a lot of stuff, and everything was name brand. I can't even think of the names because I'm so disconnected from that. For example, our winter coats, I had ZeroXposur, which is like a Sears brand. She had a ton of North Face. I was like "Oh, those look nice." Because I got a winter coat scholarship, I went to North Face to buy something. I was like, "What? Hell no!" It kind of helped me realize, "Oh, wait. She has a ton of this stuff like nothing." If I have nice stuff, it was on sale, a gift, or to be perfectly honest, I got it at a thrift store.

Miranda's eyes were bigger than her budget. When she entered the North Face store, she did not expect that the jackets would cost so much more than her ZeroXposur jacket, which went for about $48. Spending that much money on "nice things," even when aided by scholarship money, was well outside her comfort zone.

While I was conducting my interviews, North Face reigned as king of the mountain when it came to jackets. Almost overnight, Canada Goose, which cost around $745 for a basic black down jacket, became the brand of choice on campus for those who could afford it. The same judgment that the Doubly Disadvantaged launched against those with multiple North Face jackets carried over to their discussions of Canada Goose. Their criticism was a little sharper, however, probably owing to the price differential between the two brands.

Yet, even the rise (or supremacy) of Canada Goose seemed short-lived. Walking around campus toward the end of my time at Renowned, I noticed a smattering of Moncler jackets, vests, and parkas, which range in cost from $995, for a sleeveless vest, to $5,710, for a parka lined with fox fur.[18]

Even book bags provided a platform to make a fashion statement. At one point, every other backpack on campus was a Herschel pack. Toward the end of the same year, a new brand emerged as a contender. Soon, the squarish Fjällräven backpacks, emblazoned with a logo of a fox, were everywhere. The "it" brand is constantly changing, and the Doubly Disadvantaged are keenly aware when their wealthier peers take up new styles.

Clothes and fashion were not the only markers of difference the Doubly Disadvantaged students talked about. They also felt uneasy when their classmates chatted about their vacations or posted about them on social media. Snapchat stories—short sequences of photos and videos that disappear immediately after being viewed—sometimes revealed lavish seats inside private planes, or chronicled students' adventures in different countries. Even the coded language of resort locations could leave students feeling like outsiders. The Hamptons, Tulum, the Left Bank, MV—casually mentioning their trips to these popular destinations, wealthy students assumed their classmates had been there, or at least knew where they were.

Not everyone knew what or where these places were and not everyone wanted to be included in these conversations. Some students balked at even hearing such destinations being discussed at all. Melanie (DD,L), with a dimple-adorned smile that quickly slid from her face, outlined her adversarial relationship with privilege and with Renowned. She recounted being caught off guard by one of her class-mates' recent trips:

> To be perfectly honest, Renowned wasn't anything that I didn't expect. I was just way more *not* prepared for it than I thought I would be. It was just a lot at once. I've gotten glimpses of what college might be throughout high school. I came to visiting weekend. I was like, "Oh, this looks cool." Then, I got here. Oh no! No! I don't know if I can do this. I don't know if I can make freaking small talk to somebody who's from a different world than I am. I encountered kids freshman year who got on a plane and flew to India for a friend's wedding in the middle of the semester! I was like, "I can't talk to you!" What am I going to say? "How was India? Did you get that paper done on the plane?" It's just so surreal. I can't talk to you. That was shocking, this totally new culture that I was just not familiar with.

Melanie's "small glimpses of college" during high school were like drinking from a water fountain. Being at Renowned as a full-time stu-dent was like drinking from a fire hydrant. Melanie felt like she could not relate to any of her peers, and she didn't think it would be possible to become friends with students who came from such a different world—students who could travel halfway around the world during the school year just to go to a wedding.

Same Stuff, Different School

Canada Goose and Moncler did not disturb the Privileged Poor nearly as much as they did the Doubly Disadvantaged. Neither did their peers'

vacation destinations or lavish purchases. They had already encountered these displays of wealth in high school. They knew that these
items and experiences were out of their price range. And they reported
not being bothered by it. Virginia (PP,B), who left a troubled middle
school to attend an elite, all-girls private school, laid out why that was
the case. Wearing an outfit inspired by nineties hip-hop, her hair in box
braids that fell well below her shoulders, Virginia told me, "Renowned
is just a continuation of high school, but with more people." Asked
about what it was like to interact with wealthy peers at Renowned, she
said pointedly, "That was my only option in high school." Students at
her high school left their belongings lying around; everything from
phones to wallets to violins that cost tens of thousands of dollars. Her
school library, overflowing with books, had forty Apple MacBook Pro
laptops for students to use at any time. She realized early on that she
was better prepared for Renowned than some of her friends were. "By
going to private school," she explained, "I was prepared for white people
and wealthy people who are here. Things like that don't really shock
me, don't really make me feel a certain type of way."

The Privileged Poor get a sense of their peers' lavish lives that goes
beyond walking through Mercedes-filled parking lots and listening in
on discussions of whether to summer on Martha's Vineyard or in the
Hamptons. They are sometimes included in the experiences themselves. For example, learning that I was to attend an anniversary gala
at the exclusive restaurant and event venue Cipriani Wall Street,
Virginia (PP,B) snapped her fingers and said, "You fancy!" Laughing,
I asked why. "Google it, Tony," she commanded with a smile. Looking
at the website, I marveled at the beautiful building, with its grand ball-
room and mile-high domed ceiling adorned with constellations. I
learned that prominent families from around the world would have engagement parties and weddings there. Laughing at the look of shock

on my face, Virginia informed me that her first trip to Cipriani was during her sophomore year in high school, for a friend's sweet sixteen party. She laughed again, remembering that her dad had picked her up in the family's old Dodge Caravan, while her peers arrived in Mercedes-Maybachs and Range Rovers. Apparently renting such spaces was common at her school. One student's family rented out space at the Waldorf-Astoria in New York City for her birthday party and gave American Girl dolls to all the guests as party favors.

Unlike Patrice (PP,L), whose lower-income peers questioned how she could feel so comfortable in rich, white places, Virginia said she "never butts heads" with poor friends who traveled different paths to Renowned:

> At the end of the day, they know where I really came from. At the back of their minds they're like, "Yeah, you went to a rich, private school but we know where you're from." For example, they were talking about one of our friend's roommates. They're like, "She wants to spend $200 on a scarf! That's crazy!" My response was just, "What am I supposed to do about that? I've seen worse." If she wants to, let her. If that's her lifestyle, let that be her lifestyle. My friends who have never experienced that would be like, "I don't understand. You just can't do that. Why would you ever do that?" Maybe because I had those experiences younger or in high school when I would say, "She's spending $1,000 on that wristwatch! Why would she do this?" As time went on, I was like, "That's the lifestyle they live."

Virginia's culture shock had already worn off. "My friends at Renowned are experiencing something I experienced years ago," she pointed out.

What might have seemed extravagant or gaudy for her peers, who were experiencing intimate contact with wealthy people for the first time, was old hat for Virginia. "They're having a thought process I had years ago in private school," Virginia said. "That's the difference; I'm a little ahead of the game."

Months later, I found Virginia on her laptop in the cafeteria. I asked if I could join her. "Sure, I'm just watching Netflix," she responded. Asking me how work was going, I told her that while Jeanine (DD,W) and I were sitting on a bench outside having coffee, we overheard one of their classmates on the phone reserving a restaurant for her family and thirty-five friends for a graduation party. The contrast between their two reactions was telling. Jeanine snorted, rolled her eyes, threw her hands in the air, and shook her head. Virginia simply asked which restaurant.

In addition to entering college already accustomed to seeing friends spend thousands of dollars in short periods of time, the Privileged Poor had the chance to go on excursions that are usually reserved for the rich. Many of the prep schools they attended offered study abroad opportunities for all students, including those on scholarship, so they were able to leave the country to learn, live, and, yes, party. They talked about visits to museums and outings taken all over Africa, Asia, Europe, and South America before entering college. When college classmates recalled trips to Marseilles or São Paolo, the Privileged Poor often joined these conversations with their own list of international destinations. Nicole (PP,B), a junior with a distinctive, infectious laugh, said, "I'm prepared to interact with rich, white people." She talked about how she navigated discussions about travel:

> People travel a lot. In conversations with a lot of women, especially wealthier women, there's a lot of talk about Europe, South America, or "Oh, I was in France two weeks ago.

Me and my family backpacked around wherever." When I was in high school, I got to experience these things with my friends. People were talking about their yacht, where they bought houses. . . . I learned how to engage in conversation, and the conversations are going in similar ways in college. Especially after going to France, too. It's really easy to play the part. Sometimes you want to hide your socioeconomic status. I've learned to hide my socioeconomic status pretty well. But as I get older, that's just part of who I am, and it's not important for me to do that anymore. Sometimes it's necessary to move up on the social ladder here to be able to engage in these conversations and to be able to say like, "Oh, when I was in France last summer I was, blah, blah" or to talk about designers.

Unlike Melanie (DD,L), who became angry after hearing her classmates talk about traveling to India for a wedding, Nicole entered Renowned having already experienced four years' worth of casual mentions of trips and large purchases by, to use her words, "dangerously wealthy" high school peers. But that was not all that Nicole experienced. Because she had studied abroad herself, Nicole had firsthand knowledge of the sights and sounds of Europe. Additionally, Nicole was able to code-switch, managing her peers' impressions of her by choosing when and how much to share about her life. She strategically chose when to chronicle her family's financial hardships and when to showcase her knowledge of France's hidden gems.[19]

⋙⋘

Familiarity breeds ease. Sociologists and education scholars have long posited that middle- and upper-class youth enjoy smooth college transitions, while their lower-class peers endure rough ones. Culture shock, however, depends less on class differences than it does on exposure to and knowledge of the norms of elite academic communities. The disparate paths that the Doubly Disadvantaged and the Privileged Poor take to college lead to drastically different experiences with culture shock, presenting new opportunities to refine our understanding of what influences college students' sense of belonging. The diverse experiences of students in these two groups do not reflect individual differences, but rather structural ones. Students who have already traversed elite academic spaces feel more at ease in navigating social life at elite universities than do those who are entering these spaces for the first time.

When students define what is or is not shocking about life at an elite university, we gain a better understanding of how their world works. More than just a picture of who does and does not fit in, we begin to see why and how some students feel a sense of belonging and others don't. In my interviews, the Doubly Disadvantaged spoke of grappling with both economic and social constraints from the very beginning of their time at Renowned. From the general culture of Renowned to specifics like dining out, clothes, and vacations, symbols of their peers' privilege contrasted with—and shed new light on—their own disadvantage. Beyond the specific brands or activities themselves, the Doubly Disadvantaged saw their peers' purchases, and their expectations for them to join in, as indications of the insurmountable gulf between them and both their classmates and the college as a whole. The boundaries they established between those who opted for "cheap" $30 lobsters instead of free food from the cafeteria, or those who purchased Canada Goose instead of Sears jackets, slowed down or in some cases prevented building bonds across class lines. Many simply withdrew from the community. Their distaste for environments like Renowned—enhanced by the negative experiences they had with their peers—could in turn affect their decisions about whether to enter similar elite settings after college.

In contrast, the Privileged Poor acknowledged their economic disadvantage but focused more on how similarities between their high school and Renowned—from everyday experiences of interacting with wealthy peers to particularities like the names of buildings—gave them a leg up on their lower-income peers. There was more at Renowned that was familiar than was different. Moreover, the Privileged Poor welcomed new opportunities to make friends with other students of color and students from poor backgrounds, since their high schools were predominately white and rich. These students were more inclined to integrate themselves into the college community, and as a result, they had access to a vast range of social and institutional resources.[20]

Although the Privileged Poor had an advantage over the Doubly Disadvantaged in navigating wealthy environments, that does not mean that social life at Renowned was a bowl of cherries. Social class remained relevant to their college experiences. They continued to face problems associated with growing up in poor households and distressed communities. Students do not stop being poor or lose all connection to their background when they enroll in college. Although the Privileged Poor faced fewer stresses associated with their college experiences, they shared stresses from home with other lower-income students.[21]

What can college administrators and educators do to help diminish the gap between lower-income and upper-income students? Although it may sound trite, we need to make a concerted effort to teach students about each other. Understanding your peers can help limit misunderstanding and exclusion. This expansion of worldview must go both ways, however. It is not just a matter of poor students adjusting to a world of wealth: upper-income students must learn to be more accepting of other students' ways of life. It is not the job of students from underrepresented groups to teach wealthy white students about their lives. Fostering dialogue about diversity means that everyone comes away knowing more about their campus and the wider community. Amherst College has a program, the Pindar Field Dinner Series, which aims to do just this—to celebrate diversity without highlighting differences. The president's office invites a randomly chosen group of students and one member of the local community to dinner, where they talk about their activities both inside and outside the college. The students have often never met each other before. These types of events, which extend conversations about diversity in the community beyond orientation week and are integrated into the rhythm of the academic year, have the potential to make connections between different members of the college and the broader community.

In addition to such programs, university administrators can do more to understand where students come from. Lumping all lower-income undergraduates together produces a distorted view of the experiences of poor students. The difficulty of adjusting to an environment like Renowned for the Doubly Disadvantaged cannot be understated. And while the Privileged Poor face some of the same difficulties, it is important to remember that their knowledge of elite academic settings helps ease their transition. Paying attention to these diverse experiences and the structural forces that influence them, such as poverty and segregation, can go a long way toward helping to design initiatives to promote all students' sense of belonging.

2

"Can You Sign Your Book for Me?"

I HOP OUT OF AN Uber, and my friend and I rush to the doors of the local independent theater. We are fifteen minutes late for a private film screening. Seeing many professors who teach at Renowned (and a few from neighboring colleges) in line at the ticket booth, we both breathe a sigh of relief. We are not the only ones running behind. While waiting, we strike up a conversation with the couple ahead of us. They explain the delay: the theater is waiting for one of the directors, who is to introduce the movie. Finally, tickets in hand, we make our way toward the theater. About halfway there, I see a familiar face, one that seems out of place among the professors and the college president: Marie, a black sophomore from an upper-class family who pulls off business casual better than most people twice her age. I wave hello. She waves back. Looking around, I notice that Marie is the only undergraduate here. I think to myself, "I was someone's plus one. How did she score a ticket?" While we all wait to be let into the theater, Marie takes a particular interest in one professor, gets her attention, and then knifes her way through the crowd with surgical precision until they are standing face to face. They exchange greetings and a friendly hug. Then they sit down on a nearby set of stairs to continue their conversation. A moment later, Marie reaches into her Longchamp bag, pulls out a hardcover book that looks as pristine as if it had just been removed from its Amazon packaging, and asks, *"Can you sign your book for me?"* The professor obliges with a warm smile. They continue talking until the bottleneck eases up. They are the last to enter the theater.

A constant refrain rings out across campus—the social call of professors at Renowned and other colleges across the country—"My door is always open." Many undergraduates at Renowned welcomed this openness. Some, like Marie, did not even wait for such offers before reaching out to faculty. The daughter of two physicians, alumna of an elite boarding school, and a legacy admit at Renowned, Marie walked onto campus already knowing the value of connecting with faculty. She betrayed an understanding, as keen as it was unapologetic, of how the bond between student and teacher is built both inside and outside the classroom. Long before I ran into her in the movie theater lobby, she told me, "I have such great fortune with my professors. I have very personal relationships with one of them, two of them actually. We go out for dinner. I go to office hours all the time. My relationships with professors and teaching assistants are all pretty good." In addition to having seen her parents develop rapport with their superiors as they worked their way up to become division chiefs at their hospital, Marie was educated in a place where personal, sustained contact with teachers was part and parcel of academic life. A theater full of faculty, deans, and the college president was no less familiar— or comfortable—a social scene for her than a night of Netflix with friends in the dorm common room.

Being at ease around authority figures in general, and being comfortable connecting with professors, more specifically, is not something that all undergraduates share, however. Students who are unfamiliar with or unaccustomed to this intimate style of engagement find the university's ubiquitous solicitations to connect with faculty odd, intrusive, and sometimes even terrifying. For some students, college is supposed to be about attending lectures, completing assignments, and studying for tests. Trying to figure out when, how, and even why personal connections are needed can paralyze them, expanding the gap between them and their professors. It undercuts their sense of belonging. Some students eventually give up. They simply avoid professors altogether.

Affluent students are typically more like Marie; they feel comfortable around professors and engage with them easily. These students know how to navigate social situations with professors because they have grown up in environments that taught them how to do so. By the time they enter college, they have interacted with adults as partners all along the academic and social journey toward commencement and beyond. They feel entitled to the time, as well as the resources, of these adults. But they are not the only students who feel this way.[1]

Scholars have argued that poor students' lack of cultural capital—a result of not having grown up in middle-class homes with middle-class norms—leads to emotionally taxing encounters with professors and "broad failures to understand faculty's expectations about the basic features of student performance."[2] But here is where I found that students' experiences at Renowned deviated from the standard story.

81

In focusing on how families transmit advantages and disadvantages to their children, researchers have downplayed the socializing force of high schools as well as the starkly different experiences of different groups of poor students. Although they may not have been born into families with inside knowledge of higher education, the Privileged Poor learn why they should connect with adults, and how to do so, in their private high schools—places where contact with teachers is a central part of the school's mission. By the time they enter college, they have come to view adults as facilitators to their academic, social, and professional goals, filling roles that those in their families and neighborhoods simply cannot. Consequently, the Privileged Poor are similar to their affluent peers: at ease and proactive in connecting with faculty, building support networks, and asking for help. The Doubly Disadvantaged, in contrast, are not. Faculty and administrators, for them, remain authority figures who should be treated with deference and left unburdened by their questions and needs. This lesson, which they learned at home, was reinforced in the distressed schools they attended.

Face time with faculty and administrators matters. During my time at Renowned, I saw again and again that forging these relationships was not just the way students got help with assignments and homework. Help on these kinds of specific tasks was just the tip of the iceberg. Relationships were a gateway for securing support for and achieving success in future endeavors. Developing rapport with key faculty and administrators was the road not just to assignment extensions, but also to letters of recommendation, on-campus jobs, and off-campus internships. And these connections also meant so much more: having a faculty member or dean in your corner often meant getting the benefit of the doubt when in a bind; or the single in the dorm with the nice windows; or introductions to corporate recruiters and help with negotiating job offers; or, like Marie, invitations to private screenings where you could meet the director of Academy Award–winning films. And the earlier students start developing these connections, the better their chances at securing such coveted benefits.[3]

But here's the rub: this expectation to be proactive in making connections with faculty often remains unsaid, thereby exacerbating pre-existing inequalities that exist between those who have already learned that they should reach out and those who have not. No manual of "dos and don'ts" or "whens and hows" circulates during freshman orientation at elite colleges. From day one, for example, professors and staff members alike casually throw around the term "office hours." They take it for granted that students know that office hours, at their most basic, are blocks of time during which professors make themselves available to students. Additionally, professors assume that students know how to make use of them and are comfortable doing so. Consequently, most professors operate according to the rule, "If undergraduates want something, they will come." Yet office hours are rarely defined, and many students have no idea how important they are beyond their stated purpose. When professors mention office hours, often only on the first day of classes, they tell students *when* office hours are. They almost never say *what* they are.[4]

In the fall of 2016 I discussed the issue of office hours with Dawn Poirier, dean of the School of Liberal Arts and Sciences at Dean College, a small, blue-collar liberal arts college in Massachusetts that "warmly welcomes at-risk learners" to pursue associate's and bachelor's degrees. She wanted advice based on my expertise about how to encourage academic engagement. I suggested that faculty at Dean should define office hours in their classes. This suggestion resonated with her, conjuring up powerful memories of what she had heard from her own students. "I made a discovery two years ago," Dawn said, "that many of my [lower-income] students interpreted 'my office hours' to be just that, my hours to spend in my office alone, [where] I was not to be disturbed. . . . Stepping back, it actually made sense that someone might get that idea." To those unfamiliar with the concept of office hours, this is a reasonable interpretation. After all, the term itself is not one you usually hear in casual conversation. Unfortunately, the logical conclusion that Dawn's students reached was the exact opposite of what professors and administrators mean by the term. This represents more than just a simple miscommunication. It highlights gaps in expectations between faculty and students about what is required to succeed in college, and it is also profoundly consequential—a roadblock to inclusion and belonging, one that impedes access to places where connections are made, bonds are forged, and information is shared.[5]

I have found that faculty and administrators across the country reward students based on how much those students engage them. This was certainly true at Renowned. Natalie, who had spent five years living in dorms as an academic adviser, shed light on how students came to be nominated for various awards, honors, and prizes (some of which involved significant amounts of money). Although all students are eligible for these honors, Natalie revealed that she and her peers tended to "nominate who they know, who they like, and who they find impressive." With a defiant yet uneasy glance up from her phone, she continued,

> I put it in that order because thoughts go straight to the students you know best. You win these prizes by what is not on your resume. . . . You are not going to know anything unless you really know that student. Students who college officials don't know are just not in the mix. Students who don't get nominated are either not known or not liked. If you draw a Venn diagram, the larger circle will hold those students who are not known.

Being on the radar of your advisers increases your likelihood of getting nominated. But "being known" means more than having them know your face and name. It is about knowing details about your family, life before college, interests, what activities you were involved in on and off campus, and your summer and post-graduation plans. Destiny, another residential adviser who attended Renowned as an undergraduate, put it simply: "The nomination process is relationship-dependent, unfortunately. It enables students who develop relationships a leg up in the process." Visibly unnerved, she lamented that "oftentimes the best candidates are not put forward; some students get nominated for more prizes more often. It is hard to tease out what is meritocracy and what is nepotism, favoritism, cronyism, or whatever you want to call it." Ties to professors and administrators proved to be almost a necessary condition for endorsement, undercutting the common belief that hard work is all you need to succeed. It is not just what and who you know, but also who knows you and how well they know you.[6]

Although Natalie's and Destiny's comments focused on honors, the same principle of "being known" applies to referrals for internships, fellowships, and jobs. The administrators I spoke with, who worked in different offices all over campus, knew this reality all too well. Molly, known for her bespoke suits and wire-rimmed glasses, directed the Career Explorations Office at Renowned. Her office hosted many events throughout the year, but it was mainly responsible for overseeing job fairs and on-campus recruiting as well as administering grants for travel and language immersion programs, unpaid internships, and other summer opportunities. Using the metaphor of "planting seeds," Molly told me that the students who developed relationships with faculty and administrators early on were in the best position to reap the full benefit of institutional resources. With her two decades of experience in college career counseling and student services, she knew that when professors write recommendation letters, the strongest letters go to the students they know best, something she impressed upon her staff at a summer training session I was invited to attend. Molly emphasized that the students her office could help the most were also those they knew the best, which included being aware of students' professional interests and their personal drives. Molly believed that creating this complete picture permitted members of her office to "pull all the levers" to help students, from securing grants for study abroad programs to negotiating their first contracts upon graduation. What Molly didn't seem as keenly aware of in our first meetings was that some students were too intimidated to come to her office or assumed that her office was not for people like them.

Academic life at Renowned, as at every university, is inherently social. Our understanding of the particulars of this dynamic, and how social class shapes it, contains blind spots. When starting my research, my goal was to answer the questions, Who is at home in this environment? Who is shocked by it? Who hits the ground running? Who stumbles? Those students who are not familiar with the unwritten rules are unaware of what they are being asked to do—unaware that a crucial part of college is more than mastering the material that they encounter in the classroom. As we will see, some students discover, to their great consternation, that they are also responsible for deciphering a hidden curriculum that tests not just their intellectual chops but their ability to navigate the social world of an elite academic institution, where the rewards of such mastery are often larger and more durable than those that come from acing an exam.[7]

86

In Chapter 1, we explored encounters between students and their peers. Here we'll explore how students interact with faculty and administrators, and how well they take advantage of resources the college provides for them. In the first part of the chapter I explore how comfortable different students are in their use of personal connections with faculty and administrators. In the second part, I address the question of how students use institutional resources and form networks with professors and staff. The final section looks at students' use of mental health resources. These issues are increasingly important, since students from a wide variety of backgrounds bring a multitude of perspectives and problems that many universities are ill equipped to handle. To help students in their transition and acclimation to college, we must first understand what kinds of help they need. One of the first steps in doing so is to get them into our offices to talk. Comparing the experiences of wealthier students with those of the Doubly Disadvantaged and the Privileged Poor can give us new insights into how poverty and privilege shape students' strategies for developing relationships with and securing support from professors and other members of the university community, along with new ideas about how best to support them in these endeavors.

At Ease or on Edge with Faculty

An act as seemingly simple as going to a professor's office hours can define a student's college career. Many of the faculty at Renowned are high-profile academics, and connecting with them—let alone enlisting one of them as a mentor—can change a student's life. Students may have read about some of their professors in newspapers before they arrive on campus. A few celebrity professors are household names, having appeared as experts or commentators in news broadcasts or even performed cameos in popular movies. Others are famous for doing cutting-edge research or for being brilliant lecturers. Some students revel in the opportunity to meet one on one with these stars and are at ease doing so; others struggle with the mere prospect of talking to their professors and seek to limit time with them or avoid them altogether.

Mine for the Taking

Undergraduates from upper-income families (UI) talked to me about interacting with the new cast of adults they found at Renowned as if it was no big deal. Reaching out for support was just what they did. They saw college as theirs for the taking. All but five of the twenty-seven students I interviewed described positive interactions with administrators, deans, and especially professors at Renowned. They enlisted them as mentors and turned to them as sources of support. They entered college inclined to seek out the help they needed, comfortable engaging with those who could assist them in securing that support, and equipped with the skills to do so.

Antoinette (UI,B), an astute freshman whose parents had both attended Renowned, reported that she was comfortable with professors right from the beginning. Her parents offered stories about their many connections with faculty during their time at Renowned; they even introduced her to two of their professors. Moving from boarding school to Renowned was, she said, a "smooth" transition. Her ease was bolstered by the fact that Renowned and her boarding school had similar expectations and rules for interacting with faculty. Although a little more effort was required at Renowned, the process was basically the same.

ANTOINETTE: At my boarding school, it was a given. The same people who were your dorm parents were your teachers. It was easier to make close connections because you're living with them. Literally. Here, it's different. You have to go seek that relationship; it's not going to come to you.

TONY: Do you feel okay doing that?

ANTOINETTE: I do. Because of my boarding school, I know it's possible. I've reaped the benefits of being close to faculty members in high school. Coming here, if I see someone who's awesome, I go. I'm in this English class that clearly has an awesome professor. I have more confidence to go to office hours and meet her in person.

Antoinette's boarding school, like Renowned, reinforced "the independence thing. You learn how to talk to teachers yourself. You learn to do what you have to do on your own and be responsible for all the things you have to do. . . . The amount that they mix students and teachers makes you feel more grown up than you are." Amplifying messages that she heard at home, her high school pushed students to be agents in their own development while it also provided ample opportunities for personal contact with and coaching from teachers. Relationships with faculty at Renowned were not as automatic because she saw her professors less frequently than she did the teachers in her high school, which was much smaller. But she felt comfortable all the same. She routinely attended office hours and requested one-on-one meetings with her professors, even as a freshman. Her ability to make these sorts of connections allowed her to become a key member of the university's Equality Center, where she led a number of initiatives aimed at bringing students and administrators together to foster dialogues about race, gender, and sexuality on campus.

Joe (UI,B), whose parents were health-care professionals, attended local public schools that catered to the surrounding middle-class neighborhoods. Like Antoinette, he regaled me with accounts of positive relationships with teachers. In high school, where he "thrived in small classes," Joe took every opportunity to demonstrate his personality and his achievements to his teachers and principal, something he claimed had helped him at Renowned. In describing his bond with one professor at Renowned, he said with a joyous smile, "I go to his office hours. I'm like his right-hand man; we're pretty cool." This relationship was carefully cultivated. Joe approached the professor; waiting on an invitation or introduction was simply not his style.

An interaction with one of Joe's teaching assistants (TA) underscores his ease not only at dealing with authority figures, but also at advocating for himself. Joe recalled a time when he thought he had been slighted out of the grade he deserved:

> I expect a lot of teachers: be compassionate, happy to help, make sure you understand and be understanding of where you are coming from, give advice. But, man, I had the weirdest encounter with a TA; it set me off. I hadn't done as well on the exam as I wanted to, so I went to her about a re-grade. Brought the idea up to her. And she was like, "That probably won't work." I was like, "I explained my point." She was like, "Yeah, but you have to say this." She didn't seem like she cared and that kind of pissed me off.

Joe, the self-proclaimed "right-hand man" to a prominent professor, was comfortable arguing for a re-grade, and he expected his TA to see things his way. A grade-conscious premed student, Joe told me he wanted an A− instead of a B+. He refused to simply accept the B+ without a challenge. Although his attempt was unsuccessful that time around, his comfort in advocating for himself would likely prove beneficial for him in the long run, both inside and outside the classroom.

Students from privileged backgrounds also felt at ease discussing social and personal matters with authority figures. Misha (UI,B), an aspiring spoken-word artist, recounted his successes in lobbying administrators to endorse gender-neutral bathrooms and housing for transgender students in all the dorms on campus. He outlined how their support of his own gender transition left him feeling both accepted and welcomed at Renowned. Calling his interactions "positive," he explained,

> I don't think I've had a bad one. I've had to meet with the housing coordinator; she was ridiculously nice. I don't know if the resident adviser counts, but the QueerPRIDE adviser is the nicest guy I've ever met. My residential adviser is nice enough, distant, but nice enough.

When invited by a dean to attend a staff meeting where senior administrators were to discuss issues facing transgender students, Misha felt empowered to talk on behalf of other students about what changes were needed to make the campus more inclusive. He valued having a seat at the table and worked to keep it until he graduated.

Beginning early in their careers at Renowned, students from more affluent families reported being comfortable connecting to administrators and professors for a myriad of reasons. They were content. They were assertive. As Brittany (UI,B) remarked, "I have no objections asking TAs for help. I never have fear. I'm a very confident person."

Moreover, reaching out was, for them, as much a part of their academic enrichment as the essays and problem sets their professors assigned in classes. They did not let many opportunities pass them by.

Unsettling Encounters

The Doubly Disadvantaged had a far more difficult time making connections with faculty. Corinne (DD,B), with an earnest look on her face, admitted that everything at Renowned constituted culture shock. Other than "the fact I'm in the same country," she said, everything was different. For the Doubly Disadvantaged, succeeding in college was about their coursework—"the work"—which they saw as paramount. They reported being anxious as they tried to navigate this new, more personal style of engagement. Consequently, they interacted with faculty less frequently than their peers. Head bowed and voice lowered, Marcia (DD,L) explained the difference she saw between herself and her peers: "Some people would call it privilege, but it's ease. A lot of the kids here just know how to act in these situations because they don't evaluate, they don't second guess themselves. I do." While others took action, she doubted if she could or should do the same.[8]

The Doubly Disadvantaged characterized the interactions they did have as tense, off-putting, and anxiety inducing. They generally lacked the desire to get to know the faculty and feared that they would stumble if they tried. Their reluctance persisted even as they realized (and sometimes saw) that their peers were reaping the benefits of forging these relationships. But a few of them did manage to overcome their fears. Lindsie (DD,B) is a case in point. Although she called her meetings with professors "awkward," and she generally avoided one-on-one interactions with them, she said of one professor, "He was cool; he was funny. I didn't talk to him, but my TA for that class was absolutely amazing. When I needed help with something or I wasn't quite sure, I would email her. She was really good at responding and saying, 'OK I understand; here's some help.'" Only a third of the Doubly Disadvantaged students I spoke with, however, reported positive relationships with professors, and sometimes even these relationships were strained.

Many of the Doubly Disadvantaged intentionally put distance between themselves and their professors. Shaniqua (DD,B), a round-faced senior with a sleepy demeanor, said that before college, she and her family were so poor that they considered anything above the poverty line to be high by comparison. They often were homeless for months on end. They lived in shelters in three different states, each one filled with addicts who repeatedly tried to get her hooked on heroin. Through all these challenges, Shaniqua developed the resolve to withstand tough times and excel academically in the four different high schools she attended, each one poor and segregated, where violent fights between rival Mexican and black gangs disrupted learning almost daily. Yet this form of resilience, which had once protected her from the ever-present disruptions of an unstable life, now handicapped her. She felt unable to advocate for herself in college.

SHANIQUA: When you're poor and you're homeless, you get used to taking what is given. You don't complain. Someone gives you a shirt, even if it's ugly, you wear it. Of course you'll be grateful. It's made it harder for me to advocate for myself. Part of me is like, "I've been given enough." It wouldn't really be good to rock the boat when you're homeless and depend on others. I make myself likable, being okay with what is given. I've gotten better but it's hard for me to advocate for myself. It's taken time to not feel guilty asking for extensions.

TONY: How long did it take you to feel comfortable?

SHANIQUA: I don't know how much of it is pressure or me feeling comfortable. Junior year was really good. I know I'm not comfortable now, as a senior, because I almost failed a class. I didn't reach out to the professor until he sent an email. Even though he said if you don't turn in this paper you'll fail, it wasn't until I got that email that I realized I needed to email him. For weeks, I just kind of sat and didn't do anything.

Unlike Joe (UI,B), the freshman who felt completely comfortable arguing with his teaching assistant for a higher grade, Shaniqua reported accepting what was given to her well into her junior year. Her strategy of withdrawing from professors placed her grades in jeopardy, and the stress of the situation paralyzed her. I ran into Shaniqua at a vending machine during the spring of her senior year, and she told me that she was wrestling with completing her senior thesis. I did not make much of her comment at first; many students around campus were complaining about their theses, as they all were due in less than a month. Shaniqua went on. She admitted that she probably should not have elected to write a thesis, since she struggled meeting deadlines. For a second-semester senior, her problem was a little more pressing than I initially realized. After a few more minutes of chitchat, she revealed the truth—she had not written a single page. Instead of keeping her adviser updated, she had left her in the dark. She eventually dropped the thesis, and her department admonished her for doing so at such a late date. Fortunately, Shaniqua was still able to graduate.

The Doubly Disadvantaged generally characterized the process of engaging with professors as emotionally taxing. Robbie (DD,W), a sophomore from a small rural town in the Midwest whose carefully coiffed hair contrasted with his casual red-and-black plaid shirt, expressed this general feeling. "I'm very much about doing as much as I can myself and only then asking for help, because I feel bad asking for help," he said. "It's hard to put into words, but I feel guilty." Robbie felt as if his issues were just that: his. Professors, to him, were not to be bothered. Similarly, Rosalind (DD,W), a rosy-cheeked sophomore, conceded that, when it came to meeting with faculty, "I'm pretty bad at it. I have not gone to office hours this year, even last year." Even after suffering a concussion in the fall of her freshman year, which made her college transition "a hot mess," she avoided her professors, residential advisers, and even her peers because she was "not very comfortable" at Renowned. She explained:

> When I got my concussion last year, it was a very long time before I talked to anyone. I had this final exam, and I just broke down. I went to my residential adviser; I broke down crying. I was like, "I can't do this." I finally had to admit that I was struggling. It had been over a month with memory problems; double vision; and concentration, sleeping, emotional issues. I had really been struggling for over a month and hadn't reached out to anyone for help because I thought I could do it on my own. But I had to finally admit I needed help. I did get assistance, but I never followed up with these people. I don't like asking for help.

In the throes of trying to study and socialize after her injury, Rose did not seek out her adviser until after she suffered an emotional breakdown. Asking for help, especially for a medical matter, placed her on edge, adding stress to an already troubled situation. The discomfort she felt at having to rely on others delayed her from seeking treatment for an entire month. She told me that, despite seeing some improvement in her physical and mental health, she stopped seeking treatment soon after she started.

Recalling encounters with faculty often brought up powerful emotions. Melanie (DD,L), a Delaware native whose long, curly hair fell past her shoulders, failed her very first college exam, just five weeks after she arrived. As was official policy at Renowned, her professor informed her academic adviser, who called her in for a meeting. She was not used to this. In high school, teachers were preoccupied with more pressing problems like helping pregnant students graduate. Melanie grew increasingly anxious about meeting one on one with her adviser. She explained,

> In high school and middle school, there was no pressure to be anybody but who I wanted to be. When I got here, I felt pressured to act in a certain way. It didn't take too well; it was rough. I probably should have decided earlier, but after two and a half years of doing pretty badly, actually terribly, I decided I needed to get away. So I took a semester off.

TONY: How often did you seek help during such troubling times?

MELANIE: Not ever; that's the issue! Talking to professors, it's difficult. Professors don't necessarily make it all that easy to meet with them, especially freshman and sophomore year. There were so many people who were always at their office hours trying to get a word in. I was like, "Yeah, I may send an email."

The attention Melanie received from her advisers after her midterm backfired, pushing her even further away from the help that could have prevented her from taking time off. As she said, "I'm not used to these kinds of things." Melanie's reluctance to reach out was not restricted to one specific time. When I probed again for specifics about why she hadn't sought support, Melanie said, definitively, and with a touch of anger: "I literally never asked anybody for help." Even when she returned to campus to finish her senior year, she was still reluctant to talk with professors any more than she had to.

Some of the Doubly Disadvantaged did adjust to academic life at Renowned. But it usually took some time. Joshua (DD,B), a good-natured junior from the South with a sharp sense of humor, experienced a steep learning curve that was more manageable once he realized something that wealthy students seemed to know instinctively: asking questions is not a sign of weakness, but rather, a way of getting what you need. "I'm a lot more comfortable now," he said. "When I got here, I was intimidated by everybody. Now, I realize that most intellectuals ask a lot of questions. That's why I've been more open to asking questions, whether it be in class or in office hours." Joshua went on to say that he connected "with professors; not just TAs." Similarly, Charlotte (DD,B), a charismatic senior from New Jersey, recalled, "My first two years were tepid. I went to office hours once in a while, but only because I really didn't understand something or if I ever really needed help. I rarely went just to talk, which they recommend us to do. I never do that, which is bad." Charlotte heard the call. She just did not feel comfortable answering it until her junior year.

The Doubly Disadvantaged find the collegiate style of interacting with faculty unsettling. It is nothing like what they have experienced before. For many, Renowned is a near polar opposite. It places them on edge. Consequently, many prefer to avoid these awkward moments altogether. And with no conversation about what is expected of them, many feel lost. Some become angry. It takes time for the culture shock to wear off for the Doubly Disadvantaged, which limits them from taking advantage of the full range of resources their college offers them.

Go Out and Get Yours

Thus far, this story may seem like the familiar one that we often find in research studies and newspaper articles about class differences on college campuses: students' level of engagement with faculty aligns with their class backgrounds. Wealthy students feel at home navigating a wealthy college, and poor students feel out of place in this new space. But the Privileged Poor do not fit neatly into this story.

Unlike the Doubly Disadvantaged, the Privileged Poor at Renowned reported being at ease when interacting with professors and deans and being familiar with the expected style of academic exchange. They acknowledged that this was not always true, but explained that their time in private school had given them opportunities to hone their skills of engagement. Moreover, like their peers from moneyed families, they did not wait around for faculty to find them. Knowing that Renowned presented them with opportunities, experiences, and information that their families could not provide, the Privileged Poor entered college seeing professors and administrators as facilitators to their academic and professional dreams and proactively reached out to them. They attributed their smooth transition to college and their comfort with faculty to the fact that they had already learned the ins and outs of elite academic environments laden with unwritten rules.

The Privileged Poor felt entitled to professors' time and resources. Ogun (PP,L), a reflective and discerning freshman, lived in Section 8 housing in a highly segregated neighborhood before college. At the end of middle school she received a scholarship to attend a celebrated New England boarding school. Her family had been unaware of this opportunity, but Ogun's middle school teacher recommended that she apply because she wanted Ogun to go to a school that would nurture her potential. At her boarding school, Ogun mingled with teachers and administrators via institutionalized practices like seated meals and monthly advising meetings (organized especially for scholarship students). Ogun said her school encouraged everyone to develop a sense of entitlement in their academic endeavors, an attitude she came to identify with strongly.

Ogun knew that not all lower-income students at Renowned had this level of confidence. Her friend Alice (DD,L), a quick-witted Latina, said, "I rarely go to school-sponsored people for things" and found it anxiety-inducing that "you have all these professors but they're not going to come find you, you have to find them." Alice learned this fact about Renowned the hard way. "It's been difficult; it's hard to find the help you want. You're too intimidated or too afraid to go and talk to people," Alice noted. Ogun, in contrast, felt "empowered to talk to professors and say, 'I want to meet with you, chat with you.'" When I asked her why she felt this way, she smiled. "My high school instilled in me that I'm allowed to do that, and it's actually my right." Ogun said her first year at Renowned seemed like her fifth year of high school, something I never heard from the Doubly Disadvantaged. She continued,

> I draw on skills I learned in high school. I have the same agenda except this time it says Renowned. My first month, I was like, "Wow, I like this." Another thing I learned was connecting with teachers. They made it okay to say, "Hey, can you meet Tuesday at this time?" I had the small classroom

experience in high school where it was okay to ask your teacher, "Can we meet about this paper?" I did that a lot my first semester here too. There was a TA, we had a final paper and he was in New York. I asked, "Can we talk?" He was like, "Sure, give me a call." I was perfectly comfortable with that. My friends are like, "You're crazy; on the phone with your TA?" Listen, I gotta go out for mine. When I talk about my fifth year, I learned to go out and get mine because I didn't have a network anywhere else. My high school was providing my network. I use the same mentality.

Continuity created comfort. Ogun enlisted others who knew more about the world she was trying to navigate—her boarding school—and where she was trying to go after graduation—college. She developed what she called a "go out and get yours" attitude that prioritized developing a support network of people who could provide concrete advice on college life. She brought both this mindset and the accompanying skillset to Renowned. Ogun came to see faculty as facilitators to her academic pursuits. They played a role that her family simply could not fulfill.

Like Ogun, Marina (PP,L), sporting a red-and-black plaid shirt, described how she contacted professors early in her time at Renowned. Leaning back comfortably on the couch in my office, she said, "Academically, definitely my first year academic adviser, I went to her for everything. I asked her so many questions. She was very helpful."

Sara (PP,L) was equally enthusiastic about connecting with faculty at Renowned. Originally from a small, predominantly Latino community in El Paso, Texas, where everyone worked in landscaping, if they worked at all, Sara received a scholarship to attend a private day school on the other side of town. Her adjustment had its rocky moments. She had to get used to not only an hour-and-a-half commute, but also a school where she was one of the few poor and minority students. Over time, she adjusted. One thing that helped with her adjustment was that her school encouraged contact with teachers by building it into students' and teachers' daily schedules:

> My high school was very nurturing. They had study hall in-corporated into our school schedules. By study hall I mean 80 minutes of time to study or free time. They're like, "Take this time to meet with teachers. They're here. They're also free."

Sara and I reviewed what resources at Renowned had been most important in her transition from high school. Quietly, she said, "I reached out to my residential adviser and I realized how much of a calming effect an adult has that perhaps a peer doesn't have." In this case, her resident adviser was a reassuring force. Thinking back on it all, with her face lighting up as she retold the story, she said, "Just talking to my residential adviser: Wow!" The comfort Sara derived from adults stands in stark contrast to the anxiety and alienation the Doubly Disadvantaged endured when encountering the same faculty and staff members.

Reveling in the fact that one of her classes at Renowned consisted of just six students and the professor sitting around a table, Emma (PP,B) remarked, "I have the privilege of being able to get to know professors. Every professor that I have gotten to know has been really, really kind, open, and pretty diligent." Whereas the Doubly Disadvan-taged resisted connecting with faculty, Emma "thrived in small classes because it gives me the ability to be more than just a name to a professor but actually to really interact and also get to know my classmates." Of the Privileged Poor students I interviewed, Price (PP,B), who attended an all-male Catholic high school on a basketball scholarship, had had the least contact with professors. It was not because he felt anxious; it was more that he made contact only on certain occasions, specifically when he was having trouble with the material or wanted extra help. "I go to office hours around paper time," he said. "If there's a topic that I just am not understanding, if I'm struggling in class, I'll go to office hours. One class, I really was struggling, a science class. I remember going to office hours to build a relationship. Just like that, she was trying to help me."

The Privileged Poor entered Renowned ready and willing to connect with faculty. They felt comfortable seeking out support, both academic and social. Like their upper-income peers, they reported being at ease with administrators, deans, and professors. The difference: the Privileged Poor's ease was learned in high school and not inherited from their families. Bolstered by their high school experiences—which put a premium on building relationships with faculty and incorporated office hours into the official schedule to facilitate these connections—the Privileged Poor brought with them to college not only an affinity for engaging with faculty and staff, but also years of practice managing relationships with adults in elite academic contexts.

Building Networks or Going It Alone

Another important aspect of students' comfort and sense of belonging at elite colleges has to do with the strategies they employ to take advantage of the many resources available on campus. This is about more than just getting better grades; it is about securing access to those intangibles that help students with their post-baccalaureate plans. Those from affluent backgrounds and the Privileged Poor take steps not only to talk with faculty and administrators, but also to enlist them to work—directly or indirectly—on their behalf. The Doubly Disadvantaged regard their peers' strategies as nothing less than brownnosing, which they consider to be morally bankrupt. For the Doubly Disadvantaged, the end does not justify the means.

Assembling My Team

The students I interviewed from upper-income families were both strategic and unapologetic in their outreach. They sought out authority figures to develop support networks and to extract key assets— everything from recommendation letters to research assistantships to access to professors' professional and personal contacts. In other words, they put their ease into action. Kramer (UI,B), a wiry junior, entered Renowned from a private high school where he built strong ties with his teachers and even met them for coffee during the summer months. Bringing with him to college this facility for making connections, he described the type of multifaceted relationship that students from similar backgrounds developed with their professors and other members of the Renowned community. Recalling his college transition, Kramer said,

> In terms of comfort level between students and TAs,
> faculty, and staff, my high school definitely helped
> me in my adjustment to college. Knowing I could just
> go to a TA to talk about a lecture or something. . . .
> Not just academic stuff. Getting life advice.
>
> TONY: How often do you do that?
>
> KRAMER: Now, not as much as I used to. It was a lot freshman,
> sophomore year. A lot of my TAs are very friendly. I
> know them on a personal level, outside of class.
> Same thing with staff. I've had lunches with TAs.

> One of my TAs was one of my tennis hitting part-
> ners freshman year. I know a lot of TAs outside of
> class. They're unofficial mentors. . . . Professors,
> less so, but there are professors I've looked to as
> mentors as well.

Kramer started connecting early and continued making connections throughout his time at Renowned. Both academic and extracurricular encounters enriched his college experience.

Kramer was not alone. John (UI,B) was visibly excited when he recounted how he had developed a "really close relationship with the freshman dean" after going to an open house reception for freshmen. Responding to the dean's remark that students could come to his office and talk to him at any time, John took him up on it:

> I went to his office, just, kind of, to talk to him, not for any
> particular reason, you know. I say, "I want to cultivate this
> relationship." I just went and talked with him. We're talking
> just like this; it was great. Every time I see him, he knows
> my name: I like that a lot. And then office hours and things
> like that, I go when I feel like I need help. My residential
> adviser: great relationship.

John entered the dean's office with the explicit intent to develop a relationship. An open call, made to the entire incoming class, was all the invitation he needed. His delight that the dean knew his name is further indication of his affinity for making connections.

These students not only connected with professors and deans but also sought out useful resources and programs on campus. Rose (UI,B), an engaging freshman from a small town in New Hampshire, immersed herself in college life by attending open houses hosted by professors, deans, and different departments around campus. She reported developing "pretty open relationships" with her advisers and being "very willing to go to them if I have problems. I've been pleasantly surprised with how eager people are to help." When asked about resources at Renowned that had been important to her, Rose outlined a diverse network of people, both peers and professionals:

> Upperclassman leaders of my preorientation program have been a huge resource. Even if it's running into them at parties, you know; they're still looking out for you. I've had lunch with some of them just to catch up on our lives. They're role models but also people I can go to for support and advice. I've also gone to peer counseling groups. I've been to the Rainbow Room for queer students. I've been to the Confidential Resource Center. They're really good at just listening when you need someone to talk to.
>
> TONY: When you need help with something, who do you talk to?
>
> ROSE: In addition to those, I turn to my academic adviser, who's really great. I was lucky to be paired with an academic adviser who really knows what he's doing and is just very much interested in his advisees' well-being. He really, actually cares, which is nice.

Rose was equally comfortable looking for a sensitive ear to listen to her thoughts or a strong shoulder to cry on. She cultivated a team of people from across the university that she relied on in times of need and stayed in touch with on a regular basis.

In a similar vein, Justin (UI,B), a philosopher who loved the hard sciences, described his strategy with two simple words: "reach out; I reach out to everyone." He was constantly pursuing contacts that allowed him to combine his academic and preprofessional goals, something that Renowned expected from all students even though such expectations were never put into words:

> Renowned is what I expected: a place of profound excess and profound wealth. Definitely try and get a slice of it. What I do really well for myself this past year, not only this past year, is reaching out to professors, reaching out to business people, reaching out to physicians. I'm interested in medicine. Reach out to public health scholars; I'm interested in public health also. This place is becoming what it should be for me, a place where I have this opportunity, the privilege to understand how the world works and how I can effect change.

Hitting the books was far from the only way Justin wished to make the most of his college years. He wanted to tap into all that Renowned offered. He looked to the full community of scholars and researchers at Renowned to help him with his on-campus endeavors as well as his post-baccalaureate projects. He even advised me that I should do the same. Justin's work on campus demonstrated his determination: one semester he hosted conversations with leading scholars and activists to discuss race and inequality that drew hundreds of students.

This group of students from well-to-do families made it a point to get to know professors and other college administrators who could advance their goals, both academic and otherwise. They described these interactions positively—and perhaps just as important, it didn't appear to cross their minds that such interactions would be anything but positive. They expected that faculty and administrators would be available and helpful, and they were generally right. As a result of building these relationships, they reaped varied benefits, from finding a tennis partner to securing a job. And they did not limit their networking to securing support for their academic endeavors. Like Justin, nearly all of them saw professors and administrators as partners in their larger journey toward adulthood, whether it related to personal growth while at Renowned or advancement after graduation.

The Dignity of the Work

The Doubly Disadvantaged expressed discomfort with the more personal, hands-on style of engagement that was expected from students at Renowned. What became clear as I talked with them was that their lack of engagement was more than simple avoidance. Their strategy was not to network. They believed that conversations with faculty should be limited to discussing academic material and viewed interactions outside these narrow bounds as sucking up. For example, Valeria (DD,L), a junior and top-performing anthropology student, identified "building relationships with professors" as one of her biggest struggles at Renowned. She described the tension between the values she had learned at home and the expectations that were placed on her at Renowned:

> My being uncomfortable going to office hours: that's the social class thing. I don't like talking to professors one on one. That's negative because Renowned really wants you to be proactive. And raise your hand. And talk. Freshman year, I didn't say a word. People who I had small classes with, if I see them on the street, I recognize them. They

won't recognize me because I didn't speak. My dad would always teach me, "You don't want to get where you are based on kissing ass, right? You want it based on hard work. It'll take longer, but there's more value to it. You'll feel more proud." That's bad in this context because Renowned totally wants you to kiss them.

The expectation at Renowned that students should seek professors' attention and curry their favor went against the foundational lessons that Valeria had learned growing up. She entered college thinking that her advancement "should be about the work." That was how her father saw the world. That was how he instructed his children to see it as well. After three years of being at Renowned, she was finally able to identify one of its unwritten rules. Shaking her head in dismay, Valeria exclaimed, "Wow! Relationships are all that matter here." Initiating relationships with faculty, especially more personal ones, also contradicted the strategies she had used throughout high school, the very tactics that made her attendance at Renowned possible. In high school, she said, "I just went to class; I didn't talk to teachers outside of class ever. I didn't feel a reason to except I guess when I had to apply to college." College counselors were "very preoccupied with students who were having disciplinary problems . . . or mental health issues," she said, and she felt like she would be intruding on their time to ask for help with the college application process. It struck me that Valeria put more stock in protecting her teachers' and professors' time than in seeking the support she needed. She was not alone.

For Daniel (DD,L), an aspiring entertainer with a dry sense of humor, the approach he had taken in high school did not work in college. Daniel remembered the relationships between teachers and students in high school as strained. "Freshman year, classes are mixed; honors and regular students were together. People heckle teachers, argue with them, text blatantly in their face, ignore them. My honors and AP classes, we got yelled at for not doing homework." Daniel did not catch his teachers' attention until junior year, when he joined Scribe, a writing club, and began to do well on assignments. He thought just keeping his head down and getting good grades would work once he got to Renowned. He was wrong.

DANIEL: I don't do office hours. I never thought of myself as an "office hours" person. In high school, I didn't talk to teachers. I walk in and sit down. I would take the test and then they'd be like, "You got a high grade. Congratulations!" I'd be like, "Oh cool. Thanks." That's how they would notice me. I didn't want to talk to them. In college, I was like, "I'll do the same thing." But no. I wasn't smart enough. And then, these kids who go to professors after class and just talk to them. I have no idea what they're talking about. I don't have any questions beyond what they're teaching. They're kiss-asses! These people want recommendations, a spot in this guy's research team. I never wanted to grovel.

TONY: Are both strategies equally effective?

DANIEL: Theirs and mine? Well, mine's not effective at all. It worked in high school but that was high school. Now that I'm here, I never would've cut it as premed because I wouldn't have anyone to write my recommendations. I'm sure their strategy worked out. They're all going to get glowing recommendations.

At Renowned, Daniel did not seek out professors and even avoided his academic dean when placed on academic probation during the fall of his sophomore year. He drew boundaries between himself and those he labeled "kiss-asses." He shared with me that he chose not to use personal connections (via his roommate's uncle) to get an internship he was interested in. When I asked him why, he simply said that he did not feel comfortable doing so. Daniel couldn't imagine just making conversation with a professor. He could only see himself, at most, talking about the content of a particular class. Finding his peers' behavior annoying and against his beliefs about how one should get ahead, Daniel chose to focus on his work, as he had in high school. College, however, ushered in new rules. He stumbled in adjusting to the social dynamics at Renowned. Like many of his peers, Daniel experienced the cognitive dissonance of wanting to succeed but feeling uncomfortable at playing the game. Even though he knew he was missing out, he could not, or rather did not, shake old habits. So instead, he gave up his dream of being a doctor.

Isabel (DD,L), a junior from the Midwest with a calm demeanor, arrived at Renowned from an impoverished suburb where school counselors told students to "dream small" and teachers battled to stem the growing heroin use among students. Isabel's school cut programs to save money. Extracurriculars were the first to go, and when these measures were not enough, the cuts grew deeper. "They started by cutting band," she said. "They cut music and the arts. Now, just ten extracurriculars remain. The lights were cut off in the hallways. The lights were turned off in the hallways! I mean, we could still see from classrooms that are lit. I thought it was normal, like intervals of darkness."

The darkness in the hallways matched, or perhaps amplified, the depression Isabel felt when she went to school every day. Interactions with teachers and administrators did nothing to lighten the mood.

Teachers told students, even those in honors classes, that it was fruitless to dream of making it beyond the boundaries of their neighborhood. "The expectations are just very low," she said. "They really did not help students apply to colleges other than the community college. They had the mentality that the local community college is where you're supposed to go. If you're going somewhere else you were delusional." Defying her teachers and the odds, she left home for Renowned. And then things took a turn she was not prepared for. Isabel felt overwhelmed. With tears rolling down her round cheeks, she remembered being "very stressed first semester. I would just cry sometimes." Reflecting on her lack of relationships with professors, which persisted into the spring of her junior year, Isabel admitted,

> It is actually a really bad thing; I still feel great hesitation talking to professors, even TAs. TAs are closer in age; you would think it is more comfortable. . . . I have never felt comfortable speaking to adults as equals or even asking them questions. It is something I have been cognizant of since I came here. I need to be able to talk to adults. How am I going to get some sort of recommendation? How am I going to ask for help? How am I going to build a relationship they say is "one of a kind" here? I can't even open my mouth.

Months after we first met, toward the end of her senior year, Isabel was still avoiding faculty, deans, and resident counselors, even when dealing with an emotionally taxing lead-up to graduation. Rather than reaching out, she used her family's hardship as a yardstick that reminded her not only that she had it better than they did, but also that she could get through anything by just plowing ahead. She noted, "Through tough times, whether it was social situations, academic, or whatever, I would always think what would my father say or do. He has lived way worse things than I lived. I keep on going. If I do not understand the material, I just keep on reading it and reading it, just keep going over. I very rarely reach out to adults here."

Ariana (DD,L), a second-semester freshman, entered my office with the look of a West Coast transplant enduring her first Northeast winter. Clearly the joys of seeing her first snow had long worn off. We chatted about the never-ending winter for a few minutes, and then I asked about life at Renowned. Before she could get more than a few words out, Ariana began taking slower and deeper breaths. Her shoulders began to shake. I realized she was crying. Her first year had left her humbled and questioning whether she was ready to be at Renowned. She said she didn't have any trouble handling the class material. It was everything else that got to her. I asked if she had sought any support. She had not. Ariana explained why she was nervous whenever she talked with professors and administrators: "I feel very self-conscious. I still don't feel comfortable speaking to school officials." She wanted to focus on her classes and get good grades so she could go to graduate school. But she needed help adjusting. After a lengthy silence and more tears, she continued, "I'm constantly wondering what's going through their mind, how they're perceiving me, which I probably shouldn't do but it's an instinct."

Well into her second year, Ariana had not developed a support network. Like Joshua and Charlotte, however, Ariana showed progress. When we had dinner together in the cafeteria during the spring semester of her sophomore year, she adopted a determined tone to discuss her growth since our previous interview the year before. She had gotten more involved on campus, she said, and had begun to see Renowned more as her own. When she spoke to a group of high school students the following semester, Ariana admitted that the culture shock of academic and social life had overpowered her during her first three semesters at Renowned. Once she had learned to ask for help—in part through working at the Equality Center, which placed her in contact with administrators, deans, and upperclassmen—she had felt more comfortable.

Ariana also began working with the Career Exploration Office late in her junior year, to find out what steps she needed to take to apply to medical school. She got a much later start than many of her classmates because she had considered such support services to be designed for "those people"—her affluent peers—not for students like her. The director told me that they were glad she had come in, though; other students, especially the Doubly Disadvantaged, came in even later than she did, when it was effectively too late to apply during their intended application cycle.

The Doubly Disadvantaged generally feel uneasy at the prospect of having to interact with professors and deans, and avoid doing so. Focusing on their classwork, these students often contrast their strategy with that of their peers who work closely with professors to advance their personal agendas. Although many of them eventually adjust to the unspoken expectations that govern academic life, at Renowned and elsewhere, they often lose out on more than a year of relationship building and access to institutional resources.[9]

Strategic Engagement

In contrast to the Doubly Disadvantaged, the Privileged Poor tend to seek out professors and administrators in similar ways as their peers from more privileged backgrounds. They generally do not feel nervous, uncomfortable, or unprepared when engaging with them. None of the students I spoke with reported any feelings of guilt. Like their peers from more affluent backgrounds, the Privileged Poor often make connections with faculty and college officials that extend beyond academics. The difference is that the Privileged Poor identify their ease as an acquired—rather than innate or inherited—skill.

In middle school, Damion (PP,B) skipped class with abandon. He confessed, "I literally don't remember studying ever in middle school. I don't remember doing homework." Why study, when the work was easy and teachers had low expectations, was his thinking. Wanting to reinvent himself, Damion entered a private high school instead of the vocational school that his three siblings and all their neighborhood friends attended. Private school, he said, allowed him "to refocus on what was important because I didn't have those social distractions keeping me from fulfilling goals I had for myself." He often reflected on being one of the only students from a minority group—either racial or socioeconomic. Feeling empowered by his mentors to speak up, Damion lobbied administrators to increase diversity at his largely white, upper-middle-class Catholic school, and eventually he "catalyzed a minority initiative. By the time I was a senior, the school built a partnership with local communities and was siphoning students from there every year." When asked to identify the resources at Renowned that most helped him overcome his initial anxiety, Damion stated, "Definitely advisers." During his senior year at Renowned, he worked with three advisers—an alumnus, a professor, and the dean of admissions—to create a college-sponsored support group for lower-income and first-generation college students like himself. Moreover, Damion brought the president of the alumni association to speak and to pledge support for connecting alumni to first-generation college undergraduates.

Nicole (PP,B), who had become used to office hours and to making close connections with faculty while she was in high school, was not shy about talking with professors outside of class. "I say, 'Let's get coffee.' I have no qualms asking a teacher for help. If I need something, I'm more than willing to go; I email often. It's valuable for your grades to know professors. I make it a point to know my teaching assistants, my professors. Since my high school had mandatory tutorial hours for teachers, I was like, 'If I need help here, I'll just go to office hours.' It wasn't a big thing." With a smile, she talked about some of the different ways she met with professors: "One of the things that I think Renowned does really well is the faculty dinner. Really nice. I have met up with faculty members at a faculty dinner, get to know them at a much more personal level. . . . These are also the faculty members that are reaching out to you, like, 'Get a cup of coffee?' I feel comfortable reaching out to them."

Similarly, Javier (PP,L) reveled in the positive relationships he had developed in his three years at Renowned. "Since I've been here, life's been meeting people," he noted. "I'm very close with the director of the cultural center; I'm close with my thesis adviser. I'm close with a professor at the law school. I've had very good experiences with the professors here."

Stephanie (PP,B), a senior, described the dense support networks that existed at her boarding school. Her teachers had hosted informal, intimate dinners, and she maintained open lines of communication with advisers who followed her development from admission to gradu-ation. Reflecting on interactions with faculty at Renowned, she offered a parable of sorts, highlighting the differences in preparation among lower-income students and indicating where she saw herself along this spectrum:

> I know what I ought to do. My friend struggles: "I don't get this; I don't know what to do." I told her what to do: "Con-tact them." That was very intuitive to me. Reaching out to

your teacher and having one-on-one time was definitely something that was at my boarding school. I didn't think it was a big deal, but the fact that my friend was like, "Are you sure I can just email them?" Not that she felt the professor wasn't welcoming, but 'cause she wasn't used to that. I arguably have an advantage. I would have been meeting with my professor for a whole semester at this point and she would have been struggling. Let's say there's two students, both struggling. One of them gets a tutor, which I figure is normal at public schools. I would very intuitively email the professor and say, "I'm not doing well. Please meet with me. This is my schedule."

Bypassing auxiliary sources of support like academic tutors, Stephanie opted to get what she needed straight from the source. Approaching the professor, with times that best fit *her* schedule, was the only option that made sense to her. This strategy was second nature by the time she entered Renowned. Some students might view it as pushy and entitled. But, as she had learned in high school, playing email tag to schedule meetings wastes everyone's time; it's more efficient to provide times in the initial email. Stephanie had gone a step further and tried to improve communication on a broader scale; she proudly recounted how she had organized meetings between students and administrators, one of which took place in the dean's residence, because she wanted to "increase student accessibility to professors and to increase undergraduate contact with graduate students to break down barriers to communication."

Clarissa (PP,B) earned a scholarship to attend a preparatory high school with a nine to one student–faculty ratio.[10] Her school institutionalized contact with teachers through office hours and by placing students in multigenerational advising networks, which, she explained, included (over)enthusiastic alumni. At Renowned, she sought out similar connections. Her relationship with her adviser demonstrated her ease at dealing with college officials on both academic and personal matters. She recalled,

> My academic adviser has been a huge resource. She's helped me with classes. She's helped me get loans. My computer broke last semester; she helped me figure out how to get a loan. Apparently, she was friends with my financial aid officer so she helped me get in contact with her and helped her to help me. She's been really great. We'll have meetings that are supposed to be thirty minutes and we'll end up there for like an hour and a half because we talk about everything.

Clarissa connected with her adviser in ways that went beyond choosing classes. Their relationship was personal, and her adviser helped her discover that some administrators have access to discretionary funds to help students through emergencies.[11]

When the Privileged Poor discussed adjusting to the expected styles of engagement that pervade elite academic settings, they referred back to their freshman and sophomore years in high school. Michelle (PP,L), who endured bouts of homelessness while at her posh day school, welcomed the close, personal contact with professors at Renowned. It reminded her of her relationships with high school teachers, who practiced a kind of holistic advising that combined academic enrichment with personal development, and who "highly suggested" that all students attend office hours. Counselors at her day school and at Prep for Prep drilled it into students that they should always reach out, not just for help, but also for advice and support. It took time, however, for her to get used to this style of mentoring. When she first entered high school, she experienced acute culture shock being around wealthy white people, and she was initially resistant to her high school's hands-on advising style. But after three years of seeing and working with the same people on everything from academic assignments to extracurricular activities, trust began to grow. In time, these connections provided stability when she did not know whether she would have a place to sleep after the school day was over. She brought these lessons to college with her.

> Freshman year at Renowned, there's a very good support system, a lot of advisers you could go to. Sophomore year, they don't help you as much. I'm really good friends with my advisers. TAs, they're most loyal to those who come to office hours, quite frankly. My adviser is great: out of ten, probably nine. Some TAs haven't been good and others have been excellent. I bother them a lot if I need help. I make it known I need help so they'd help me. So that would probably be a seven. There is this microeconomics professor who's really legit. I would love to get to know him better. He's super chill. We got along really well. We chilled, had a good talk . . . best buds.

When they entered private high school, usually in ninth grade, the Privileged Poor were surprised by expectations about how they would relate to their teachers. By the time they entered Renowned, however, interacting with faculty was just another school routine. Accustomed to frank, open conversations with her high school teachers about everything from being homeless to choosing where to study abroad, Michelle already had an affinity for connecting with faculty. Building on these positive experiences, she developed a relationship with her economics professor that went beyond supply and demand curves. An economics major interested in finance, she continued to build on this relationship after the semester ended.

The strategies of the Privileged Poor are more like those of their wealthier peers than like those of the Doubly Disadvantaged. Instead of withdrawing or waiting for authority figures to come to them, the Privileged Poor actively reach out to them and enlist them as facilitators to help them reach their goals.

Reducing Burdens or Adding Stress

College is not all about the books. Connections with faculty do not just result in extensions on papers and advice about internships. Access to emotional support and professional help is sometimes needed. I observed that the way students at Renowned enlisted different officers of the university to navigate these stressful times was often a manifestation of their most basic instincts of how they should (or shouldn't) relate to those in positions of authority.

As other researchers have found, students are often less willing to talk about mental health problems than about other aspects of college life. But I was able to gain insight from the testimonies of three students—Carol (UI,B), Elise (DD,W), and Patrice (PP,L)—who each faced hardships resulting from family troubles early in their college careers. These students' strategies for seeking help—in this case mental health support—were nested within their larger repertoire for engaging faculty, deans, and others at the university.[12]

Carol (UI,B), a down-to-earth double legacy, called Renowned "easy" to navigate, a feeling reinforced by many trips to Renowned with her parents and years of socializing at her elite day school in the Midwest.

Family troubles, however, disrupted what was shaping up to be an otherwise "pretty seamless" college transition. Her parents' divorce—and subsequent fighting—undermined her mental well-being, especially when her father, the noncustodial parent, began dictating what major she should choose and which extracurricular activities she should get involved in. Head lowered, she revealed, "My dad's a very difficult person to deal with. He has his own way of viewing the world that doesn't always match up with what's actually happening. There is a lot of drama and stress coming from my father that affected my experience here." Tensions ran high; the stress associated with being an intermediary between her parents disturbed her sleep, lowered her desire to socialize, and hampered her ability to concentrate on coursework. Carol reached out for help:

> My resident adviser, freshman year, was really close to us; I
> felt really close to her. When I was going through stuff with
> my dad, towards the end of freshman year, she was the first
> person I went to. Interacting with her was really productive.
> Similarly, the other resident counselors I know really well; I
> like talking to them. Seeing them is awesome. Our dean,
> I was also really close with. . . . The counseling center has
> been really useful. Freshman through sophomore year, every
> single one of the counselors there was really helpful, again
> for all the reasons with my dad. It definitely had an effect on
> my experience here. Having that resource was really helpful
> to me.

Carol crafted a diverse support network, from her residential adviser to a team of counselors who provided professional support. She purposefully worked to maintain relationships with her trusted advisers and other college officials over the course of her time at Renowned.

In contrast, Elise (DD,W), a junior whose bright, blond hair contrasted with the dark rings under her eyes, did not feel comfortable turning to anyone, let alone building an entire support team. She made it to college on her own. She worked "40 hours a week between two jobs" in high school so that she could buy books and SAT flashcards and help her mother with the bills. Still, she and her family lived through six evictions and numerous disruptions in utilities. Toward the end of high school, her family disowned her because they regarded her plan to go away to college as equivalent to desertion. She lamented that Renowned was "completely, completely different. My high school didn't prepare me at all for Renowned." Thrusting her hands in the air, she exclaimed, "Is there anything similar?" Reflecting on her time at Renowned, Elise revealed unaddressed health issues, which included an eating disorder, insomnia, and problems concentrating, all of which continued to slow her integration into college life. She explained,

> I have focus problems. I'm getting ready to start Adderall. In high school, you have structure. Here, you don't. All these things going on back home, my family is like, "You abandoned us!" All this stress in the back of your mind and you're supposed to sit down for five hours and read Weber? Go to class and discuss Rousseau? It's hard to focus when there's so much going on. I need to be working or I can't afford next semester. There's so much going on! Then depression and not sleeping, it became so hard to get to class, to do any work. Last week was the first week all year I've

been to every single class. Not everyone else has all these things going on. But you can't always go to your professor and say, "I have all this shit going on." In the real world, it doesn't matter your mom is dying, you still need to perform to the same level as others. If you can't, then you're screwed. It's such a stressful thing to think about.

The idea of seeking support did not provide Elise any solace; she saw herself as different from everything at Renowned and drew boundaries between herself and those who could potentially help her. "When I need help," she said, "I don't have anyone to turn to. I don't have a support network. I'm on my own." This feeling persisted even though mental health counseling was covered by the student health plan, and she had access to just as many resources as Carol and every other student at Renowned. But she was reluctant to make an appointment. "I don't know if I feel really comfortable around anyone," she said. "It's intimidating." Even when dealing with the stresses of her sister's recent eviction, a parent's hospitalization, and her grandfather's passing, she kept everything bottled up. She said she was "in denial" about losing her grandfather. "I've shut down my emotions. Eventually it's going to get too much and I'll break down, but I'm hoping that'll happen over spring break. Although, yesterday, in class, we were talking about cancer and old people. I just started crying, I couldn't help it." A few weeks later, Elise began seeing both a psychiatrist and a psychologist when another public outburst of pain caught the attention of her professors, prompting an intervention. But that was only after she had been at Renowned for more than two full years.[13]

Like Elise, Patrice (PP,L), a freshman, grew up in a single-parent home and knew the disruptive power of evictions. Patrice's family also disowned her for leaving home, but this had happened several years earlier—when she left for boarding school. Patrice came to rely on the academic community where she lived and studied. Her teachers and counselors facilitated her adjustment to life in a rich, white, academically challenging school. Like Michelle (PP,L), she began to trust these adults and to look to them for support while she worked through family troubles. These deeper connections with adults, which initially felt alien and unsettling, were inevitable in a small boarding school, where "everything was very structured; faculty were coaches, dorm parents, teachers, and club sponsors." She put these learned strategies to use when she discovered, soon after she arrived at college, that child protective services had removed her siblings from home. This news left Patrice emotionally exhausted. She stopped eating regularly and lost ten pounds in a short period of time. To manage this turmoil, Patrice sought help:

> I was a mess; I was trying to keep it together. I got a lot of help from my resident counselor. I got a psychologist. That helped a lot. The dean of students, I talked to him during the week when I found out. I always had to be on the phone to find out what was going on at home. I couldn't go because then I couldn't come back. It was a legal issue with child services and I was seventeen. My siblings, they're under the custody of the state. I would have been too had I gone back and I would have had to testify against my mother. I got a lot of help. A few assignments, my professor said I didn't have to turn in that week so I could focus on myself. I was freaking out: "Oh wow, I just got here. I don't know anyone. Now I'm freaking out." I never freak out; I'm big on keeping it together.

Whatever family issues are going on, I center myself and do work. This time I couldn't. . . . We kept having dorm meetings about mental health. There's so much here for you! I was able to email my professors, tell them what was going on, and talk to the dean. People care about you. It's a big place but people want to make your experience good. That's why I love Renowned even more.

Family problems hit Patrice before she had even received her first homework assignment. Recognizing the toll it was taking on her, she not only sought out mental health services, but also enlisted her professors and residential adviser so she would not fall behind on work. Moreover, unlike the Doubly Disadvantaged, who generally reported being uneasy engaging with faculty, Patrice appreciated it when "my professor kept up with me . . . and sent me things. I have really bad anxiety; she sent me meditation things."

Patrice and I crossed paths months later. She was on the phone and visibly upset. It turned out she had missed the start of an exam because a medication her psychiatrist had prescribed caused her to oversleep. Although clearly worried, she put a plan into action: she called her therapist, informed her residential adviser, contacted the teaching assistant, and was en route to the professor's office to explain her absence in person.

The college gates do not keep out pain and cannot shield students from life's problems. Carol, Elise, and Patrice all faced stressors from their family situations that made life at Renowned difficult. While Carol and Patrice chose to seek professional help that lightened their load, Elise elected to shoulder the burden alone, allowing those problems to deepen. Elise's attitude is understandable given what we have already learned about the Doubly Disadvantaged. If an undergraduate feels uncomfortable attending office hours to ask questions about a research paper, how likely is it that she will ask for help for an emotional problem?

❧

From asking for academic help to developing bonds with mentors, making connections with college staff—professors, administrators, advisers, and others—is the surest way to gain access to the abundant resources available at elite institutions. To not avail oneself of these resources means to not get as much out of college as one can. In a 2015 commencement address at the Martin Luther King Jr. College Preparatory High School in Chicago, then First Lady Michelle Obama emphasized this point. Obama, a first-generation college student who went from a public magnet high school in Chicago to Princeton University, said that as she got to know her college classmates, she "realized that they were all struggling with something, but instead of hiding their struggles and trying to deal with them all alone, they reached out." Her classmates got both the help they needed and the assistance they wanted. "If they didn't understand something in class, they would raise their hand and ask a question," she explained. "Then they'd go to professor's office hours and ask even more questions. And they were never embarrassed about it, not one bit. Because they knew that that's how you succeed in life." She began to do the same thing, and over time, her emotional well-being and her academic experience both improved.[14]

Part of the hidden curriculum at a college like Renowned is that students are expected to ask for help, whether it be assistance with homework or emotional support. Such behavior is, for better or for worse, how students get access to institutional resources as well as social support. None of this is explicitly stated; it is assumed that students already know what to do. But not all students have had a chance to learn how to navigate mainstream institutions like colleges before they actually enter them, and colleges should not assume that they have.

Even someone who is able to learn these invisible rules still needs specific skills to apply them. For an upper-middle-class student who went to the best schools, is used to conversing with adults, and feels confident of their place in the world, engaging with professors and administrators is second nature. But not all students can say the same; many students, especially those from poor families, have not had the opportunity to practice, let alone master, these skills before they take a seat at a seminar table or lab bench.

Experience and exposure are powerful teachers. Like their peers from upper-income families, the Privileged Poor enter college primed to engage with faculty members and other college officials. They have learned and, equally important, practiced how to approach and form relationships with faculty in high schools that emphasized independent thinking and prioritized contact with teachers. The Privileged Poor have had years of experience showing up for office hours, attending informal dinners, and having casual conversations with faculty by the time they walk across the freshman quad to their first college classes. Students from upper-income families see faculty as partners along their academic journey, while the Privileged Poor come to see them as facilitators of their advancement. Students in both groups reap benefits from their assertive behavior.

For the Doubly Disadvantaged, in contrast, college is like a new world filled with foreign rules. With no explicit directions for when or how to engage professors, these students experience anxiety when they realize that they are expected to have close contact with college officials. They may withdraw from faculty despite seeing the benefits their peers get for reaching out. To them, college officials are authority figures who should be kept at a distance and treated with deference.

Their parents have often reinforced their reluctance to curry favor. The Doubly Disadvantaged express strong faith in the idea of meritocracy—believing that focusing on "the work" is enough for success—but they actually stand to lose the most for believing so. Good work may bring recognition, and hard work may be rewarded, but academic performance alone is not always how you get ahead or get what you need in college.

Even for those students who eventually learn how the system works, the lag can be consequential. Alice (DD,L) was still uneasy even during her senior year, when she plucked up the courage to ask me, "Tony, how do you navigate these rich, white places?" The first two years of college set the foundation for undergraduates' academic and social development. Early and sustained contact allows professors and administrators—who, among other things, serve as gatekeepers to internships, fellowships, graduate school, jobs, summer travel, and many other opportunities (both publicized and unpublicized)—to get to know undergraduates' personal stories, interests, and qualifications.[15]

As the stories of Carol, Elise, and Patrice suggested, students' academic support strategies inform how they seek out mental health support. Those who are already comfortable with faculty and administrators are equally at ease accessing counseling and other forms of support when they need it. Their strategies are not a unique set of behaviors, but are rather part of their larger cultural toolkit.

In our conversations, students spoke in general terms about their interactions with faculty and rarely brought up issues of race. This could be due to the open-ended nature of the interviews. I did not specifically ask about the race of faculty members or administrators they were talking about, since I was trying to understand their overall style of academic engagement and ease at navigating the social side of academic life. Additionally, the topic may not have come up because three-quarters of the faculty at Renowned are white, with some departments being almost exclusively so. This is not to say that race did not and does not matter. I hope that future researchers will pick up the mantle and look into factors that I was not able to explore, including how the race, gender, and academic discipline of university faculty and staff affect lower-income students' comfort or likelihood to engage with them.

To provide more effective help for the most disadvantaged undergraduates, colleges need to take into account the diversity of cultural resources they bring with them to campus. A number of steps, some of which have already been put into place at a few institutions, could help less socially prepared undergraduates make the transition to both academic and social life. Some colleges, such as Bates College, Georgetown University, and Williams College, have summer and preterm orientation programs that bring admitted students to campus before they begin their first semester. These programs are particularly powerful ways to provide knowledge of the campus and, equally important, those who populate it. Enlisting faculty as instructors and mentors for such programs can present opportunities for students to get to know them in a lower-stakes setting.

Learning how to interact with faculty and other college staff cannot, of course, guarantee a successful college career. Nevertheless, the opportunity to practice this skill in a welcoming community could be immensely helpful in removing some of the social barriers that the students at Renowned identified as hindering their academic integration into college. Two studies investigating best practices at the most successful community colleges in Texas, carried out by the Pell Institute for the Study of Opportunity in Higher Education, found that first-generation college students who participate in summer and / or orientation programs are more likely to develop relationships with faculty than those who do not participate. At the University of Maryland, Baltimore County, administrators coach students in the Meyerhoff Scholars Program—a scholarship program for minority students interested in the sciences or engineering—how to ask questions when they first meet with a professor. By doing so, the program hopes to achieve its broader aim of getting students accustomed to advocating for themselves and feeling comfortable in interactions with authority figures.[16]

Freshman orientation could have a bigger impact if it was not focused just on the students alone but included their larger social circle. After all, the transition to college is a collective one. Colleges could use this time to bring in undergraduates' off-campus networks, such as their families and friends at home, and make them aware of what resources are available (and the associated costs if there are any) as well as what expectations are most prevalent on campus. Instead of just sending parents instructions about how to donate to the annual fund or how to purchase care packages for their children, colleges could also send out directed mailings describing what college life is like and what the college sees as the most successful strategies for navigating it. This kind of program could help a wide variety of students and their families. International students who did not attend American schools, for example, would benefit from a primer on the customs of American higher education and the specific rites and rituals of their particular campus.[17]

Other steps should be taken to demystify the hidden curriculum. Professors and administrators alike need to ensure that all students know what office hours are. By outlining the basics of office hours instead of leaving them largely undefined, we might be able to help more students get the support they need and develop social relationships that will help them in the future. The definition would not have to be uniform across an entire university. Some professors want to limit conversations during office hours to discussing coursework, while others may want to engage students on questions related to industry or internships. Barry Mazur, a mathematics professor at Harvard University, began defining office hours for his students in order to explain what that one hour block every Wednesday afternoon is for. He wrote on the board, and also on the syllabus, "You are INVITED to come to these office hours even if you have no question or problem you want to ask about; we'll consider specific problems that people bring up, but if there's none (or if there is extra time) we'll discuss general issues about the material we are doing in class."[18]

While Mazur focuses on course content, other professors may be interested in talking with students about their transition to college or about how the course relates to campus life and national events. Rebecca Kissane, professor of sociology at Lafayette College, defines office hours on her syllabus as an opportunity to talk about a variety of topics:

This semester I will hold office hours on Mondays and Wednesdays from 3:00–4:00 pm and Fridays from 1:00–2:00 pm. This means that during those hours, you need not have an appointment to talk to me—just stop by my office during that time. Office hours are a time when you can come to ask me for assistance in understanding course material or assignments, or they can merely be an opportunity to chat with me about the course or how the course relates to current events, college more generally, or anything else you want to talk about with me. Do not feel like you need to have a "good" question or reason to come to office hours—you can just pop in to say hello if you want! And, if you cannot make my office hours because you have a conflict, I'm happy to meet with you at other times—just make an appointment.

Kissane communicated her own view about the value of office hours to her students. What she—and her students—did during that period matched not only the larger aims of the course, but also the kind of professor that she wanted to be.[19]

Some professors opt to hold meetings at coffee shops or restaurants close to campus. This change of location could help both students and faculty feel more comfortable talking about a fuller range of topics. Any professor who chooses this strategy must inform students in advance that she will pick up the tab. Students have been known to decline to meet with a professor at Starbucks because they could not afford to go there but were reluctant to say so.

Many colleges and universities, especially those with a strong liberal arts culture that promotes faculty–student interactions, support such endeavors. For example, Amherst College hosts a program called Take Your Professor Out (affectionately called TYPO for short), where a group of students invites a professor to dinner at a local restaurant, paid for by the college. Renowned adopted a similar program after meetings with various deans in which I discussed ways to increase academic engagement. Programs like this help to blur the lines between the academic and the social.

Colleges must perpetually ask whether their practices and policies help or hinder students, and must work to create opportunities for success for all those who walk through the college gates. Understanding how students gain access to institutional resources and supports—and the hurdles that get in their way—is a first step. Being explicit about the types of relationships that are expected between students and faculty, as well as making clear that all are invited to enter the spaces where these bonds are forged, is another. It is these basic building blocks that we must return to if we are to truly foster inclusion for all students.

3

"I, Too, Am Hungry"

WITH THE SETTING SUN AT MY BACK, I hustle to catch one of the three chartered buses parked outside Renowned's main gate, which will take me—along with ninety students—to "Young, Gifted, & Black," the end of the year celebration for the Black Students' Union. I get on the first bus and see many familiar faces. Everyone here is a student, save for one resident counselor, the bus driver, and myself. We start catching up about work and life. Naturally, talk turns to the must-see TV show of the moment, *Scandal,* and Olivia Pope's many misadventures. Someone then asks what I did over spring break, which was two weeks before. "Besides catching up on sleep," I say, "I cooked, 'cause usually I eat with y'all." I extract my phone from my pocket to show off pictures of my new favorite dish: salmon and shrimp and grits. I describe the meal as my phone gets passed around, explaining how I season the seafood with black pepper, cayenne, and crushed red pepper; Lawry's Seasoned Salt; and lemon juice. And then I mention the grits, with pepper jack cheese melted in. The uproar is instantaneous. From three rows back, someone yells, "Where was my invite?" Another shouts, "Way to leave me out; you know I was here. No love!" Oh, the shade that was thrown my way. Joshua, a fit young man with a joker's smile as broad as his muscular shoulders, stares me dead in the eyes and says, with a straight face that lasts only until he gets the last word out, "Well damn, Tony, *I, too, am hungry.*"

We all shared a laugh after this talk of food as the bus rumbled through winding city streets, but then the conversation turned somber. The lively reaction from the students was not solely a response to my burgeoning culinary skills or my lack of sharing. Rather, something more serious was afoot. Students' responses reflected a troubling reality that many of them, and others at Renowned University, had to contend with each March: the university's policy of closing all cafeterias during spring break.

With comedic seriousness, Joshua (DD,B) had adeptly appropriated the "I, too" campaign slogan that swept colleges around the world in the spring of 2014. In that campaign, students of color at various campuses put together multimedia projects documenting insults and offenses that had been directed their way by white classmates—some intentional, some not. Joshua's quick reaction switched the focus from the interpersonal to the institutional. He highlighted the painful fact that a university with a multibillion-dollar endowment, where the cost of attendance surpasses $60,000 a year, suspended all meal services during spring break. Partly because of the assumption that all students leave campus. Partly to save money. Most students at Renowned were oblivious to this policy, since they were at home or on vacation somewhere. But for those students who stayed on campus, usually because of circumstance rather than by choice, the absence of the food service was keenly felt.[1]

A particularly brutal irony is that one of the largest donations to Renowned in recent decades was made in the name of recruiting poor, academically talented youth. The closing of the cafeterias distressed exactly those students the college had so eagerly worked to bring to campus and left those very same recruits suffering from food insecurity—not knowing where their next meal was coming from. Little did Joshua realize that in choosing Renowned as his academic home, he would confront an old truth he had learned when living in an abandoned barn after his family had been evicted from their home: hunger hurts.[2]

Chapters 1 and 2 focused on the differences between the Doubly Disadvantaged and the Privileged Poor, specifically in how they experience and manage encounters with their peers and their professors. We have seen that lower-income students' divergent trajectories to college—and specifically the formative experiences they had in their drastically different high schools—shape their knowledge of and strategies for navigating elite academic institutions like Renowned.

But a focus on cultural resources paints an incomplete picture of the problems poor students face. For example, scholars who have discussed spring break have looked at how lower-income students feel inadequate because their affluent peers take trips to places they can't afford and may not even have heard of, and talk about them after returning to campus.[3] But what I found in my research at Renowned was that although poor students mentioned travel in other contexts, when they talked about spring break woes, they did not discuss their peers' excursions at all. Instead, both the Doubly Disadvantaged and the Privileged Poor talked about something more basic: surviving. They described how they scrounged for sustenance. They recounted how they rationed their provisions. They narrated how they effectively starved themselves as they tried to stretch every morsel of food they could get their hands on.

Even though the Privileged Poor adapted to relationships with peers and professors at Renowned incredibly well, they were still poor; there was still no way to bypass the pervasive structures and policies that are built around access to money. An empty pocket meant an empty stomach. Material differences between students loom large when the stakes are this high.

What does it mean to be materially poor at Renowned? Unlike other facets of college life, where the Privileged Poor report experiences similar to those of their affluent peers, being poor on a rich campus is something that both the Doubly Disadvantaged and the Privileged Poor wake up to every day. Moreover, university policies and practices can exacerbate social difficulties that cause structural exclusion: pushing poor students to the margins, thereby reminding them of their difference—often in ways that connect to racial inequalities on college campuses and in the nation as a whole. The cumulative effect is that to disadvantaged students, Renowned feels like a place that—both intentionally and unintentionally—works against affirming them as full members of the college community.[4]

In this chapter, I focus on practices at Renowned that demonstrate how certain college policies and programs shape daily life in highly visible ways, especially for poor students. These practices are easy to overlook, easy to write off as manifestations of the humdrum, day-to-day happenings of various university offices. Yet it is in the university's policies that we see, in many ways most plainly and painfully, not only the disparities between the haves and the have-nots, but also the gap between the lengths a university can go to make its education accessible and the blind spots that keep it from making that education truly inclusive. Our understanding of how poverty and inequality influence college students' experiences will remain incomplete if we do not document, examine, and reckon with these practices and the boundaries they create—boundaries between lower-income students and their peers, as well as between poor students and the university as a whole. While affluent undergraduates are generally unfazed by or unaware of these practices, *both* the Doubly Disadvantaged and the Privileged Poor bear the burdens and emotional scars of the feelings of marginalization that they generate.

Renowned's hiring of students as janitors, through its Community Detail program, established a clear-cut distinction between students who had to work and those who didn't. Scholarship Plus, a program developed by the college to help students afford social events, created separate spaces even as it tried to promote integration. And cafeteria closures during spring break left those students with the least amount of financial support to fend for themselves. Poor students saw these practices—and the social stratification they engendered—as tears in the fabric of social life that indicated to them that although they might be at Renowned, they were not of it.[5]

The three practices I highlight here are those that students mentioned most often during interviews because they had the largest impact on them. Two of these practices have recently been modified at Renowned, in part because of my advocacy. But all of them are worth detailed exploration because they reflect a mindset that is still prevalent at Renowned and elsewhere, and because similar practices are in place at many colleges and universities across the country.

Let Them Be Maids

The first program I examined, Community Detail, is a janitorial service administered by Renowned that was offered as one of four preorientation programs for incoming first-year students. It also served as a work-study-eligible, on-campus job throughout the academic year. The work paid well and had flexible hours, but the social costs were high. Talking with students who participated in Community Detail, I found that many of them viewed it as Renowned's way to push students from disadvantaged backgrounds into doing manual labor.[6]

Preorientation

The end of summer is typically signaled by a slight chill in the air, back-to-school sales, and for anyone near a college campus, roads clogged by returning students driving U-Haul vans. At Renowned, fall brought another familiar sight: small groups of teenagers walking around campus wearing odd-looking cylindrical backpacks and carrying what appeared to be white baskets. At first glance, it looked like they had dressed up in *Ghostbusters* costumes for some sort of team-building game. On closer inspection, the backpacks turned out to be eleven-pound vacuum cleaners, and the baskets were actually buckets filled with soap, gloves, brushes, and cleaning products. These students were incoming freshmen on their way to clean dorm rooms that had recently been vacated by the hundreds of students who flock to Renowned in the summer for academic programs and athletic camps.

What the students found waiting for them in those rooms was revolting. They told me stories of having to pick up soiled tampons and used condoms, mop sticky floors, sweep up dead cockroaches and rats, scoop vomit from sinks, and pull out hair stuck in clogged drains. Their welcome to Renowned: dirt, grime, and trash.

During the days before freshman orientation, Renowned offered students a choice of exciting programs that were billed as a way to get to know the campus and their fellow students. Students who wanted to come to campus early chose among several options: Summit Seekers for hiking, Vamonos Van Gogh for the arts, CiViC for volunteering and social engagement, and Community Detail for, well, cleaning. Summit Seekers and Vamonos Van Gogh both charged a fee. CiViC was technically free, but there were small costs for incidentals. Community Detail was the only program that paid participants. It was also the only program centered on physical labor. The others all focused on the life of the mind through creative expression and self-exploration.

Community Detail was not always a preorientation program. It had been added relatively recently, chiefly to meet administrative needs rather than student demands. Nancy, a no-nonsense assistant dean who oversaw freshman orientation at the time of my study, confirmed this. For decades, Community Detail operated a separate, standalone program organized by the Department of the Physical Plant. When Renowned increased the amount of financial aid it granted to students, the number of students working fell below what was needed to ready the dorms for freshmen to move in. With their student workforce numbers down, administrators at the physical plant lobbied the office of the dean of freshmen, and other offices that organize orientation, to move Community Detail into the family of preorientation programs.

Some administrators contended that adding Community Detail to preorientation would increase the options for students trying to find a program that matched their interests. And it would also provide students with money to help start their college careers. But there's the rub. For poor students, the money constrained their choice. They felt they had to choose the program that not only did not have a cost, but also would offer payment. And once they did so, they were pushed into an introduction to their new home that was starkly different from what their better-off peers were experiencing.

Madeline (UI,B), bespectacled and wearing a bowtie, believed in community engagement. She inherited this drive to give back from her mother, who was an administrator for the local school board. In high school, Madeline spent much of her time outside of school volunteering for different causes in her small town. She wanted to continue this kind of work. When she received her orientation pamphlet, she was excited to find CiViC, which aligned with those ideals. After comparing her experience with the accounts of her classmates who had participated in the other programs, she knew she had made the right choice:

> I heard that Community Detail was awful, cleaning the week before school started. I have a lot of friends who did it. In one sense I was considering doing it myself; then I got into CiViC. The nice thing about CiViC is that it's practically free. If I did Vamonos Van Gogh, I would have had to pay tuition. CiViC is nice because it's economically inclusive; they cover your room and board for the whole week. They want to make sure that it stays that way; that's really important to their mission. But students who need the $600 feel obligated to do Community Detail instead of something more enriching.

For Madeline, Community Detail was just one of four options she could choose from at her leisure. The stories she heard from friends who accepted Renowned's offer—$600 for seven days of cleaning—were the evidence she needed to confirm that, for her, the money would not have been worthwhile.

When Nicole (PP,B) received the pamphlet listing the preorientation programs, her heart saw a few intriguing options. Her empty pockets saw only one. As she spoke about her time with Community Detail, she shifted toward the front of the couch, growing more animated as she explained the sense of constraint and difference that the program had evoked for her:

> Community Detail is really problematic. Poor students come to this institution and the first thing that they see are dirty dorms they have to clean. I have had several conversations with friends about this. When we got here, we felt like in order to be successful here we needed to clean. I think it's really unfair that students who are lower-income go into Community Detail whereas wealthier students are doing Summit Seekers and going climbing. Or playing instruments. Or doing artsy things with Vamonos Van Gogh. Orientation very much placed the idea of poor students doing menial jobs and wealthier students having the privilege to explore the arts, explore different things. Community Detail is cleaning, menial work. My friend was like, "I don't understand; what's the problem with Community Detail? I needed the money." I was like, "That's the issue. If you need the money, you're going to do Community Detail." I signed up for Community Detail.

Nicole's anger was palpable. Coming to Renowned gave her firsthand knowledge of experiences she had grown up hearing about while sitting at her grandmother's knee: what it's like to be a black woman cleaning up after wealthy, white people.

Some students I spoke with, Nicole's friend among them, saw Community Detail not as a problem, but just as a way to make money. A few students argued that it built character, especially for freshmen who had never had to do similar work before coming to college. Callie (DD,W) offered a mixed review. Aside from the day when she refused to clean a room where she found "16 live cockroaches in the shower," she noted that Community Detail "was pretty good. I worked with a couple of girls who I really liked. They were nice and friendly. Was disgusting, but it was good. I got paid; it wasn't as much of a bonding experience that you hear people have when they go on Summit Seekers obviously, you know, when you camp in the wilderness for a week." But Callie was one of only a small minority of students who saw Community Detail as a positive or neutral experience. Most students echoed Nicole and viewed the program as "really problematic."

Although generally reserved, Miriam (PP,L) became animated discussing how she felt she had been sold a bill of goods: "I hated Community Detail. I thought it'd be cool. It was advertised like, 'You get to meet kids ahead of time and see the college campus.' I'm like, 'I definitely got to see the college campus all right! And I was blowing dust out of my nose for a week—a week!'"

This is not to say that the prospect of earning $600 did not entice some students from privileged backgrounds. It did; but not many. During my time at Renowned, on average, 60 percent of Community Detail participants came from just 15 percent of the student body: those on full financial aid. In other words, poor students were four times overrepresented in Community Detail. And the true numbers may be even more lopsided, since they do not take into account how long wealthy students actually participated in Community Detail. Several former participants of the program, and one of the program managers, told me of wealthy students in designer clothes who worked for one day and then stopped after finding out exactly what they were expected to do. Poor students, however, generally did not have that option. Instead, they protested in the only way they knew how: via social media. The days before school starts were often accompanied by a flurry of Snapchats showing dirty rooms, with captions reading, "When you're tired of slaving away on the PLANTATION . . ." or "Why do bad things happen to good people?"

Students quickly discovered that the sticker price of the preorientation programs did not reflect the full cost, and the pay for Community Detail was also misleading. All of the programs came with hidden financial expenses. Some were quite high. The advertised price for Summer Seekers in 2015 was $535. But the cost would quickly go up for the fledgling outdoorswoman who did not already own hiking boots, thick wool socks, a sleeping bag, or any of the other mandatory items on the equipment list. Freshmen were told that they could rent gear, including long underwear, for a low fee. But at the same time, participants were strongly advised to break in their hiking boots over the summer. And not everyone is comfortable wearing used clothing. Buying the mandatory equipment for Summit Seekers would add at least $800 to the original price.

Community Detail, by contrast, advertised that it paid $600, but the devil is in the details. Community Detail did not provide meals, and checks were not distributed until after the conclusion of orientation. Students complained to me that these aspects of the program were not mentioned in the information provided to them in the general flyers describing the different preorientation programs. Ariana (DD,L) was leaning toward Community Detail "because you're paid for it," despite her father's advice that "Es mejor trabajar con la cabeza, que con la espalda" (It is better to work with your mind than your back). The money was less enticing, though, after her father did some sleuthing and found the fine print: "My dad was like, 'But you have to pay for all your meals; it cancels out.' I was like 'Oh, that's true.' The area is pretty expensive." Food costs, assuming a modest budget, would reduce the $600 windfall to just over $400.[7]

School Year

The socioeconomic division of the college community according to who did or did not do physical labor continued once classes started. Community Detail created more strain during the academic year than during preorientation because rather than cleaning empty rooms to get them ready for the upcoming academic year, those working Community Detail now entered dorm rooms occupied by their peers, with the specific task of cleaning the bathrooms.

The demographics of students who worked Community Detail were not as readily available for the academic year program as for the pre-orientation program. One complicating factor is that some students performed Community Detail as a way to fundraise for their clubs. Instead of the student receiving the money for hours worked, the funds went into the club's coffers. Based on my interviews with students, conversations with others on campus, and my own observations, however, I concluded that the socioeconomic makeup of the Community Detail workers was about the same during the school year as during preorientation, especially during students' freshman year.

Both Privileged Poor and Doubly Disadvantaged students worked a range of jobs while at Renowned, but Community Detail offered perks that many lower-income students felt unable to pass up, including flexible schedules that allowed students to set their own hours and higher hourly rates than many other campus jobs. One student told me, "It pays better than my job in the admissions office. And hours are completely flexible. You can work as many hours as you want. You can listen to music. You can clean with a friend." Some popular jobs, like shelving books in the library, paid $12 an hour during the period of my study. Serving as a professor's research assistant paid the same. Administrative offices paid $10 an hour for clerical work. But the hourly wage for Community Detail was almost $14. Why would the least intellectually challenging job pay the most? Marcia (DD,L), with uncanny wit, explained this discrepancy (which students were very aware of) in blunt terms: "The higher pay says nobody wants to do that."

In addition to learning about subatomic particles or debating the merits of Marxism, some undergraduates also mastered protocols for entering rooms so as to clean up after their classmates. One day when I was walking down a dorm hallway on my way to meet a student, I ran across Dante, a student whom I had met in passing but had not seen for a while. He was standing with a bucket that held two plastic spray bottles, a roll of paper towels, a few heavy-duty sponges, and blue plastic gloves hanging off the side. As I got closer I heard him call out, while rapping on the door hard enough for those inside to hear, "Knock knock. Community Detail. Knock knock. Community Detail." The routine nature of it seemed oddly familiar; this was the same protocol used by maintenance teams and technology specialists at Renowned when they came by the office to fix the radiator or a computer. There was no answer, so he entered the room with keys supplied by his supervisors.

Not only did this routine seem similar to what happens elsewhere on campus, but it's much like the system of hotel cleaning services. The knock on the door is the same, and so is the wording from management about what to expect. Notices posted in the dorm hallways about Community Detail explained that patrons should expect "polite, professional, respectful" employees and provided instructions for "how to contact us with any comments or concerns" about the "service you received."

Affluent students generally dismissed Community Detail as an option for on-campus employment (if they worked at all), but some of them felt uneasy about the dynamics. As Carol (UI,B) noted, "Community Detail, other students cleaning my bathroom, it's like Cinderella. You're living in the dorm with them but then they clean your bathroom. It's awkward." Her middle-class status, which she acknowledged, protected her from having to clean toilets, but that privilege had a cost. She did not want to be seen by her new peers as the evil stepsister.

Jose (DD,L) was unable to sit still as he talked with me about Community Detail; for him, cleaning dorm rooms reproduced the same inequalities of power that he had experienced at home. Jose's mother was a domestic worker who cleaned the homes of white, affluent families in the neighboring town. Since she couldn't afford a babysitter, she took young Jose with her when she had to work on weekends and at night. Although he sometimes reaped benefits, like an old Xbox system that one of her employers was throwing away, he also had some demoralizing experiences. One day he and his mother drove in their beat-up but reliable car to one of the houses in the hills that his mother had cleaned for three years. They began working shortly after saying perfunctory hellos. About halfway through their shift, one of the client's children got upset about something and cursed at Jose's mother. Jose felt powerless to do anything. He could not remember now what had caused the outburst, but the words this child spat at his mother, and the feeling he had when he heard them, stayed with him. Choking back tears, he remembered, "those little kids talking shit to my mom—I was so close to going off on them in big ways but because of the dynamics of my mother's work, I wasn't able to." Knowing that any response would cost his mother her job, he bottled up his anger.

This paralyzing sense of powerlessness resurfaced when he took a job with Community Detail at Renowned:

> Community Detail hurt me. It was literally painful. Emotionally, it was painful to have to relive experiences I've lived for the past eighteen years, cleaning these people's rooms, cleaning these people's bathrooms, literally cleaning up their shit, poop, feces. I don't know how you wanna describe it but I couldn't do it again. It hurt. My mom was still doing the same thing back home. I couldn't do it. I-I-I—it was—I wanted to, I wanted to have my mom feel like her hard work was paying off. You know, my mom always said, "I don't want you to ever do this when you are older." My mom wasn't able to guide me through education; my mom has a sixth-grade education. She's been a farm laborer since she was five, literally five years old. She was in the crop fields, *los campos.* She told me, *"Sembrando semillas"* [Sow seeds]. I was like, "Mama, okay. You think education is important; I'm gonna do what I can." I wanted my mom to feel like her hard work was worth it.

Even after enrolling at Renowned, Jose was not able to avoid the kind of manual labor that his mother never wanted him to experience again. The ability to work extra hours and the relatively high hourly wage allowed him to help his family financially when money was tight. Jose worked Community Detail regularly during his first two years at Renowned, but he only did so sporadically during his final two years.

When parents discovered that their children were working Community Detail, it sometimes led to heated confrontations. Michelle (PP,L) faced criticism from her mother when she heard about her campus job: "She was like, 'I worked so hard for you not to do those jobs and you're doing it at Renowned. What is wrong with you?'" Michelle explained to her mother that the money she sent home to help pay the rent, catch up on overdue bills, and put food in the fridge came from all the jobs she held on campus, but mainly Community Detail.

Community Detail also created divisions on campus. When setting up the program, administrators had hoped that it would repair rather than deepen rifts between students, specifically between those from rich and poor backgrounds. On one cloudless Friday in September, I was called into a meeting with Joseph and Marcus, the director and supervisor of Community Detail, respectively. When the conversation turned to interactions between students who worked Community Detail and those who didn't, Joseph argued that in addition to providing jobs, one of the reasons for (and benefits of) the program was that it prevented students from affluent backgrounds from hiring a professional maid or a cleaning service to clean their dorm rooms, which he assured me had happened. He and Marcus sincerely believed that such displays of affluence would make poorer students feel as if they did not belong at Renowned. What played out in the dorms did not align with their wishes, however. The students working Community Detail said their classmates often regarded them not as peers, but just as people who cleaned up behind them.

Stacy (DD,B) prided herself on being defiantly independent. After leaving an abusive home to live with her extended family, she pushed herself to make it to college. She earned a full scholarship to Renowned (and a host of other colleges). Stacy's financial aid covered her tuition, but not her other expenses. In order to raise money for a service trip with one of her clubs, she took a temporary job with Community Detail. Although this option helped Stacy go on a trip she never thought she would be able to afford, her interactions with other students while on the job left her feeling angry, hurt, and questioning her place at Renowned. We talked about one particular experience in great detail. As she started to answer, she punched her right fist into the open palm of her left hand, over and over again for emphasis.

It's like having a maid, a student maid! The ones who don't have to work can just chill and be here. I have to do this. This is the only job I can have. To clean up after you is strange. A restroom, urine and feces, is the worst of the worst. . . . To have to get on your hands and knees and scrub their toilets, it says a lot about the divides here between who has to work and who doesn't. To be like, "I have to clean your shit because I can't afford to go to school." The first restroom I cleaned, I was like "What is going on?" Community Detail comes every three weeks.[8] The fact that they don't clean in the interim is just nasty. They let their bathrooms get dirty because they know Community Detail's going to clean it up. One girl walked past yelling, "Community Detail, YES!" Her restroom was so bad. Why did they let their restrooms get so disgusting? . . . That just shows how they feel: Community Detail is their maid. I don't think they understand that students do this not because they want to but because they have to. So bad. The room was a mess, but I'll focus on the bathroom. There was underwear all over the floor, multiple pairs. The floor was just dirty. Lift the toilet seat and there was feces all over the toilet seat, tissues on the floor, toothpaste on the sink, empty beer can in the bathtub. . . . The most disgusting thing was the feces all over the toilet. It was hard to clean. There was just so much stuff on the floor; we had to move their underwear out of the way. I don't know how they could go in there and use the bathroom every day.

What happened later upset Stacy even more. When she was in class a few days later, she realized that she was sitting near the student whose bathroom she had cleaned. Throughout the lecture, she kept looking over to make sure it was the same person. It was. Still frustrated by the state of the bathroom, and now distracted in class, Stacy confronted her classmate. Her classmate's response shocked Stacy more than the filth. Stacy took on a sing-song, Valley girl voice to imitate the young, white woman: "Oh my god, that was you. Thank you! Yeah; sorry. I had stomach flu last week." Stacy explained why this angered her further: "She knew it was bad. Her saying that to me let me know that she knew her bathroom was a mess. You said you had it last week—why is your restroom still like that? Just shows they wait for Community Detail. 'We can do whatever because we know Community Detail's going to clean it.' That's just sad. These are students, your peers. You're just like, 'Oh they have to clean it anyway.' They don't care." As Stephanie (PP,B) noted, "Community Detail contributes to a toxic mindset, which is insensitivity to other students."

The students who worked Community Detail often told me of being distracted by troubling interactions long after their shifts ended. One day on a bus on the way to lunch, I saw Guadalupe and Marisol sitting toward the back of the bus off by themselves. I noticed that Guadalupe was consoling Marisol. Marisol, her eyes puffy, had tears streaking down her face. She was telling Guadalupe about her most recent Community Detail shift. Marisol had entered the dorm room as usual.

Even though she made eye contact with the occupants and recognized one of them from class, they ignored her the whole time she was there. A few days later, one of the students walked up to Marisol as she was crossing the freshman quad and said, "I don't want to get you in trouble or anything, but you missed a spot. Next time can you scrub under the toilet?" Marisol was so shocked that she didn't know how to respond. She felt isolated, alone, and powerless. She called a friend and ranted for an hour. That unexpected exchange had occurred two days before; but her pain and anger were still boiling over. Marisol had discovered two things that are often overlooked. Students who worked Community Detail were judged by their peers, not their professors—for their cleaning ability, not their academic performance. And the burdens of the job did not end when the shift was over.

Race adds another angle to students' work with Community Detail. White students who worked Community Detail often reported feeling that the job revealed their status as being poor. The prevailing assumption on campus was that white undergraduates were wealthy, and that no wealthy student would work Community Detail. Elise (DD,W), a bubbly blond with soft blue eyes who could pass for middle class with her thrift-store J. Crew finds, noted that Community Detail "presents a lot of opportunities for humiliation." Disowned by her family and fully supporting herself in college, Elise worked a number of jobs on and off campus to make ends meet. Yet Community Detail made her feel the most stigmatized. "Students who don't need money are not going to do Community Detail," she explained with a grimace. "Knowing that someone works Community Detail lets you know something that you otherwise wouldn't know: their financial aid status, their socioeconomic class. Just seeing someone you won't know his or her background. It's not fair that Community Detail gives it away." Community Detail, according to Elise, removed students' ability to decide for themselves what to reveal about their class background.

In addition to feeling outed as poor on a rich campus, Elise discussed how working Community Detail added stress to an already difficult situation:

> Community Detail is really gross. One room, the floor was covered in used condoms. It was the lacrosse team. It was nasty, but it was more just how dismissive people were. There was never like, "Thank you for cleaning my bathroom." It was like, "Here's my bathroom. Go to work." They just completely ignore you. It's dehumanizing. You're going in, putting in this effort, yeah you're getting paid, but you could do other jobs and get paid. You're cleaning someone's bathroom and they don't even acknowledge your presence. It can be very disheartening. Sometimes I get frustrated. One time I was in a really bad mood so every bathroom I left I'd be like, "You're welcome!" And scream it into the suite and slam the door. . . . Students on campus aren't very respectful. I don't think they realize someone's not working Community Detail because they can't get any other job. Just think about it, the people working Community Detail, it's someone who's on financial aid. These are people that are in college, but not only are they having to deal with the academics of Renowned, but also to find time to work, to make money. People don't realize how difficult that can be or how much more of a burden that can be. I've heard so many people complain about Community Detail— "They didn't clean my bathroom very well." Go clean your own bathroom then.

Outing and dehumanizing: that was what Community Detail meant for Elise. Elise saw Community Detail as giving away her social class status, which would otherwise go unnoticed because many of her peers assumed that she was middle class. Elise was not the only white student to mention this shielding that being white provided. Because many undergraduates, and even some deans, assumed that white undergraduates were affluent, lower-income whites were able to pass until placed in situations where their class background was brought to the forefront. When Elise reluctantly mentioned her Community Detail shift to others, the mask of her middle-class status fell away.

For black and Latino undergraduates, the situation was quite different. The assumption in their case ran in the other direction: people expected them to be from a lower socioeconomic class. Antoinette (UI,B), who was the daughter of a trustee at a prestigious boarding school and a double legacy at Renowned, recalled her peers—both in high school and at Renowned—asking how much financial aid she received. That her answer was "none" raised eyebrows. Seeing black and Latino students doing manual labor did not upend assumptions; it cemented them. For these students, Community Detail carried the added weight that they were engaging in stereotypical manual labor in a wealthy academic setting where most students were affluent and white and most janitors were Latino and black. Moreover, this history of domestic service was not so distant from students' home lives. Like Nicole (PP,B) and Jose (DD,L), roughly one-third of the black and Latino undergraduates I spoke with reported having family members who worked as house cleaners, maids, custodians, or janitors.[9]

Allusions to *The Help, The Jeffersons, Devious Maids,* and *Spanglish* often came up when students discussed how Community Detail evoked stereotypical images of the type of work minorities do. Ogun (PP,L), quick-witted and engaging, argued that Community Detail created worrisome power dynamics, and being Latina only complicated the situation: "Going to someone's room who is my lab partner or in class with me and I'm coming in as the typical 'Latino cleaning person' cleaning their bathroom, the power structure in that situation makes me uncomfortable." Many black and Latino students complained that working Community Detail made them feel—to borrow from James Baldwin—as if their color was their uniform, or perhaps their uniform was their color. A very light-skinned, biracial Latina, who could pass for white and admitted not knowing Spanish, shared with dismay that one of her peers said her work with Community Detail was "the most Hispanic" thing about her.

Echoing Ogun's frustration, Javier (PP,L) saw the "shaming" attached to Community Detail as neither unintentional nor without consequences, and he connected it to the few memories he had of his father from childhood. "I grew up with my mom; my father was incarcerated," he said. "There's one early memory of me watching basketball with him. My next memory is him in an orange jumpsuit." Before his father went to prison for his twelve-year sentence, however, he imparted a lesson on respectability to his son that Javier never forgot:

> My dad used to say, "Do you know why they have big windows on buses? It's to humiliate minorities." That's what Community Detail is. It's like, "Give the dirtiest job to the kids who can't afford other things." And a lot of them are minorities.
>
> TONY: Can you speak a little bit more about why you think Community Detail is humiliating?
>
> JAVIER: Because, say I was to knock on someone's door. I'm like, "Yo, can I clean your bathroom real quick?" I'm going to clean the toilet that you just threw up on this

past weekend when you're partying like crazy. Let me just clean that for you. And then just add the fact that I'm a minority reinforces that stereotype that all Spanish people do is clean and mow lawns. That's what they're good for. Explicitly that might not be what they're thinking, but to some level implicitly that's what they are.

Working with Community Detail was an additional reminder of how constrained Javier's experience was at Renowned compared with that of his more affluent peers, making him feel less than a full member of the community. These restrictions bothered him. In his eyes, his more affluent, white peers had two types of freedom that he did not: the freedom to fully experience Renowned without the burden of economic hardship and the freedom to be seen as just another student. When he entered a dorm room as "the help," both of these freedoms were lost to him.

Many students were aware that Community Detail had a variety of hidden costs and few benefits. Marcia (DD,L) explained some of the reasons why she made the difficult choice to quit:

> It's a total signifier. Even as a freshman working in upperclassman dorms where I didn't know the people whose rooms I was cleaning, it felt weird. I felt really weird whenever I would say, "Community Detail is here" and they would direct me to the bathroom. It's a very interesting dynamic between two students. That was part of the reason I stopped. Another reason was it got really inconvenient. I would change clothes. I literally put on a uniform. I would put on clothes I didn't care about, that it wouldn't be gross for me

to be cleaning someone's bathroom in. It got annoying having to go to class, go back home, change, go clean, come back home, change back into normal clothes. That was very inconvenient. . . . I think it's totally fine for students to work, but they're working as research assistants. They are working in the admission office. They are doing things that are prepping them in some way and building their resume. It's just so weird, honestly. The more I think about it like the weirder it gets.

Marcia highlighted one of the key differences between Community Detail and other jobs on campus: the lack of transferable skills and experiences that employers, graduate schools, or fellowship committees would identify or even value. There is a difference between working in a research lab or a library and cleaning toilets. Even seemingly small things, like having to change clothes before doing her job, were additional burdens she had to bear.

One white alumnus of Renowned contacted me after hearing about my study, wanting to share a memory about Community Detail that had stuck with him since he had graduated thirty-five years before. Renowned had been whiter and wealthier then. A student from a working-class family, he had worked his way through college just as he had in high school. Initially, he did not mind Community Detail, seeing it as just a job. One interaction during his freshman year changed that for him. A classmate of his, whose room he cleaned regularly, presented him with an envelope at the beginning of winter break. Inside was some cash—his Christmas bonus. In that moment he realized that his classmate regarded him as his servant. He left for home dispirited.

Both the Doubly Disadvantaged and the Privileged Poor likened Community Detail to a forced choice made attractive by their limited funds. Relatively high wages and flexible hours were often too good to pass up. But for almost everyone I talked with, the burdens of the work eventually outweighed the benefits. For those who began the program during preorientation, Community Detail undercut their ability to affirm their academic identity before classes even began. To students like Nicole, Renowned's message was loud and clear: in order to be successful, she first had to clean. The resulting "customer service" relationship had added significance for black and Latino students, a significance rooted in America's segregated past, in their families' current situations, and in longstanding racial stereotypes about who does the manual labor of life and who does the more rarified mental labor.

A Separate Line for You

As colleges become ever more diverse, they sometimes adopt new policies to accommodate the new groups of students they are admitting. Understanding that laptop computers are near-essential tools that still carry a hefty price tag, many colleges, from the University of California, Davis, to Dartmouth College, offer laptop purchasing assistance programs. Some simply purchase computers outright for students. Colleges in places where students endure months of freezing rain, sleet, and snow, like Amherst College, sometimes offer a winter coat fund. Renowned supplied both types of help, offering financial support for the purchase of both laptops and coats.

Administrators at Renowned decided to do even more to help out low-income students, acknowledging the smaller but perhaps more consequential expenses of attending cultural and social events on campus—from celebrations hosted by student groups, to movie screenings, to talks by celebrities. In a moment of forward thinking, Renowned created the program Scholarship Plus to remove money as a hurdle to participating in the life of the college. Most undergraduates who received full financial aid were eligible for the program, which provided five free tickets per semester to campus events during my time at Renowned.[10] The program was designed to increase students' connection to the college and their sense of belonging. A bonus of Scholarship Plus was that it served as a clearinghouse for information on school-sponsored social events. In fact, it was often the way undergraduates learned about some of the less-publicized events. Students who qualified were quick to make use of it. The few affluent students I spoke with who knew about Scholarship Plus spoke highly of it as well. One student, when asked if she received Scholarship Plus, joked, "I don't; wish I did." Another said, "It's a great thing to have available; it allows students to go to things they usually can't go to if they have to pay for it." Jose (DD,L) generally agreed. "To be honest man, let me tell you," Jose said, "if it wasn't for Scholarship Plus, I wouldn't know what it is like to be at Renowned." The opportunity to see performances by dancers from his mother's home country of Venezuela was a dream come true. But for Jose, and other poor students who accepted Renowned's generous offer to support their integration in college life, this dream had nightmarish elements.

Imagine entering the cavernous foyer of a campus theater. You see two wooden tables positioned at nearly opposite ends of the room. One table sits next to the main entrance near the well-manicured front lawn. The other table is next to the scuffed-up back door, which leads to an alley full of broken-down cardboard boxes. Hundreds of students are in line to buy tickets. You notice that there are two lines, one at each table. The line nearest the main entrance is long and noisy, filled with smiling faces and idle chitchat about classes and weekend plans. The students are a diverse group, but mostly white. When they get to the table, they dig out their wallets and pay $15 for their ticket.

The other line, near the back door, is considerably shorter. Although equally boisterous, it is much less diverse. Most of the students are black or Latino, with a few Asian and white students sprinkled in. Instead of money, they pull out their college ID and announce to the ticket collector, and anyone within earshot, that they receive Scholarship Plus. In reality, most say that they "PLUSed" their ticket, a shorthand they have adopted to expedite matters. The ticket collector checks their name off a printed list. The students then enter the theater through a small side door, while their peers enter through the theater's main door, half a football field away. You say to yourself, "Well look at that—a rich line and a poor line!"

Now, this observation is not completely accurate. Undergraduates in the general line could well have received some, little, or no financial aid. But given that Scholarship Plus was effectively a means-tested program, there was a much narrower economic range in the Scholarship Plus line. And because of the nature of economic inequality in the United States, the implementation of this program resulted in separate lines and separate entrances largely segregated by race, effectively creating a colored, "poor-door" policy.[11]

In their attempts to foster inclusion, administrators at Renowned had no desire to recreate images from the Jim Crow South with its segregated bathrooms, water fountains, and lunch counters. Those who oversaw the program told me that they believed allowing students to pick up their tickets separately at the event would minimize any potential stigma or "awkwardness," to use one administrator's words, that poor students would feel if they had to ask for a Scholarship Plus ticket in the regular line. But for anyone standing in the theater foyer, or in any of the many other places where students used Scholarship Plus, the image of segregated facilities was unavoidable.

Both the Doubly Disadvantaged and the Privileged Poor regarded Scholarship Plus as one part blessing and one part curse. About a fifth of the students I spoke with reported not being bothered by using the separate Scholarship Plus line. They were immensely proud of having overcome obstacles and of making it into Renowned, and they saw no shame in accepting financial assistance to attend expensive events that they viewed as luxuries, regardless of how tickets were administered. Callie (DD,W), for example, lived just two towns over from Renowned in a working-class white neighborhood with its fair share of problems, from drugs to dropouts. Many people from her community, at least those who had jobs, worked as groundskeepers and mechanics at Renowned, but none had attended it. She had grown up in its shadow, something that inspired her to enter Renowned as a student and not an employee. As she reflected on Scholarship Plus, she said that the separate line "doesn't bother me personally; I feel very, 'Hell yes I have Scholarship Plus!'" It was not that students like Callie were wholly uncritical of how Scholarship Plus tickets were handed out; they did not necessarily see its implementation as a fatal flaw. Other students, however, were not so forgiving.

Although thankful for the ability to attend plays on campus that she otherwise could not afford, Ogun (PP,L) readily outlined what she saw as the good, the bad, and the ugly of Scholarship Plus:

> It's embarrassing; I have experienced embarrassment because of how they hold tickets at the event. I love Scholarship Plus, but the fact that you can't have access to the ticket until the day of the event and you have to go to the Scholarship Plus line and you have to say your name, it's uncomfortable. Honestly, for me, I know that's my situation and it's something

that has to be done. I've had practice with things like this in high school. For me, it's awkward that they have a Scholarship Plus line and a regular line so you know who's where. Ideally, for me, you could pick up Scholarship Plus tickets at the ticket counter beforehand so now everyone's there and everyone has a same thing. Instead, I'm picking up a ticket for Ogun. They know. It says, "Scholarship Plus." There's a bit of shaming. It's the same at the food stamps office, welfare office, where I am vulnerable. Even though I go here just like you, I am vulnerable again. "I need a Scholarship Plus ticket please." Or it's like when they put condoms at Walgreens in a drawer and you have to ask someone to open the condom drawer. It's a shaming thing. What messages are we sending?

Ogun wanted to enjoy events at Renowned in the same way as her classmates. Scholarship Plus helped her get to the events, but not to experience them as her peers did. Its implementation also brought up some underlying pain that had begun at home and continued to trouble her at Renowned. Having to stand in a separate line from her peers evoked memories of being belittled by caseworkers while she translated for her mother at the welfare office. She believed that the implementation of the program was intentional. Ogun blamed Renowned for, as she put it, shaming her for using the very program that had been created for students like her. Separate lines and identifiably different tickets prevented her from feeling as valued as her classmates who could pay their way through Renowned.

Poor students' suspicions that the administration regarded them as "less than" their peers were not wholly unfounded. Some college officials publicly called Scholarship Plus "a handout." At one point during my study the director of an undergraduate dorm, Maxine, sent an email message out to the entire dorm in which she argued that students should not be able to use Scholarship Plus for dorm events because it was unfair to the students who had to pay for the events. When Vivian (DD,L), who lived in this dorm, saw the email message, she felt disbelief first, and then anger. The fact that the dorm director said that poor students had been given enough in their financial aid packages and did not need any additional help erected a boundary between Vivian and Maxine that never came down.

Along with undercutting students' sense of belonging, Scholarship Plus undermined efforts to build community. Sometimes it even got in the way of budding relationships. Lindsie (DD,B), normally high-spirited, looked a little deflated as she recounted an experience that had occurred a few weeks into her first semester at Renowned. When she went to an on-campus party that she used a Scholarship Plus ticket to attend, she noticed that a young man she had been interested in since orientation was the person checking names at the door. She was neither ashamed about receiving Scholarship Plus nor embarrassed about being from a poor family. But she wanted to reveal those personal facts to her peers in her own good time. She nearly left but decided against it. She did not, however, pursue the young man further.

Because the Scholarship Plus ticket tables were not labeled, confusion sometimes ensued when the lobby became crowded in the minutes before showtime or the start of a party. To achieve some order, every so often the ushers would yell out into the crowd, explaining which line was for those buying tickets and which line was for Scholarship Plus. Manuel (DD,L) abhorred this practice. He found himself attending everything from contemporary ballet performances to Irish music festivals because Scholarship Plus gave him access to "things I've never even thought of before." On the night he used Scholarship Plus to attend a friend's fashion show, however, he felt outed, ostracized, and "othered":

MANUEL: Scholarship Plus is a problem, though, in terms of outing people. My first and second year, it was traumatic. That was a time when it was really difficult to admit where I was coming from; I was ashamed of what I was coming from. So being in that line, saying Scholarship Plus, I dunno. It was like being on a welfare line, or social services.

TONY: You are not the first person to use that analogy.

MANUEL: You know, I think of it as food stamps, honestly. In terms of being a similar stigma like, "Those people who are mooching off Renowned's money." I feel like I'm on welfare. Scholarship Plus here isn't a bad thing, it's just the way the stigma, the way it's gone about, the way the people, the students who give out the tickets go about it.

TONY: How do they go about it?

MANUEL: It's blatant. . . . There is a distinction in terms of where I'm using the tickets. If I'm using it at black and Latino events, I think the reception is much warmer, generally. . . . But, if I go to a non-black, non-Latino event, I feel like, generally, the reception of Scholarship Plus is much colder and really judgmental. A particular situation that stands out from some of my Scholarship Plus experiences is when they yell out, "Scholarship Plus tickets over here!" Yeah. When the event's about to start, people get mad and try to get into the place, it gets really crowded and ticket takers are trying to make sure people get their tickets, and so it's usually like, "People who have paid already, over here. People on Scholarship Plus, over there!"

From the look on his face, I could tell that Manuel was embarrassed. The method of ticket delivery added social costs to what was otherwise a free ticket. Many students were aware of this and made attempts to reduce the stigma associated with the program. Student groups implemented Scholarship Plus with more sensitivity when hosting their own parties or shows. The leaders of some student groups prominently placed "Scholarship Plus Eligible" on flyers and encouraged upperclassmen to talk openly about using Scholarship Plus as a way to turn it into a positive aspect of campus life rather than a source of shame.

The Doubly Disadvantaged and the Privileged Poor enjoyed the opportunities Scholarship Plus allowed them to have, but the social costs associated with it sullied their experience and eroded their relationship with the college. Some students, like Ogun (PP) and Miguel (DD), likened the program to government aid, with its history of shaming the "undeserving poor." They saw the attempt to separate out poor students as purposeful, which further undercut their sense of belonging. Even the administrators of the program recognized that it had problems. In a revealing moment of honesty, Marshall, the dean of student affairs, put his head in his hands when he was talking to me about it and admitted that he sometimes wondered if the implementation of the program was damaging the very thing the program was intended to increase: social integration.

Scratchin' and Survivin' during Spring Break

For the nine days of spring break each year, the policy at Renowned was to close all on-campus eateries. Students, especially those from poor backgrounds, loathed this policy. Again and again during our conversations, both the Doubly Disadvantaged and the Privileged Poor made statements that were tantamount to accusing Renowned of negligence. They entered the college having been promised that money, or rather their lack thereof, would not be a barrier to full membership in the community. But every March, they found themselves forced to pay for basic necessities because of the antiquated belief that all students leave campus during spring break.[12]

As was the case with Community Detail and Scholarship Plus, cafeteria closings during spring break generally did not trouble students from more privileged economic backgrounds. Walking around campus in the weeks just before and after spring break, I heard students swap stories of where they were going or where they had just returned from: Vail for skiing, Europe for backpacking, Mexico for partying, the Caribbean for tanning. I joked with one student who had just returned from Puerto Rico, and was still wearing his straw hat, that he looked more like one of my cousins than his own white, New England kin. Six days in the sun had given him a golden glow. Stories of private planes for those who dislike flying commercial percolated to the surface. So did tales of staying in second (or third) homes in remote locations so as to avoid crowds of tourists.

Some students preferred a different form of relaxation. Brittany (UI,B), the daughter of two senior-level corporate executives, opted to spend time with her family and meet up with old friends during her first spring break. She wanted nothing more than to have her family all to herself, she said:

> Spring break; it was great. I was in Texas. I didn't invite anyone. Just with my family. I have friends at home, high school friends, so I hang out with them. But I spend a lot of time asleep and with my granny, my mom, my dad. Family time. My family is really close and that's what I prefer. I was like, "I wanna spend time with my family."

Brittany regaled me with details of lounging in her pajamas and being pampered by her grandmother. This was actually her second trip home in short succession. Earlier in the spring, her mother had summoned her home for Easter, which fell just before spring break itself. This summons annoyed Brittany. "I told everyone; it's ridiculous," she complained. "It was a week before spring break." For Brittany, the annoyance was not because of the cost of two round-trip tickets. She just did not want to make the two long trips so close together.

For lower-income students, the challenges of spring break were entirely different. The poor students I spoke with did not focus on where their peers were going, an aspect of social life that scholars of higher education have often written about. Rather, they focused on what it meant to not know where their next meal was coming from and on the strategies they employed to find enough food to eat. Looking uncharacteristically stern, Valeria (DD,L) stated, "There's always famine during spring break."

When asked about Renowned's policy to close the cafeterias, Nicole (PP,B) said, "I think it's stupid. It's stupid. It's particularly interesting that spring break is the only time the cafeterias are closed." She continued:

It is the most blatant break where privilege and wealth play a part in whether or not you leave this institution and go to your house. It's a problem that Renowned is not feeding students; one of the reasons a lot of the students probably aren't going home is because of money and you're just making us spend money to stay here. It doesn't make sense. That's my feeling. . . . They don't understand what it means to be here and the ramifications of being here under circumstances like spring break, and not being able to go home, not having money to eat. Freshman year, I literally had no money. I just could not eat anything.

Spring break was a luxury that Renowned forced students to purchase, even though many students could not afford it. Nicole saw spring break as distinctly different from other breaks because it was unencumbered by familial or religious obligations to be home. It was also the only mid-semester break during which the dining halls were closed. For her, the ability to go home or on vacation during spring break was simply a sign of privilege.

Coming from the gym on the Monday at the beginning of the break, I ran into Nicole entering a dorm, but not the one she lived in. She was carrying six plastic bags, three in each hand, loaded with everything from sandwich meat to cans of beans. Taking a detour, I entered the dorm with her. After she dropped her bags on the common room table, I noticed that her fingers had ridges in them where the bags had dug into her hands. She shook her hands to regain feeling in them. A simple hello then turned into a two-hour conversation in which she told me that she had had to walk a long way to shop for food because the stores close to campus were too expensive for her already limited budget. To top it all off, the kitchen in her dorm was locked during the break, so she had to carry her groceries, as well as pots and pans, across campus to a different dorm.

Many students claimed that Renowned did not announce the closing. This is not technically true. During the month before the break, the calendar that Dining and Hospitality Services posted on its website did show the dates of the closure. This website, however, was not one that students frequented very often or that was updated regularly. At the time I was conducting my interviews, the website often contained incorrect or outdated information and was not easy to navigate; there were many links you had to click to find out about openings and closures. Although some information was there, it was buried. Moreover, the dorms did not broadcast the closures until a week or two before spring break. One dorm did not send out a notification until the Monday of the week that the break was to start.

Students were bitter about this policy and the way Renowned delivered the details about spring break. After Marcia (DD,L), a California native, heard about the closing a few days before break started, she felt blindsided by the news. Her confusion quickly turned to anger. When I asked Marcia what she did over spring break, she laughed a hard, mirthless laugh. "I stayed here," she said, with a look indicating that I should have known what her answer was going to be. I asked her why the laugh. She replied,

> Because I remember a week and a half before spring break when I found out that the cafeterias weren't going to be open. I called the Office of Financial Aid, honestly. I don't know if they had anything to do with it, but I was so upset. I was like, people who stay at Renowned during spring break have reasons to stay: athletes who have to, international students

who can't fly home, or just students who can't fly back home. There is usually a reason we're here and, for a lot of us, that is a financial reason. How are you going to tell me that I'm not going to have a place to eat for a week? I was so upset. It sucked. I wasted so much money.

TONY: What did you eat?

MARCIA: Carrots, hummus, apples. What else? Bagels. Nutella. Once in a while, well not once in a while, often, I would say, "I'm tired of this." It would have been nice to leave the room to go eat, so sometimes I would spend money. A lot actually. It was so unhealthy. I was so mad that I have to go and buy food. It did get really expensive.

Marcia found herself ill-equipped to deal with the closings on such short notice. She could not afford a regularly priced ticket home to California, let alone a last-minute one. Marcia scrounged for food that was relatively cheap, easy to find, and easily stored, but leaving her room to eat would require something that she had very little of: money.

I met Miranda (DD,L), who favored a Goth aesthetic, during her junior year at Renowned. We had crossed paths a number of times, but had never been formally introduced to each other. She was heavily involved in the Latino community and stayed incredibly busy. When we finally had a chance to sit and talk, she told me about her struggles getting to Renowned. From her underperforming high school, with a nearly fifty percent dropout rate, to financial troubles at home, she had overcome a lot to make it to college. She was proud of it. She felt fortunate to be at Renowned. But that did not mean that she was not critical of her college. Miranda was most critical when we spoke about spring break. She lamented that she had spent so much money that week, money that she didn't really have. "I should have just gone home. That's how I felt. It was annoying. We don't have a kitchen. So it's really frustrating." She could not have afforded to return to New Mexico, though. She managed to scrape by, but it was difficult, especially since, like Nicole, she didn't have a kitchen in her dorm. Showing her frustration, she threw her hands up in the air as she sat in my office and yelled, "What the hell are we supposed to do?"

Miranda's words, heavy with emotion, stayed with me. They seemed to return with renewed force as I spoke to other students. Tracey (PP,L), who dedicated her time at Renowned to advocating on behalf of her fellow first-generation college students, offered intimate details about her life from the moment she entered my office. Although she was not normally very chatty, she spoke readily about her situation. We discussed the domestic violence she had witnessed in her home and in her neighborhood. We talked about her fears about whether she belonged at Renowned. When the conversation turned to spring break, her entire demeanor changed. No longer lounging, Tracey moved to the edge of the couch. She began to slowly rock back and forth. She became more soft-spoken. I'm not sure if she was aware of it, but her arms even shifted to cover her stomach. Tracey told me that the combination of the cafeterias closing and her severely limited funds—she came to college with $14 to her name—had forced her to live on just one not-very-healthy meal every day.

Weeks later, our paths crossed in front of the library. During what I thought was a casual conversation, Tracey revealed why she hated talking about spring break. Trying to make ends meet, she had taken on additional shifts at her campus job but had not been able to increase her food consumption beyond that single meal. One day toward the end of spring break, when she was alone in her room, Tracey found herself on the floor, not knowing how she got there. She had fainted from lack of food.

Even students whose families lived nearby did not always escape the problem of spring break. A number of lower-income students reported having been disowned by family members because of their decision to attend Renowned, especially when they chose Renowned over the local state or community college. Damion (PP,B) hailed from a town less than an hour away by public transportation, but tensions between himself and his father prevented him from going home for most of his time in college. "It's bad," he said about Renowned's policy of closing the dining halls. "Renowned's really oblivious to the fact that a lot of people can't go home during spring break." He explained how he and other students felt: "The fact that you likely can't go home because of financial reasons and then you're taking away the security of having food to eat. You're only hurting them further."

Months after my interview with her, I met for lunch with Elise (DD,W). She joked that the last time we had gotten together was over food during spring break. She was right: I had treated her to dinner almost a year before. Elise's experience of spring break was different from that of the other students because she suffered from an eating disorder that she had just begun getting treatment for. Concerned that disruptions in accessibility to food could trigger a relapse, Elise's nutritionist scheduled an appointment with her right before spring break. "My prescription was food; they gave me cans of soup," she said dryly. Although thankful for this assistance, she "hated" having "to live off of $0.67 ramen from Walgreens" when the soup they gave her ran out. Elise's experience shows how problematic closing the cafeterias can be for undergraduates' mental and physical well-being.[13]

Anger combined with disbelief sometimes erupted when we touched on this policy during interviews. Anne (PP,W), annoyed and looking like she was at her wit's end, imploringly asked me, "You're going to make them do something about this, right? Seriously, this is absurd!"

College students across the country are nothing if not resourceful. The students I spoke with adopted different strategies to cut costs. Almost all upperclassmen described how they stocked up on bread, deli meats and cheeses, cereal, bagels, milk, fruit, peanut butter, and jelly from the cafeteria in the days leading up to break. Several students told me about considerate cafeteria workers who helped by setting out bags of cereal and loaves of bread for them. I witnessed this informal support firsthand as two black cafeteria workers, Martha, an older, motherly woman who spoke with a calming voice, and Joey, an ardent basketball fan who was around my age, rolled out carts loaded with already opened bags of bagels and granola for students to take with them. Jose (DD,L) was thankful for their generosity. "I take bread from the cafeteria. It is *Survivor* for a week," he joked. "Peanut butter is my best friend over that time even though I break out in pimples because peanut butter is that oily. I wish I could go home." Students added to their diminishing stocks of food with whatever they could afford to buy after their confiscated goods had gotten stale or there was simply nothing left.

Many poor students used strategies they had learned at home but were not expecting to have to call on after they arrived at a wealthy college like Renowned. Michelle (PP,L) knew what it meant to live on limited funds. That was her life before college. She stated proudly that her family "may not have had everything but we were rich in love; that was really what matters in the end." But as she continued, her emotions and words told a slightly different story. "We actually got evicted from our apartment. We became homeless. I wrote my college essay about that, that struggle, which is terrible because your mother is crying every day." Finding themselves living on the street was not a one-time occurrence for Michelle and her family. She experienced periods of homelessness throughout all of high school. "We never knew if we had a home. We're about to get kicked out from my friend's place, just series of things." Unbeknownst to Michelle, this painful past would help her through her unpleasant present. I asked her what she had done during spring break:

MICHELLE: Last spring break I stayed here. I didn't want to go back home and burden my mom with having another person in the room. It's really super small; smaller than this office. So I stayed here with my friend from California. She couldn't go back. We hustled. We went to a food pantry. Got tons of food. It was awful to live off of that for a week.

TONY: What do you think about the fact that the cafeteria isn't open?

MICHELLE: It's an issue. They should keep it open because so many people can't go home. We already have unstable home circumstances. It's hard to support yourself if you don't have the money to feed yourself. That should definitely be addressed.

I witnessed another strategy when I took students I had interviewed out to eat during spring break. I decided to treat them to a meal at a local restaurant that none of us had been to before. The rationale was two-fold. First, I wanted to alleviate some of the worry of finding food, if only for one meal. Second, I wanted updates since our previous meeting. (I guess there was actually a third reason: I wanted to try out these spots, too.) The first thing I noticed was that only one student ate all of his food. Even after mentioning that our late lunch or dinner was the first meal they had had all day, students ate slowly and asked for at least half of their food to be wrapped up to take home. At first, I thought they did not like the food and were too polite to say anything. But then I learned otherwise. They assured me that they had had fun and enjoyed the food, but they wanted to save some for later. They turned one meal into two.[14]

Renowned made very little attempt to assist poor students who stayed on campus during break, other than referring them to a guide to budget restaurants in the neighborhood that the Office of Financial Aid published every year. This online guide, which identified inexpensive places to eat and shop and provided other tips for those on a tight budget, was provided specifically to students on significant financial aid, although it was available to everyone. Students pointed out to me that it was incongruous that the office that published this guide was the same office that knew exactly how little money they had, and thus should know that even these "cheap eats" were out of their price range.

Contrast this with the college's treatment of student athletes, who were provided with a per diem if they were required to be on campus during spring break. The athletic director confirmed to me that, in 2014, athletes received a daily allowance of $35. And sometimes they received even better treatment. Cindy, a member of the heavyweight crew team, told me that each day during spring break, the team received a catered breakfast at the boathouse that included "bacon, eggs, oatmeal, hash browns, fruit, bagels, pastries, and different juices." While Cindy was receiving free food, Michelle was venturing to food pantries and Tracey was fainting from lack of food. Renowned made sure its athletes had enough to eat, but left its neediest students to fend for themselves.

The practice of closing dining halls during spring break is widespread. In 2015, I examined spring break closure policies at the colleges and universities that have adopted no-loan financial aid policies. I discovered that just one in four kept their cafeterias open for students to use without restriction during spring break. Several colleges not only closed their dining halls, but also charged students a fee to stay on campus. Connecticut College charged students $40 for meals and $70 for housing. Smith College charged $80 for the week. St. Lawrence University charged $175 for housing. Still other colleges shut down completely. Fairfield University was one of the few that provided a justification for this practice. Housing is closed during recess, its website said, because "most American students go home for these academic breaks, while others plan vacations."[15]

Food insecurity is a national problem. We usually focus on how it affects children, for good reason. According to Hunger Is, an advocacy organization, one out of six children in the United States are food insecure. Less well known is that many college students across the country face a similar situation. During the past decade or so, hard data have been coming in about the extent of this problem. Studies of colleges across the country have shown disturbingly high levels of food insecurity, ranging from 20 to 36 percent of students. In 2015, a report commissioned by California State University chancellor Timothy White found that 20 percent of the 475,000 students in the state system were food insecure. Two-thirds of first-generation students at George Washington University struggled to secure food at least once a month, and 20 percent faced this challenge three or more times per week.[16]

In 2015, I presented my research on food insecurity at the second meeting of IvyG, a conference organized by first-generation college students at Ivy League and other elite colleges and universities. During the question and answer period, a young white woman, with a pixie cut, wearing a Columbia University sweatshirt, stood up to ask a question. She announced her name and her class year. And then she paused. "Do you see gender differences in spring break strategies?" she asked solemnly. Looking at me as if for courage, she rushed on before

I could answer the question. She described her own strategy, which was to increase her online dating activity in the lead-up to spring break in order to secure dates for the following week. Relying on the gendered norm of men paying for the first date, she knew she could secure a few meals in this way. She was treating Tinder as if it were OpenTable. Many of the students in the audience shook their heads in sympathy.[17]

Although none of the students I formally interviewed at Renowned mentioned a similar approach to securing meals, a handful of women admitted in casual conversations that they too had done so in a pinch. In light of the increased attention that sexual assault on college campuses has been getting, administrators should be aware that an unintended consequence of spring break dining hall closures is that they are pushing some students, especially young women, into potentially dangerous situations.

Spring break reminded lower-income students not only of their disadvantage, but also of their peers' privilege. It was a contrast that university policies facilitated. Most of these students talked about the closings in terms similar to those of Callie (DD,W), who called the practice "pretty terrible . . . royally unfair." Closures proved to be an obstacle for both the Doubly Disadvantaged and the Privileged Poor, since neither generally had the resources to leave campus. Some did not have a place to return to even if they could afford it. Closures placed additional and unforeseen financial burdens on already financially strapped undergraduates, adding to the stress associated with being poor at a rich college. "Spring break is the real *Hunger Games*," Valeria (DD,L) quipped, and the odds are *never* in poor students' favor.

❦

Renowned has dedicated significant sums of money to financial aid so as to open its campus to all students, not just those from rich families.

But once students arrive on campus, those from less-privileged families still often feel excluded. The students I interviewed attributed the subtle reminders of social class to university policies that highlighted rather than downplayed class differences. These policies pushed lower-income undergraduates to the margins, effectively creating separate and unequal spaces. All groups of lower-income students had the same experience. Black, white, and Latino. Male and female. Doubly Disadvantaged and Privileged Poor.

Students do not engage with their peers and professors in a vacuum; they traverse a campus filled with policies that govern many aspects of their daily lives. These policies often emphasize class differences, amplifying students' feelings of difference and undercutting their sense of belonging. The three policies featured in this chapter all left lower-income students unsettled, hurt, and sometimes angry. Poor students—whether they come from prep schools or not—pay the price for university policies that effectively make money mandatory for full citizenship in the college community.

The Community Detail program, in which some students were hired to clean other students' rooms, undercut poor students' sense of belonging. In the classroom, all students were supposed to be equal; but when poor students scrubbed rich students' bathroom counters and toilets, their relationship mirrored worker-client relationships in the outside world and set up a hierarchy between them. Moreover, Community Detail did not affirm the students' academic identity or provide them with resources to advance their careers. The work, unlike jobs with academic programs or even in libraries, did not foster contact with faculty, deans, or other administrators. Community Detail might indeed teach valuable life skills, as some students noted, but not the kinds of skills we expect students to gain from attending an elite college.[18]

Even though lower-income students of all races discussed feeling excluded because of being poor, race often underscored these differences. The chagrin that poor white students experienced when their
social class was revealed by their inability to afford everyday life at Renowned did not affect students of color. But black and Latino students
found that Community Detail and Scholarship Plus singled them out
in racially stereotyped ways that were connected with the long, troubled history of exclusion that their own family members had experienced both in the labor market and in public spaces.

There is a silver lining to this dark cloud: formal policies and
practices are more easily changed than attitudes and preconceptions
(although as I learned with my advocacy work behind opening the
cafeteria during spring break, it still is not easy). As a first step, faculty and administrators should be examining the democratic implications of manual labor jobs like Community Detail on a campus
that purportedly privileges the life of the mind. They should also
recognize that the economic carrot attached to Community Detail
borders on coercion for economically strapped undergraduates. And
they should ask themselves what alternatives exist. Instead of hiring
undergraduates, colleges could hire trained, professional janitors to
do the work. Or, simpler still, students could clean their own bathrooms. Instead of having lower-income undergraduates serve as personal maids for their peers, colleges could provide on-campus jobs
that foster skill acquisition, contact with faculty and administrators,
and opportunities for enrichment. Bryn Mawr and Haverford Colleges, for example, host the Students as Learners and Teachers
(SaLT) program, where students are paid to collaborate with faculty
as "pedagogical partners" to enhance innovative teaching at the
colleges.[19]

Renowned is not the only institution that places students in manual labor or service-orientated positions. Purdue University and the University of Connecticut hire students for janitorial services. Amherst College, Brown University, and Princeton University hire students to work as servers or cleaners in their cafeteria and eateries. As at Renowned, these jobs attract lower-income students because they often have the most flexible work schedules, higher hourly wages, or both. It is time for all colleges and universities to rethink such programs.

Scholarship Plus, the program that provided free tickets to events for low-income students, is a good example of how program implementation is as important as the idea behind the program itself. Organizations taking steps to remove barriers to access must be careful when putting policies into place, to be sure that they do not inadvertently undercut the very goal they are trying to advance. In the case of Scholarship Plus, I suggested to a dean at Renowned that tickets could be delivered electronically through students' college IDs, so that students receiving this benefit would not be stigmatized by having to stand in a separate line. An electronic system would allow undergraduates to enter events by simply swiping their ID at a card reader and could save the college money by removing the costs associated with paper tickets. Although this specific suggestion was vetoed, my overall goal was achieved: there are no more separate lines at Renowned, at least for entry into university-sponsored events. Students can now print their tickets at home after receiving an email from the box office.

With respect to spring break cafeteria closures, an obvious solution is to keep at least one cafeteria open to all students who stay on campus—athletes, international students, and lower-income undergraduates alike—free of charge. This change would even remove the need for piecemeal solutions like supplying undergraduates food on a case-by-case basis and giving per diems to athletes. But this solution is not easily instituted. Partly because of money. Partly because of prerogative.

From my own experience trying to advocate for a new spring break policy at Renowned, I learned that change can happen, but it takes time and perseverance. When administrators at Renowned told me they didn't know how many students stayed on campus during spring break and weren't sure how to find out, I suggested that they look at how many students accessed the dorms the previous year during spring break. Of course this would only be a ballpark figure, but it was better than nothing. The numbers shocked them. Roughly one out of seven students stayed on campus during spring break. Now, not all of these students were poor. Thesis writers, athletes, international students, and those who had academic or work-related reasons to stay around were included in that number. Still, the fact that so many students remained on campus caused some administrators serious pause.

Documenting how many students were on campus over break was not enough, however. When this information was presented to senior-level administrators—those who control the purse strings of the university—two additional hurdles arose. First, some administrators questioned whether opening the cafeteria was the right solution. If students knew the cafeteria was open, they argued, more of them would stay, which would be an added cost to the university. The second hurdle centered on the question, "When is enough enough?" One administrator suggested that the school already provided plenty of financial aid. She asserted, I was told, that she did not see the point in opening the cafeterias since they were closed when she was an undergraduate.

Some colleges, Renowned among them, are trying to do better. After a year of lobbying administrators, the dining halls at Renowned remained opened during spring break for the first time in 2015. Although administrators have subsequently experimented with different ways to ensure that students have enough food during the break, they have committed themselves to providing support during this period. In addition, Renowned expanded support and programming during the Christmas holiday portion of winter break. My work with Connecticut College is further evidence that things can change for the better. The college's policy had been to charge students who stayed on campus over the break for both food and housing. Jefferson Singer, dean of the college, worked not only to remove the cost for housing, but also to open the dining hall to lower-income students free of charge.

For colleges and universities that have adopted expansive admissions and financial aid policies, the testimonies in this chapter should serve as a wakeup call: admitting students and giving them financial aid is not enough to make an inclusive campus. Community Detail, Scholarship Plus, and spring break do not exhaust the list of practices at Renonwned that unevenly burdened and negatively affected lower-income undergraduates' college experiences. Neither are they the only kinds of policies that make poor students feel like second-class citizens in this first-class world. Colleges and universities must adapt and change to accommodate a more diverse student body. Understanding the contours of students' social world is a critical first step toward inclusion, as well as a crucial step toward deepening our understanding of the difference between access and equity.[20]

Conclusion

BEYOND ACCESS

"Keep, ancient lands, your storied pomp!" cries she
With silent lips. "Give me your tired, your poor,
Your huddled masses yearning to breathe free,
The wretched refuse of your teeming shore.
Send these, the homeless, tempest-tost to me,
I lift my lamp beside the golden door!"

—EMMA LAZARUS, *The New Colossus* (1883)

As I CHRONICLE WHAT college life is like for today's undergraduates, nearly twenty years after the first no-loan financial aid policies were instituted, I wonder about the next twenty years. I wonder about the next generation of students who will, like me and those whose stories are the lifeblood of this book, benefit from an education that far exceeds what their families could afford. More and more elite colleges, standing sentinel, offer a twenty-first-century update to Emma Lazarus's *New Colossus:* a beacon promising hope to all those who are determined and striving, who have grand dreams and unrelenting drive, yet find themselves held back by a lack of money. These institutions invite youth from humble means to walk through their elaborately carved gates, to find a new home in their hallowed halls.

But the realities of undergraduate life at Renowned, and at many other colleges across the country, reveal a tension between proclamation and practice. Changes in financial aid have ushered in significant demographic shifts, bringing the rich and the poor together in ways that are happening nowhere else in this country. Citizenship in any community, however, means more than just being physically present in a certain place. It is about a feeling of belonging in that place, a feeling that shapes your sense of who you are. The stories in this book force us to see the painful truth that access is not inclusion.

Diversity should not be celebrated the day a college publishes its admissions statistics only to be put on the back burner once the next crop of students arrives on campus. The four years that follow their arrival matter just as much. Diversity must be continuously cultivated. The elite college must change, adapt, and grow right along with its changing student body.

Adopting no-loan policies was a bold step to remove economic barriers to entry and to increase access for underrepresented groups. These policies of replacing loans with grants and scholarships open the door to students from economically disadvantaged families. Policies that admit students regardless of their ability to pay for college reduce the economic factors that have typically pushed students to disengage from academic and social life on campus, like their need for external loans or full-time, off-campus employment. And yet, as we have seen, financial aid does not cover all costs, and an absence of loans does not solve all problems. Talking with undergraduates at a need-blind, no-loan institution like Renowned helps us to recognize the many other factors that, even when access is possible, get in the way of full inclusion.[1]

What steps could be taken to ensure that the more diverse groups of students now being admitted are also becoming full members of the college community? The stories that students at Renowned shared with me, some with smiles on their faces, some with tears streaming down their cheeks, reveal what is missing in our current attempt to diversify our campuses. My hope is that their experiences will inspire discussions about how social class—both in its symbolic and its material dimensions—operates in college and what it means for students during their undergraduate years as well as after graduation. Their stories open a window onto the varied backgrounds of low-income students, their struggles once they enroll in elite colleges, and the changes we can make, both on campus and beyond, to help them succeed.

Lessons from the Past: The Diversity of Low-Income Students

Researchers and college officials too often treat all lower-income students alike, as an undifferentiated group of students at risk, thus flattening out the vast differences in social preparation for college among students from economically disadvantaged backgrounds. One consequence of this flattening is a simplistic account of what it means to be a poor student in college. To understand students in the present, colleges must first understand their past. Scholars and university officials alike must be conscious of where students come from—and what they have been through to get to college—if they hope to make sense of why each student experiences the next four years as they do, and how they navigate—or fail to navigate—life inside the college gates.

Our approach to understanding the social life of lower-income undergraduates must match the complexity of "the poor" themselves. One dimension of that complexity that I have highlighted throughout this book is the distinction between the Doubly Disadvantaged and the Privileged Poor. This distinction—between low-income students who have gone to prep schools and those who have not—illustrates the shortcomings in much of the current work in sociology, which focuses on the importance of family background in perpetuating class structure. The belief that how children are socialized is determined by the class status of their birth family leads to a rigid idea of how students do or do not acquire cultural capital as they approach young adulthood. The transmission of cultural capital from parents to children is not the whole story, as this account of student life at Renowned makes plain. It is crucial to look not just at the home, but also at the full breadth of experiences that shape a student and her capacities. I advocate an approach that takes into account the constellation of institutions and influences that play a role in students' strategies for negotiating their college years. I believe that we must examine students' experiences in their neighborhoods and high schools, since these are "gateway institutions" that fuel inequality. Highlighting the dissimilarities between students' lives before college and in college— instead of just differences between students' familial resources— deepens our theoretical understanding of what shapes undergraduates' everyday experiences and gives insight into practical ways to best prepare for the new diversity that colleges now so ardently seek out.[2]

The contrast between the Privileged Poor and the Doubly Disadvantaged makes it clear that high schools are immensely powerful socializing forces, shaping students' academic identities immediately before college as well as their capacities for engaging with and belonging to whatever institution they join after they graduate. Moreover, moving beyond a focus on the family enables us to detect the historical legacies of race, particularly the segregation and concentrated poverty that are endemic in the neighborhoods and schools of disadvantaged black and Latino students, and the ways that these enduring manifestations of racism amplify class differences.[3]

My own membership in what I later came to call the Privileged Poor gave me firsthand knowledge of the crucial importance of both family and educational background in the transition to an elite college. Two worlds collided when I transferred from the local public high school to wealthy Gulliver Prep. As I became familiar with my new world, I developed a different understanding of social class and race, of privilege and poverty. It was training for Amherst College that went beyond what my family or expensive books about college life could ever teach me. My experiences at Gulliver did not just show me how to manage relationships with peers who came from much more money than I did and with faculty who had advanced degrees; they also gave me a preview of how to manage relationships with my family and friends back home.

The Privileged Poor know a hybrid reality. They know the dangers of distressed communities and worry about the people they love who still call those places home. They also know the joys of burying their feet deep in foreign sands while studying a second language, and they know which fork to use when being served a multicourse dinner at the Biltmore or the home of an alumnus. But this new knowledge doesn't replace the old; it sits alongside it. The Privileged Poor still know what it feels like and what to do when the eviction notice gets taped to the front door or when the sound of gunshots precedes the spray of bullets. Although they have developed, to borrow from the sociologist Shamus Khan, an ease of privilege, they have not entirely entered the world of those who have known privilege from birth; their security in knowing how to navigate elite spaces is punctuated by poverty and its often debilitating corollaries.[4]

Although one of the major goals of this book is to document the existence of the Privileged Poor and describe their experiences, I am concerned with developing a better understanding of the experiences of all lower-income undergraduates. The stories we have heard from Ariana, Elise, and Shaniqua show us what it is like to be a Doubly Disadvantaged student at an elite college. These students experience a huge jump when they arrive at college, in everything from social expectations to cultural norms. They come from places that are often poor, distressed, and segregated, with little understanding of how adults can be seen as peers. In college, the people and customs are different. So are the rules that dominate social and academic life. The Doubly Disadvantaged come to see college not as a land of unbridled opportunity, but rather as one littered with new lessons of social and economic constraint and new reminders of the vast gulf between the world they came from and this new world that they don't fully belong to. On top of these social and cultural differences, they must also contend with the bleak reality of living with empty pockets in deep-pocketed institutions, as well as with the endless problems of poverty back home.[5]

Understanding students' disparate precollege and college experiences would be enhanced by greater exchange between scholars who study (higher) education and those who study urban (and rural) poverty. A greater grasp of how structural inequities are rooted in neighborhoods and schools would deepen scholars' insights into the challenges that students contend with en route to as well as in college. University faculty, staff, and administrators must become more aware of these issues as well, so that they can craft policies to help students' integration into campus and be prepared to deal with the problems that their students may face.

As new groups of students arrive at college—especially elite colleges like Renowned—colleges' connections to once-overlooked communities also expand, grow, and deepen. One consequence of these new ties is that they bring various inequalities into sharper relief. Some neighborhoods and schools protect youth from harm, while others place them right in the thick of danger. Students from poor backgrounds—especially black and Latino youth, due to pernicious patterns of segregation and concentrated poverty—must contend with high rates of crime, violence, disorder, and other social ills in their neighborhoods and schools that continue to influence daily life in college. These students may also lack stable housing: one in ten of the students I interviewed at Renowned had faced homelessness at some point before college. There are practical lessons to be learned—especially for faculty, deans, resident advisers, career advisers, and other administrators—in studying the way these social forces affect students' trajectories through college. For example, though everyone experiences loss in one way or another, losses can be of a very different kind for the poor and racial minorities than for wealthy and white students. Segregation and poverty increase the likelihood of a student losing someone they know to violence while in college. Ogun dealt with this reality in her first year, when a friend of hers was killed. Mental health and counseling centers should be just as well equipped to help a student through the loss of a grandparent as to aid a student whose cousin was caught in the crossfire between two rival gangs. The same principle holds true for poor students from rural backgrounds as they contend with loss from a farming or a mining accident, black lung disease, or the growing opioid epidemic.[6]

Awareness of the many structural inequities in our society, and the ways those inequities affect students' lives, can lead to improved policies, practices, and outreach on our campuses. Whether you are a professor of education, an administrator in the bursar's office, or a mental health counselor, you should come away from this book with greater insight into the complex lives of the students who walk through your door. I have highlighted that complexity by introducing the categories of Doubly Disadvantaged and Privileged Poor and showcasing the subtle ways in which social class shapes students' daily lives as they march toward graduation. But as their unique voices make plain, there is considerable variation with each group. My goal is not to inspire a deterministic way of thinking among professors and other college officials. Rather, I aim to outline the broad contours of these students' divergent experiences in the hopes that it will help us better appreciate the incredible variety of experience and capacity found within these groups and prepare for *all* those who enter the college gates.

Speaking openly about poverty and inequality in America—their origins and their manifestations—and how it plays out on the college campus can help the students themselves make sense of their experience. In 2015, I delivered a lecture at Amherst College on diversity at elite colleges. At the end of the talk two sophomores, Maya and Tonya, approached me. Tonya said something that I did not expect to hear: "Your terms give us a language to speak about our differences." She had been able to go to private school because of a grant from the Wight Foundation, a New Jersey nonprofit organization that places students in boarding and day schools. Maya had gone to the local public school in Newark. Although they bonded over being from neighboring communities, they fought about their experiences at Amherst. Maya said she often felt lost. Tonya spoke about how she did not. Maya did not think Tonya was sympathetic enough, while Tonya wanted to focus on making the most of Amherst and not on how different it was from home. They noted that the terms Doubly Disadvantaged and Privileged Poor placed their disparate experiences not only in the context of what happened when they got to campus, but also within a larger context of how inequalities in their neighborhoods and disparities between their high schools shaped how each of them experienced Amherst. It helped them move the conversation from one about individual differences, which made their debates seem like personal attacks, to one about social inequities.

The Here and Now: From Admission to Inclusion

We already know, thanks to the work of scholars who study economic stratification, that graduating from college has a big payoff in terms of lifetime earnings. We need to acknowledge all of the ways that a college can help or hinder that process. What about students' social and emotional well-being? Do students take advantage of all that the college makes available to them? In other words, we must know more about the role of colleges as mobility springboards, how they aid students' future successes or deepen their hardships. It is through studying the everyday experiences of those who eat in the college's cafeterias, walk on its lawns, learn in its classrooms, and chill in its dorms that we begin to gain insight into this process.[7]

Too often we think about those youth who make it out of distressed communities and into college—especially elite colleges—as having already won. These young people, we assume, hold a golden ticket. Yes, making it into an elite college almost guarantees that you'll graduate: Renowned, like its peers, boasts a very high graduation rate. But graduation rates do not tell us of students' experiences in college, their trials or their triumphs. After all, it is one thing for students to graduate. It is another for them to do so whole and healthy, ready for whatever the next adventure brings.

Just because students are admitted to an elite college does not mean that they will take advantage of all the connections and resources they have access to on campus. Some of the students I talked with at Renowned, like Nicole and Michelle—mostly the Privileged Poor—advocated for themselves, built support networks, and availed themselves of the myriad resources and opportunities that the college provided. Others, like Valeria and Miguel—mostly the Doubly Disadvantaged—became isolated and withdrew from the college community, neglecting to take advantage of institutional resources and supports. We may think of students who advocate for themselves as simply individuals who are more engaged, more invested in their education, and perhaps, more deserving of our support—without investigating how these differences came to be and how they map onto existing cultural norms within the university community. It is the responsibility of scholars, professors, and administrators to understand not only how poverty and inequality shape how students move through college, but also how colleges amplify differences between students on a daily basis.

Contrasting the experiences of the Privileged Poor with the Doubly Disadvantaged can help us see how much an elite college is defined by exclusion. Within every elite institution there is a hidden curriculum full of unwritten rules, unexplained terms, and a whole host of things that insiders take for granted. It is no surprise that universities—often without even realizing they are doing so—tend to reward students who enter college already familiar with these rules. That practice in turn amplifies differences in precollege experiences rather than narrowing them, and rewards insider knowledge rather than ability, or drive, or talent. University faculty and staff need to assess all of the tasks we perform each day and ask ourselves whether these are helping our students or hindering them. That assessment may seem absurd, but the voices of the students in this book show that it is not. Let us start with the most commonly used words, which are rarely defined or explained: syllabus, liberal arts, prerequisite, internship, fellowship, credit, and the like. For anyone who is not used to being around a college or has not attended a prep school, these words are foreign, even alienating. Something as simple as professors describing the purpose of office hours in the first class of the semester could be a step on the way toward making explicit the tacit expectations that permeate so many facets of college life.[8]

The insights gained from studying the day-to-day reality of college life do not just deepen our understanding of differences between the Privileged Poor and the Doubly Disadvantaged. Throughout this book I have also focused on the similarities between these two groups—on the features of college life that handicap disadvantaged students but not their more affluent peers. All poor students, for example, must scrounge for food in a land of plenty when cafeterias are closed during spring break. Michelle went to food pantries. Jose stole food from his own cafeteria. Researchers know what happens when students are "too hungry to learn" in primary and secondary schools, and some policies have been enacted to provide food for young students who need it. Yet there is a dearth of research on food insecurity in higher education; its prevalence and its effect on academic and social outcomes are unknown. We do know, however, that scarcity taxes our mental resources. It causes a person to focus on managing the situation at hand, drawing one's attention away from other tasks and negatively affecting cognition and behavior.[9]

Students' experiences in college affect not just their performance in school, but also their life following graduation. After four years of classes and parties, internships and lectures, some undergraduates are more comfortable than others at the thought of moving into an environment that is similar to what they experienced in college—either in terms of demographics or elite status. In a study of professionals in workplace settings, the psychologist Valerie Purdie-Vaughns and her colleagues found that people who encounter signals that an environment is hostile toward their group of identification—whether being a member of an underrepresented racial group or being a woman—are likely to avoid similar settings in the future. This phenomenon would hurt the Doubly Disadvantaged most: if students believe that the college recruited them, promised them an academically challenging yet socially enriching experience, and then intentionally made them feel like outsiders when they arrived, they would shy away from taking jobs in professions where the same pattern would play out. William, who became disheartened after hearing his peers discuss "cheap" lobster lunches, wrote off not only all social clubs on campus, but also the for-profit sector that he believed was for "those people"—investment banking and management consulting. This matters not just for the individual mobility and prosperity of these students, but also for attempts to diversify the professional world, and for the nation's capacity to tackle the most complex problems facing society.[10]

Understanding how inequality shapes feelings of inclusion or exclusion among members of nontraditional groups has import outside of university settings. Employees at firms and organizations that have increased outreach efforts to recruit, hire, and retain more diverse staff face similar problems as do universities trying to diversify their student bodies. These companies also have cultural norms that new employees must adapt to—their own version of the hidden curriculum—and many of the rules for advancement are left unsaid. If you are at ease with the gatekeepers, you have a better chance of getting the job. Just as some students are more comfortable developing relationships with professors, some graduates will be better than others at creating a network of peers and mentors at work. The ability to create such a network shapes a new employee's access to information, guidance, and other resources that enhance mobility within the organization. Making unsaid expectations known to all is as important in the organizations, companies, and firms that students enter upon graduation as it is during their college years.[11]

Looking Forward: Policy Solutions

The differences between the Privileged Poor and the Doubly Disadvantaged highlight how unequal opportunities constrain disadvantaged groups long before and during college. While the Privileged Poor come to Renowned and other elite colleges from high schools where teachers have advanced degrees and the ability to share their expertise with students, the Doubly Disadvantaged have attended schools where teachers divide their time between fighting for basic materials and breaking up fights. Should we conclude, then, that the best solution would be a massive increase in funding for poor students to attend private schools? Support for such an approach is increasing nationwide and has been championed by U.S. Secretary of Education Betsy DeVos. But this solution would have lasting negative consequences—namely, a systemic disinvestment in public education. Funneling poor youth into private schools is not social policy. It is an abdication of responsibility. Programs like A Better Chance and Prep for Prep, which place lower-income students into preparatory schools, as well as initiatives at private schools that provide scholarships for poor students, are well-meaning efforts, but they benefit individuals rather than the collective. For every student who is chosen for one of these programs, several others stay behind in underfunded schools. They reward the few rather than raising up everyone. The use of federal dollars to place students in private schools, instead of improving public education, further disenfranchises public schools, removes funds from districts and schools that are already financially strapped, and sidesteps the problems plaguing the education system.[12]

The nation needs what sociologist Patrick Sharkey calls "durable investments"—significant and lasting efforts to transform public education, especially in underfunded, under-resourced communities. The answer is not to pluck the lucky few out of their distressed communities and place them in an environment of abundant resources; the answer is to bring those incredible resources into distressed communities. When lower-income students have access to resources similar to those of their wealthier peers, they can and do acquire—and later use—the skills needed to succeed in college and other mainstream institutions. The Privileged Poor provide compelling evidence for this. The Privileged Poor students at Renowned whom we met in this book moved through college in ways similar to their wealthy peers. These students' remarkable achievements are possible not because they are better or more worthy than the other poor kids on their block, but rather because they have worked incredibly hard *and* have had access to incredible resources. We should strive to make those resources the norm. Closing this opportunity and resource gap, however, would require addressing the entrenched structural inequalities that handicap America's forgotten neighborhoods and neglected public schools. That entrenchment is so deep, and those inequalities so vast, that radical change can seem impossible. Our current political leadership has not demonstrated either the spine or the vision for instituting that kind of broad change.

But the bleak prospects for innovative federal policy should not make us throw up our hands in despair; there is still a great deal that we can do at the level of state, county, and city policy, and within individual institutions. High school administrators, for example, can foster a college-going culture in their schools and provide students with strategies for navigating college once they arrive. Several promising innovations have already been instituted, including scaffold advising, a program that integrates students into support networks of adults with advanced degrees and allows them to engage with adults as equal partners rather than as authority figures. Additionally, developing a curriculum that promotes self-empowerment and encourages engagement with adults can not only engender a college-going culture, but also help youth craft academic identities that align with the cultural and social norms of college life. In his examination of public schools in California, the sociologist Hugh Mehan found that these structural changes can work. I believe that it is also important to keep class sizes small so as to allow teachers to engage in intense academic coaching. I have discussed with teachers, counselors, and secondary school principals the idea of using the same kind of terminology in secondary schools that colleges and universities use on their campuses. For example, some schools have begun calling conferences with teachers "office hours" and have invited families to join in, so that the family is not only involved but is exposed to the new language as well. Some of these changes require greater funding for public education and commitment to institutionalizing practices similar to those found in private schools. Some do not. With changes such as these, we could narrow the gulf between the public schools that are required to serve students from disadvantaged backgrounds and the colleges that will give those disadvantaged students the best chance to create a new life.[13]

Efforts to help prepare high school students better for college life are not enough, however. One way to help students would be for granters of college fellowships and scholarships like the Gates Scholarship to allow direct cash transfers to students to make up the gap between estimated financial need and actual expenses. A dedicated portion for food, housing, and incidentals would go a long way toward helping students feel more financially secure. But the greatest need is for colleges and universities—especially elite ones—to review and revise policies that make life difficult for poor students or exacerbate the divisions between students from different backgrounds. In earlier chapters, I have suggested some concrete changes that could be made: defining office hours, to narrow the gap in cultural knowledge between those who already know what they are when they enter college and those who don't; creating employment opportunities like SaLT that connect students to professors, to foster academic engagement; and making sure that students have access to food throughout the entire academic year, to combat food insecurity and remove hurdles that disproportionately burden poor students.

Food insecurity was a concern that came up repeatedly in my interviews at Renowned and is a chronic problem among undergraduates all across the country. It must be addressed if we are to reduce inequity among students. Some colleges are starting to make changes. I have worked with Renowned to make sure students have access to food during spring break. Administrators, seeing how much it helped students, expanded the program to include winter break as well. Connecticut College no longer charges students to stay on campus during spring break. Some colleges, like Virginia Commonwealth University and Columbia University, have opened food banks and pantries for students. These are steps in the right direction, but they are not enough. Opening a food bank is like putting a Band-Aid on a gaping wound. We need national policy changes to help students across the country, not just at particular colleges with the resources to establish support systems like food banks. Two policy changes in particular would help alleviate economic strain for poor students: expanding Supplemental Nutrition Assistance Program (SNAP) eligibility to college students, and increasing the amount of money given to students via Pell Grants. Making more nutritious food available to students would benefit their health and also free them from taking on extra work shifts that keep them from academically and socially enriching activities like guest lectures and study groups.[14]

⊷◦◦⊶

When James Baldwin reflected on America, his home, he noted, "I love America more than any other country in this world, and, exactly for this reason, I insist on the right to criticize her perpetually." We must all exercise this essential right. For everyone who attends college, yesterday, today, and tomorrow, remember that your college is your home. Amherst—as different as it was from poor, segregated Coconut Grove—was mine. Wherever you go, you have the right to be there, and you have the right to criticize it. You are its citizenry. You may not feel this way at first. Feeling attached to such a rarified place is not easy for some students. Advocating for yourself may not be easy. Yet college is a time to develop and grow, and sometimes growth is uncomfortable. For those of you who entered college thinking you would never have a seat at the table, let alone the right to share your thoughts, opinions, and feelings, use your time in college to discover and hone your voice. For those of you who entered college having already done so, know when to step up to be counted and when to step back so that others can do the same. In the spirit of Baldwin, dare to demand as much of your college as your college demands of you. With your help, we can push our colleges and universities, as flawed as they are wonderful, to reach beyond access and toward inclusion.[15]

Appendix

IN THIS APPENDIX, I describe how I conceived of and carried out the research project that serves as the basis for this book. I also describe some of the more personal aspects of the interview process and reflect on the lessons I learned along the way.

The Study Site: Renowned University

"Renowned University" is a pseudonym for the university where I did my research. It is an elite college in the northeast United States with a long history of educating academically gifted youth. I have chosen to use a pseudonym for several reasons. First, my focus is on documenting the complexities of social life on campus and exploring the policies that influence daily life, and I do not want the identity of the university to be a distraction. Second, the conditions I have identified are common to selective colleges across the country; I hope to remove the temptation for college officials at other universities to say, "We are different" and ignore the conclusions I have reached about how to make campuses more inclusive communities for underrepresented groups. Third, by agreeing not to name the university, I was able to secure conversations with and data from institutional research.[1]

There are some disadvantages to focusing on a single institution, but there is always a trade-off between breadth and depth. Concentrating my inquiry on one college allowed me to understand students' lives in a way that would not have been possible with a larger comparative project. When studying inequality and how it affects students' daily lives, the details make all the difference. I had the opportunity to attend parties, share meals, and sit on stoops and talk with lots of students—both those whom I formally interviewed as well as those I did not. Immersing myself in the daily hustle and flow of Renowned also meant that I could have conversations with administrators, deans, residential counselors, and professors, all of which gave me a richer sense of campus life. An added bonus of locating my study within one site is that it permitted me to observe responses to local and national incidents dealing with race, status, social class, sexuality, politics, and gender in real time. Events that occurred during my study period, from 2013 through 2016, included the murders of Michael Brown and Eric Garner and major Supreme Court cases involving marriage equality, affirmative action, and immigration. Hearing students' ideas and thoughts about these larger issues was invaluable; it allowed me to understand their lives and world in a new way.[2]

Like many elite colleges, Renowned University has adopted need-blind and no-loan admissions and financial aid policies. During the time of my study, about two-thirds of undergraduates were receiving some amount of financial assistance. On the other end of the economic spectrum, roughly one-third of the undergraduates at Renowned did not qualify for any financial aid at all because of their families' annual household income and assets. An independent student newspaper reported that almost 15 percent of the incoming freshman class in 2017 came from families that earned more than $500,000 a year. But these statistics do not capture the full reality: many undergraduates at Renowned come from some of the wealthiest families in the world. During the time of my study, white undergraduates were the largest racial group, at nearly 50 percent, followed by Asian American students, at 20 percent, and black and Latino students, at roughly 12 percent each. More than three-quarters of the faculty identified as white. About 13 percent of undergraduates were the first in their family to attend college.

Academically, Renowned is one of the most highly ranked and selective universities in the country, accepting less than 10 percent of applicants. The middle 50 percent of SAT scores are between 2000 and 2400, which is at about the 92nd percentile. Current undergraduates enter as U.S. Presidential Scholars, Gates Millennium Scholars (now the Gates Scholarship), National Merit Scholars, Hispanic Scholarship Fund Scholars, or recipients of other sought-after fellowships and awards. Like clockwork, graduates go on to win Beinecke, Fulbright, Marshall, Mitchell, and Rhodes scholarships, to name just a few.

Renowned is almost exclusively residential; over 97 percent of undergraduates live on campus. After their first year, during which all students live in freshman-only dorms located on the freshman quad, students enter upperclass dorms. The dorms are tight-knit communities that serve as hubs for social activities, both formal—from movie screenings to cultural celebrations—and informal—from impromptu cookie study breaks to late nights in the cafeteria. Renowned also houses academic advising in the dorms and pairs students with residential counselors who help them with everything from choosing classes to handling breakups. Consequently, all undergraduates are immersed in a common social world, are exposed to the same social and cultural norms that govern campus life, and have access to the same campus resources and support services. This aspect of residential life, as well as the other features noted above, made Renowned an ideal place to examine what the sociologist Mitchell Stevens and his colleagues call the "experiential core of college life" and to investigate what makes some students experience the same campus so differently from others.[3]

The People

Once I had secured Renowned University as the site of my research, I set out to collect as much data as I could. It was clear that I needed to talk to a lot of people if I truly wanted to understand Renowned and its students. So I immersed myself in the community. I ate in the cafeterias. I attended social gatherings and informal events hosted by different student groups, like television show screenings. I volunteered to moderate discussions on social class, race, and inclusion, sponsored by both undergraduate clubs and university offices. I also built rapport with college administrators by attending workshops, presentations, and demonstrations on campus.[4]

I became the person whom the leaders of various student groups came to when they needed a moderator or panelist to provide context for current events, like the killing of Michael Brown, or for upcoming events, like the Supreme Court case on affirmative action. Some of the events I moderated became part of the semester lineup for these groups. For example, I hosted open discussions on shadism / colorism—how the color of one's skin affects social life and mobility—for black, Latino, and Asian American affinity groups, who wanted to encourage cross-cultural conversations about the issue. These public events were particularly interesting because I saw a different dynamic among students. The debates that happened during these events took on an academic vibe, whereas much of my other time with students, from midnight conversations in common rooms to joking around in the cafeteria, was more relaxed and unrestrained. During these events, I was able to observe which students sat together and which students snapped their fingers in support of someone's comments. Afterward, students often sent me text messages or emails, which allowed me to better understand their views, and I would often follow up on these exchanges with casual conversations on campus or at local cafés.

Scandal-watch parties became an important weekly event, not just for the fun of watching the lead character, Olivia Pope, navigate the backchannels of DC politics, but because the viewing room where we gathered became a safe space. Roughly forty to fifty students piled into the common room every Thursday night. Sometimes there were a lot more. We would watch *Scandal* and then talk until around midnight. Conversations would slowly shift from discussing what happened during that week's episode to larger issues—from being a member of an underrepresented group at Renowned to interracial dating and police shootings.

I recruited students for my study in three ways. First, through participation in both private and public events, I befriended student leaders of on-campus affinity groups. After I explained my project, these students would forward an invitation to sit for an interview through their group's email list. The majority of students whom I eventually interviewed (56 percent) reported first hearing about the study in this way. Second, I introduced myself to undergraduates at public events on campus and personally invited them to participate in the study. I recruited 26 percent of the students I interviewed in this way. Third, I asked students who interviewed with me to refer other students who they thought would like to participate or would benefit from participation. This process, called snowball sampling, generated the remaining 18 percent of interviewees. Most students introduced their friends to me at events around campus or cc'ed me on emails.

This immersive way of meeting students helped me become a known name and face around campus. The boundaries between researcher and subject became increasingly blurred as time went on. Students became comfortable with me and let me into their lives, beyond the immediate realm of my research. I met many parents and a few siblings, in person and even over FaceTime. I would receive text messages and phone calls inviting me to offer perspectives or help—from social activities to personal emergencies—from students with whom I maintained relationships after they graduated. One tool that I used was to invite students to meals at restaurants away from campus. These off-campus interactions permitted students not only to update me on what had been going on since our formal interview, but also to speak more freely, without time constraints. Being away from campus put us all in a familial setting.

I decided early on that I would pay students for participating in the study. I saved money in advance so that I could conduct the research on my time and on my terms before I received funding from grants. In determining how much to pay, I believed that it was important to offer an amount that would entice students to participate and would also respect their time. But I did not want to offer so much that students would see it as an offer that they could not refuse, especially if sitting for interviews made them uncomfortable. I decided to pay at a rate comparable to the hourly rate of on-campus jobs in the library, as a research assistant, or on Community Detail, which was about $12–$15 per hour. Given that I expected the interviews to last from one and a half to two hours, I elected to give students $20 per interview.

Once I decided on a pay rate, a different set of concerns arose. First, what would I do if an interview lasted longer than two hours? I wanted to be able to let students talk and not have to cut them off. A number of interviews did last for more than two hours; one extended to just over four. But my funds weren't unlimited. I decided that I would pay $25 for any interview that lasted over two hours. Even though I couldn't compensate the longest interviews at the same hourly rate as the shorter ones, I felt that this solution showed respect for the students' time.

Second, what if an interview ran so long that I could not complete it before the next one began? Because of the structure of the academic calendar and my wish to gather the data expeditiously, I usually conducted four interviews a day (at 9 AM, 12 noon, 3 PM, and 6 PM) and did not have the option to allow students to speak for longer than two hours and forty-five minutes, because I had to prepare for the next session. I structured each interview to cover the student's life before college first and at college second, so that if a student was particularly thorough in their answers about experiences at home, in their neighborhoods, and in high school I could ask them if they would agree to a second interview (which I informed them they would be paid for); then I would not have to rush them through their experiences navigating life at Renowned. In all, twenty-five students completed their interviews over two sittings, and three completed them over three sittings.

Overall, I conducted semi-structured, in-depth interviews with 103 black (B), Latino (L), and white (W) undergraduates who were born in the United States and who fell into three different social categories: upper-income (UI), Privileged Poor (PP), and Doubly Disadvantaged (DD) (see Table 1). I also did two years of ethnographic observation of undergraduate life at Renowned. I limited the investigation to the

Table 1   Social and Ethnic Classification of Students

Social Classification	Black	Latino	White	Total
Upper Income	27	0	0	27
Privileged Poor	9	11	1	21
Doubly Disadvantaged	13	29	13	55
Total	49	40	14	103

experiences of native-born undergraduates so that I could examine how exposure to the manifestations of structural inequalities particular to the United States—segregation, joblessness, poverty, and so on—shaped undergraduates' college experiences. I conducted all the formal interviews in an office on campus that allowed the students privacy.

To gain a more nuanced understanding of how lower-income undergraduates' trajectories to college shaped how they navigated Renowned, I knew this meant going beyond studying black students. I made a special effort to include Latino students for four reasons. First, much of the literature on inequality and undergraduate college experiences focuses on comparisons between black and white students or on class differences within racial groups, and I wanted to expand beyond these studies. Second, Latinos are the largest minority group in the United States, making up 17 percent of the U.S. population in 2013. Third, black and Latino undergraduates are exposed to poverty and segregation before college in ways that are similar to each other but are distinct from the experiences of most white and Asian American undergraduates. Fourth, boarding, day, and preparatory high schools, as well as elite colleges and universities, target lower-income Latino youth alongside African American youth for their diversity initiatives. In contrast, I did not seek to formally interview upper-income Latino or Asian American undergraduates. Most of the upper-income

Latinos I encountered at Renowned had been born outside the United States; thus, although their perspective was interesting, it was outside the bounds of my research. I decided not to recruit and formally interview Asian American undergraduates in order to keep the project to a manageable size. My sampling strategy permitted me to explore (1) intraracial, cross-class comparisons between black students, to see how class influenced the experience of Renowned for those in the same racial group; and (2) intraclass, cross-racial comparisons between lower-income black, white, and Latino students to see how race shaped student experiences.[5]

A word on racial / ethnic classifications and terminology is needed. Students' racial / ethnic classifications are based on self-identification. The Latino students I interviewed did not refer to themselves as belonging to any particular racial group, such as black, indigenous, or white. They primarily used the term "Latino" rather than "Latino / a" or "Latinx," which some people prefer as a way to avoid using the masculine "o" ending for groups that include both women and men. Following students' predominant usage, I use "Latino" for the ethnic group as a whole and for an individual male student and "Latina" for an individual female student.

I interviewed 27 students from upper-income backgrounds (UI). I use "upper-income" as a broad category to designate undergraduates from more advantaged backgrounds. Upper-income students came from families where one or both parents had degrees and worked in white-collar positions. Many of their parents were doctors or lawyers. I realize that this classification is very broad, including students from middle-class, upper-middle-class, and upper-class backgrounds, and I do not intend to convey a false sense of homogeneity among those who are not poor. But my primary aim is to explore the often-overlooked differences within lower-income students. Our understanding of the experiences of children from middle- and upper-class families, and, to some extent, the diversity therein, is far more developed in the litera-ture on higher education than is our understanding of the diversity within children from poor families.[6]

I interviewed 76 students from lower-income backgrounds, which I defined as students who were the first in their family to attend college, or who reported receiving significant financial aid. (On average, over 80 percent of their tuition was covered by scholarships.) These students reported receiving Pell Grants. They also reported experiencing dis-ruptions in services at home, and almost all had endured economic hardships. I classified the 21 lower-income students who had attended a private high school as Privileged Poor (PP) and the 55 who had at-tended a public high school as Doubly Disadvantaged (DD).

Of the students I interviewed, 70 identified as female and 33 identi-fied as male. The ratios were roughly equivalent in the three social classifications (Privileged Poor, 77 percent female; Doubly Disadvan-taged, 70 percent; upper-income, 68 percent). This gender imbalance mirrors that of black and Latino undergraduates at Renowned and at elite colleges more generally. The sociologist Douglass Massey and his colleagues found that in selective colleges, the ratio of women to men is 2:1 for black students and 1.18:1 for Latino students.[7]

Because my study included only one lower-income white student who was Privileged Poor, I am limited in the claims I can make about racial differences within this group. Lower-income white youth who attended private high schools are a small, hard-to-find population on elite campuses. These students do participate in pipeline programs, but at a lower rate than their black and Latino counterparts. There are two possible explanations for this disparity. First, lower-income white students are not targeted by diversity initiatives at boarding, day, and preparatory schools in the same way that black and Latino students are. Second, geography may play a role: students who live in cities—where black and Latino populations are larger—may have more opportunities to attend private schools than those who live in rural communities.

I supplemented my primary data by conducting the same interview with 12 undergraduates who did not fit the strict criteria for the study. These were students who had contacted me to share their perspectives, and I did not want to turn them away. Their experiences also deepened my understanding of students' day-to-day reality. Three of the 12 were lower-income Asian American students, 7 had immigrated to the United States as children (6 Latino, 1 black), 1 was an upper-income white student, and 1 an upper-income Latino student. Their testimonies generally matched those of the larger sample. For example, Piper (PP,A) adopted the same strategies for engaging faculty and administrators as did other Privileged Poor students, and she also had to reckon with food insecurity during spring break. Similarly, Spencer's (DD,A) accounts matched those of the Doubly Disadvantaged in withdrawing from college officials and also in going hungry during spring break.

In order to build rapport, I started each interview by asking the student to choose a pseudonym. This was one of the first things we discussed after they signed the consent forms to participate in the study. They often grew excited when talking about why they chose the names they did. Most of the students said they chose particular names because they wanted to be able to identify themselves when the book was published. Some were students' own nicknames from home, while others were those of relatives or friends they were particularly close to. Beyoncé chose this opportunity not only to make it easy to locate herself in the book, but also to show how devoted a fan she is of the performer. Conversations about names proved to be a funny and helpful way to break the ice.[8]

I structured each interview in roughly the same way. In the first part, we discussed their lives before college, both inside and outside school. I followed a targeted life history approach to investigate their depictions of and experiences in their homes, neighborhoods, and schools, and any clubs and organizations they participated in. In the second part, we focused on college experiences; I asked about their transition to college, interactions with college officials, living in the dorms, and day-to-day lives.[9]

For both parts of the interview, I began by asking general questions in an open-ended manner, in order to allow the students to identify their most salient experiences and to feel like they were active participants in our conversation. I then asked more probing questions. I started by asking students about their family, neighborhood, and high school. Then I asked more specific questions, such as, "If I were to take a walk down a street that you frequented, what would I see?" The answers to these questions provided me with a general understanding about where students came from and what they had been through before coming to college. The primary source of data for Chapter 1, on culture shock and fitting in, came from students' answers to questions about their transition to college, interactions with peers, and assessment of fit. I asked students to discuss their first month at school and then followed up with questions such as, "Tell me about moving in and meeting your roommate." I also asked, "How much of a culture shock was coming to Renowned?" The primary data source for Chapter 2, about interactions with faculty and administrators, was students' responses to the request, "Tell me about your interactions with college officials." They would typically describe encounters with or perceptions of professors and other authority figures at Renowned. In

Chapter 3, on socioeconomic divisions, the primary data came from students' discussion of college programs like Community Detail and Scholarship Plus, in addition to their descriptions of what they did during spring break. I intended from the beginning to ask about spring break because it is common in the literature to assess social exclusion in this way (scholars have argued that students often feel like outsiders because they cannot afford to go on fancy trips), but I added questions about the specific college programs because they quickly emerged as formative experiences for many students across campus.[10]

Given my status as, on the one hand, a black man who was a first-generation college student, and, on the other, an authority figure (in the students' eyes), I gave a lot of thought to researcher effects. Would my identity influence students' willingness to talk openly with me? And would it influence my own subsequent analysis? I do not believe that the students I interviewed withheld essential information. In fact, many divulged details about their lives that their family and closest friends—both at home and on campus—did not know. Students outed themselves to me in numerous ways—as homeless, transgender, queer. On average, interviews lasted almost two and a half hours. Students provided intimate details about their lives before Renowned, and they were equally forthcoming about their college experiences, talking about everything from how they felt about their professors to whether they fit in on campus. I made a point to remind students that the interview was confidential. Many of them said that the interviews "felt like therapy," or said our conversation was one of the few times at Renowned that they felt someone cared about their story rather than just about what they were majoring in or what career they wanted to pursue. I believe that students came to see me as providing an emotional outlet for them—more as someone who could empathize with them than as a researcher.[11]

Bearing Witness

I began my project with a certain amount of bravado. In graduate school, I had listened to seasoned ethnographers tell tales of spending full days making observations and doing interviews, followed by long evenings writing up their notes or speaking them into a tape recorder. With some trepidation, I hoped to follow this model. I crafted an ambitious schedule that involved conducting interviews at 9 AM, 12 noon, 3 PM, and 6 PM, then heading out to a *Scandal*-watch party or a campus event or meeting in order to catch up on what had been going on while I was shut away in my office. Instead of taking notes late at night, I created a summary checklist with blanks that I filled in during the interviews. I recorded observations around campus as they happened, using my phone and voice recordings. Limited by an academic calendar that restricted data collection to just the ten weeks of the semester when students were available to talk (excluding move-in week, final exams, and holidays), I wanted to collect as much data as I possibly could. My friends began to comment on my "crazy schedule." I took their comments as a sign that I was doing something right. Suffice it to say, I learned that bravado could get in the way of self-care.

About halfway through the project, I woke up one night sweating and feeling out of breath. That week, I had conducted interviews that were particularly powerful and depressing. One student revealed that her mother, who was being physically and emotionally abused by her father, would call her several times a day just to have someone to listen to her tears. Another student said that he and his siblings had been victims of abuse, and he avoided going home at all costs. Other students told stories of having to hit the floor after hearing bullets fly through their windows or about running all the way home from school so as not to be sexually harassed by the seedy men who frequented their neighborhood. I heard tales of forced homelessness and being disowned by parents.

These stories made me remember events from my own childhood that I had not grappled with for some time—all those many manifestations of exclusion and poverty that I saw every time I walked to the corner store. I began to have dreams in which I was a character in the memories that I had just heard. I saw fists coming toward my face. I stood alone in places that seemed vividly real, though I know I'd never been there. It was like watching a whole season of a television series flash through my head, dramatic scenes bursting forth one after the other. The fear, hurt, and pain grew with each new scene. Eventually I opened my eyes in a dark room that, thankfully, was wholly my own.

Strong emotions welled up again and again, sometimes months after an interview, as I remembered a particular detail or listened to the recording of an interview. Ariana (DD,L) began crying as she responded to what I thought was a very innocuous opening prompt—"Tell me how you got to Renowned." People back home, she told me as the tears welled in her eyes, had asked her how she could possibly justify going off to Renowned and leaving them behind. I wanted to recall not just what students said, but how they said it. Words often left their mouths weighed down by suppressed tears and emerging fears; other times the words leapt from their lips, as they were desperate to be rid of them. Eventually, after too many bad dreams, I decided to schedule no more than three interviews in a day. I felt more alert and was able to take time for meals. When I had a larger gap in my schedule, I would leave the office to attend lectures or simply walk around campus to observe everyday interactions. I often ran into students whom I had interviewed, and it was nice to see them outside the confines of my office.

When I started my fieldwork I had a sense of how intellectually challenging it would be, but I had no idea how emotionally challenging it would prove. It is now clear to me that I have learned as much about myself, and the burdens of fieldwork, as I have about my students. Self-care is incredibly important when doing any kind of research project, but especially when doing qualitative research. The stories that researchers hear are not just heard. They are felt. If we are doing our jobs well, we carry them with us long after the interview has ended. Some haunt us. Some inspire us. We need to be prepared to deal with testimonies that are often laden with pain and isolation.

An Active Observer

I began my data analysis by listening to interviews to develop major themes while a professional service transcribed them. I then used ATLAS.ti, a computer program that allows you to tag blocks of text from interviews and field notes with labels. I would, for example, use the label "engagement" when students discussed how they engaged with authority figures, and "structural exclusion" when they mentioned university policies that made them feel excluded from the community. This program allowed me to identify and organize major themes that emerged as I was reading transcripts and listening to the interviews.[12]

As I began to develop ideas and themes, I bounced my ideas off colleagues and friends. I shared drafts of chapters with colleagues, the students I had interviewed, and administrators from across the university. Their feedback allowed me to learn more about what was happening on campus and if any policies had been changed. I repeatedly discussed my findings with students as a way to respect their stories and the relationships that we had built. Whenever I was invited to give a talk elsewhere, I took the opportunity to practice the talk in front of students at Renowned so they could respond to how I presented their stories. They corrected the occasional error and sometimes challenged me about how I was framing the talk. These conversations enabled me to keep up to date on their lives and other events on campus that had to do with the topic of that lecture. When the New York Times accepted my opinion piece "What the Privileged Poor Can Teach Us," I called Alice (DD,L) and Ogun (PP,L) to ask their opinions on the quotes from them that I wanted to include; they confirmed my choices, but more importantly, they told me that the patterns I discussed were still evident.[13]

Although my focus was primarily on students, I also met with a number of administrators at Renowned. As with students, I use pseudonyms for them in this book. I requested conversations with staff members who worked in career services and counseling services, and with deans of student life who worked with affinity groups, clubs, and other student organizations. When Renowned created a committee to examine diversity among students, the chair invited me to sit in on meetings and present my research. These encounters largely confirmed what I had found in my interviews with students. I also presented findings at public forums and departmental meetings focused on how to better engage first-generation college students.

One of the most beneficial meetings took place during a retreat for the university's career center, whose staff were keen to understand how to encourage lower-income students to apply for internships, fellowships, and jobs earlier in their time at Renowned. In that retreat, we developed a plan to provide "cluster meals," where several university offices would combine efforts to host dinners for students during the part of orientation when the cafeteria was closed. We were making the best of a bad situation: if the college was not going to open the cafeteria, at least these offices would have a captive audience to hear about the resources available to them. These structured dialogues, along with informal discussions with undergraduates around campus, suggested that my analysis captured not only the experiences of the students in my study, but also those of undergraduates not in the sample.

Toward the end of my two years of dialogue with administrators, I noticed that they had begun to use the terms I had introduced to refer to different populations of lower-income students. "Privileged Poor" and "Doubly Disadvantaged" started to show up in their reports and during their retreats. Although the college was largely welcoming of my approach, however, I sometimes found myself caught in the middle when students and administrators were on opposite sides of an issue. I ended up deciding to cope with these situations by letting my findings speak for themselves. In conversations with deans and other administrators, I used material from my interviews and notes to give them a picture of how students perceived the situation on campus. When they asked me, for example, about the effects of closing cafeterias and other services during spring break, I told them that Michelle (PP,L) had gone to a food pantry, and Tracey (PP,L) had fainted in her room. I also reminded them that for some students, home is a place of harm, not comfort. Keeping the relationship a reciprocal one, I gave them the opportunity to confirm or deny the patterns that I had detected. In the case of spring break, administrators confirmed that roughly 1 out of 7 students remained on campus. The combination of hard data and my qualitative accounts of what it was like for students who stayed on campus eventually convinced the administration to change its policy and keep the dining halls open during spring break.

My role in contentious campus controversies was not always so straightforward. One day a group of students, primarily students of color, initiated a surprise protest in memory of the black men and women who had recently been murdered at the hands of police officers. Their protest was designed to disrupt a long-standing tradition in which hundreds of students gather at midnight to celebrate the end of term. Administrators were worried about what might happen if student protestors faced off against their partying peers. The dean of students called me into his office around 6 PM that day. He, several other deans, and the deputy chiefs of the campus police had assembled for an emergency meeting, and they asked me for suggestions about how to prevent the scene from devolving into a fight. I decided the best course of action would be to call and text the student leaders I knew to be involved. I asked them what they needed from the school and relayed that information to the deans in the office. Over the next several hours, I would leave the dean's office each time my phone rang in order to have private conversations with the students. Then, as I walked back in to inform the deans of what was going on, the phone would ring again. We finally came to an agreement, which allowed the students who wanted to protest ample space to do so, without police inference. Campus police would remain, however, to provide them protection. Although I helped create a workable compromise, I had to choose sides. My primary concern was with the well-being of the students.

The night of the protest was indicative of a struggle I felt throughout the process of my research project. In order for this project to succeed, I had to maintain a primary allegiance (for lack of a better word) to my interviewees. Otherwise, I risked becoming just another authority figure whom they would either ignore, mistrust, or use for little more than a recommendation letter. But at the same time, I needed to maintain relationships with the administrators at Renowned, in order to push Renowned and other colleges and universities to better understand the difference between making a college accessible and making it inclusive.

(Aiming for) Apples to Apples

Much of my project focuses on differences between two groups of lower-income students who have had different high school experiences before enrolling at an elite college: the Privileged Poor (those who have attended prep schools) and the Doubly Disadvantaged (those who have attended distressed public high schools). But for my conclusions to be valid, the students in these two groups must be pretty much the same except for their disparate high school experiences. If they differed in some other way, then that factor, rather than their high school experience, might explain their different responses to college. In this section I discuss selection bias—that is, whether, as I examined differences between the Doubly Disadvantaged and Privileged Poor, I was indeed comparing apples to apples.[14]

I first documented the existence of these two groups, using both qualitative and quantitative data, when I examined undergraduate life at another elite private college, which I called Midtown College. In that study, I showed that the two groups were similar on many baseline characteristics associated with negative college transition and acclimation experiences.[15]

The two groups shared several crucial elements: economic hardship, familial instability, and limited parental resources and knowledge about college. They also had a similar level of exposure to segregation, disorder, and violence in their neighborhoods and primary schools. Using data from interviews I collected with students and from the National Longitudinal Survey of Freshmen, as well as information about where the students lived and what schools they attended, I showed that their experiences diverged once the group I call the Privileged Poor entered preparatory high schools. I also provided evidence that, for the most part, the Privileged Poor and their families did not seek out these schools, but rather discovered them from flyers, extrafamilial networks, and independent solicitations from programs—like A Better Chance, Prep for Prep, or the Wight Foundation—that place students from underrepresented groups into private schools. I found that although the Doubly Disadvantaged did have access to some enrichment programs that helped them prepare for college, these programs did not remove students from their high schools. Examples include the LEDA Program (Leadership Enterprise for a Diverse America), South Central Scholars (now the SCS Noonan Scholars), and the Schuler Scholar Program, as well as competitive college access programs like Questbridge, which matches successful applications to highly selective undergraduate institutions.[16]

It is important to note that my investigation of campus life at Renowned focused solely on those undergraduates who have successfully graduated from high school, passed the stringent admissions selection process, and decided to matriculate. I cannot speak of the experiences of the Doubly Disadvantaged and Privileged Poor who did not make it to college. When comparing the experiences of the Privileged Poor and the Doubly Disadvantaged at Renowned, however, I am confident that the differences I have found are a consequence of their different high school experiences, rather than any other difference between the groups.[17]

First, as in my study at Midtown College, the Doubly Disadvantaged and Privileged Poor at Renowned gave similar accounts of family and neighborhood dynamics as well as exposure to poverty and segregation in their elementary and middle schools. Second, I did not select students based upon their precollege experiences. The only criterion for participation was having been born in the United States. Third, I asked all students to discuss how they came to participate in and to detail their experiences with any enrichment programs (such as

Questbridge) that assisted them when applying for scholarships or to college and / or any pipeline programs (such as Prep for Prep) that placed them in private high schools with the intention of providing them access to college. Both types of programs seek out academically gifted youth who are lower-income and / or minority. I found that both the Doubly Disadvantaged and the Privileged Poor participated in auxiliary programs and reported discovering them primarily from sources outside of their families.[18]

For the Doubly Disadvantaged, the most common way students reported finding out about enrichment programs was through direct outreach by different scholarship and college access programs (18 percent) and through teacher recommendations (11 percent) (see Figure 1). These students were identified as academically talented by staff at their school or by getting a high score on a standardized test at the state or national level. A small number of the Doubly Disadvantaged (11 percent) reported independently seeking out programs that would help them gain access to college after they realized that their families had limited resources or would not be able to support them in going away for college. For example, Elise (DD,W), who had been disowned by her father and whose mother was in debt from medical bills, recalled how she discovered Questbridge:

I was looking for scholarships my junior year and I went to websites like Scholarships.com. And Questbridge, they had something for the summer before senior year. I missed the deadline for it but I went on the Questbridge website and realized it was something that I wanted to do. You know, it's free, free scholarship to college and it'll help match you with full financial aid.

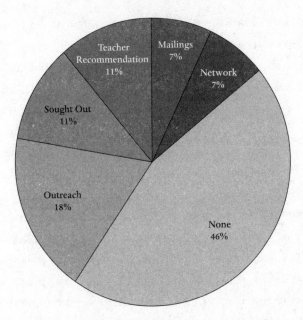

FIGURE I. Mode of discovery for the Doubly Disadvantaged

Almost half (46 percent) of the Doubly Disadvantaged reported not participating in any program, either because they were unaware of them or because their school counselors actively discouraged them from applying. Joshua (DD,B) regretted not participating in any programs after he heard about the experiences of some of his college classmates. "My school actually didn't present these things to me," he said.

The vast majority (90 percent) of the Privileged Poor I interviewed at Renowned reported that neither they nor their families had sought out scholarships or programs for them to attend private schools. Indeed most of the students reported that they were the only one of their siblings to attend private school. For half of the students, this choice was the result of teacher recommendations (30 percent) and outreach by the programs and private high schools themselves (20 percent) (see Figure 2). For example, Sara (PP,L), whose parents worked as landscapers and had limited English proficiency, said, "I was fortunate that, in sixth grade, someone came to my public school and talked about the private schools in my hometown. Due to that, I entered my private high school. That place was so nurturing for me." Two additional pathways were important: direct mailings from private schools and pipeline programs (15 percent) and sport scholarships (15 percent). Patrice (PP,L) noted that Prep for Prep reached out to her middle school:

> Prep for Prep always sends packages to schools to hand out to kids, but they never gave them out. They don't think parents would let their kids go away, so they never gave them out. But I was close to the counselor and I saw that on her desk once and I was like, "Hey! I kind of want to do this." She was like, "Oh, are you sure your mom would let you? I don't know if this middle school prepares you for that. But you're smart!"

The two varsity athletes in my sample who earned scholarships to private schools were both male and played football and basketball in high school. In informal conversations with other athletes, both men and women, I discovered that they had also been recruited and received scholarships to attend private high schools. In contrast with the Doubly Disadvantaged, who often reported being members of several different enrichment programs, the Privileged Poor generally reported working with only one program aimed at helping them gain access to college, because their high schools had a team of administrators who handled that kind of work. Some told me that they didn't learn about programs like Questbridge until they got to Renowned because their high school

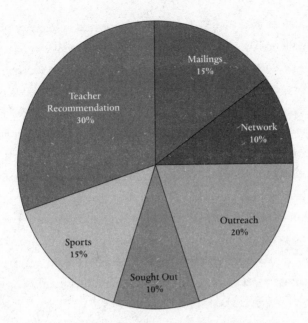

FIGURE 2. Mode of discovery for the Privileged Poor

counselors were not very knowledgeable about scholarships for disadvantaged minority high school students.

A final factor that could confound my comparison between groups of students is that an attitude or family environment found among the Privileged Poor but not the Doubly Disadvantaged might explain both why the Privileged Poor found it easier to interact with professors and peers in college and why they attended private school in the first place. Perhaps Privileged Poor students would have been better at navigating social hierarchies in elite environments even if they hadn't attended private high schools first. I do not think this is likely, however, given the very specific nature of the knowledge that is transmitted within elite high schools and the limited exposure to such environments in students' personal networks before they enter these schools.

My work at Midtown College and Renowned University provides strong evidence that the differences I have observed between the Privileged Poor and the Doubly Disadvantaged has to do with their disparate precollege experiences rather than with differences between them before high school. This work points out the shortcomings of treating lower-income undergraduates as a homogenous group of at-risk students. Studies that do so cannot properly measure the effects of inequality and poverty on college experiences, and as a result, they lead to biased understandings of how class and culture reproduce inequality in college. I have documented large differences between the Privileged Poor and the Doubly Disadvantaged, and both groups are represented in increasing numbers at elite colleges and universities. It is important for scholars to fully explore and document their experiences and recognize their distinctiveness.

Notes

Introduction

1. William Bowen and Derek Bok, *The Shape of the River: Long-Term Consequences of Considering Race in College and University Admissions* (Princeton, NJ: Princeton University Press, 1998); Jenny Staletovich and Patricia Borns, "West Grove: The Miami Neighborhood That Time Forgot," *Miami Herald*, April 6, 2013, http://www.miamiherald.com/news/local/in -depth/article1948901.html.

2. Tressie McMillan Cottom, *Lower Ed: The Troubling Rise of For-Profit Colleges in the New Economy* (New York: New Press, 2017); Susan Choy, *Students Whose Parents Did Not Go to College: Postsecondary Access, Persistence, and Attainment. Findings from the Condition of Education, 2001*, Report no. NCES 2001-126 (Washington, D.C.: U.S. Department of Education, National Center for Education Statistics, December 2001), available at https://files.eric.ed.gov/fulltext/ED460660.pdf; Jennifer Engle, Adolfo Bermeo, and Colleen O'Brien, *Straight from the Source: What Works for First-Generation College Students* (Washington, D.C.: Pell Institute for the Study of Opportunity in Higher Education, December 2006), available at https://files.eric.ed.gov/fulltext/ED501693.pdf; Caroline M. Hoxby and

.

Christopher Avery, "The Missing 'One-Offs': The Hidden Supplies of High-Achieving, Low Income Students" (Working Paper 18586, National Bureau of Economic Research, Cambridge, MA, December 2012), http://www.nber.org/papers/w18586; Jolanta Juszkiewicz, *Trends in Community College Enrollment and Completion Data, 2015* (Washington, D.C.: American Association of Community Colleges, 2015), available at https://files.eric.ed.gov/fulltext/ED557990.pdf; Shankar Vedantam, "Elite Colleges Struggle to Recruit Smart, Low-Income Kids," *Morning Edition,* National Public Radio, January 9, 2013, http://www.npr.org/2013/01/09/168889785/elite-colleges-struggle-to-recruit-smart-low-income-kids.

3. Anthony P. Carnevale and Jeff Strohl, "How Increasing College Access Is Increasing Inequality and What to Do about It," in *Rewarding Strivers: Helping Low-Income Students Succeed in College,* ed. Richard D. Kahlenberg (New York: Century Foundation Press, 2010), 71–190.

4. Raj Chetty et al., "Mobility Report Cards: The Role of Colleges in Intergenerational Mobility" (Equality of Opportunity Project, NBER Working Paper no. 23618, revised, July 2017), http://www.equality-of-opportunity.org/papers/coll_mrc_paper.pdf. See also Gregor Aisch et al., "Some Colleges Have More Students from the Top 1 Percent than the Bottom 60. Find Yours," *New York Times,* January 18, 2017, https://www.nytimes.com/interactive/2017/01/18/upshot/some-colleges-have-more-students-from-the-top-1-percent-than-the-bottom-60.html. Elite professional schools for business and law have similar numbers; see Daniel Fisher, "Poor Students Are the Real Victims of College Discrimination," *Forbes,* May 2, 2012, https://www.forbes.com/sites/danielfisher/2012/05/02/poor-students-are-the-real-victims-of-college-discrimination/.

5. Karen W. Arenson, "Senate Looking at Endowments as Tuition Rises," *New York Times,* January 25, 2008, http://www.nytimes.com/2008/01/25/education/25endowments.html; Nicholas Hillman, *Economic Diversity among Selective Colleges: Measuring the Enrollment Impact of "No-Loan" Pro-*

grams (Washington, D.C.: Institute for Higher Education Policy, August 2012), available at https://files.eric.ed.gov/fulltext/ED534615.pdf.

6. Shapiro quoted in "Princeton University Further Increases Its Support for Students on Financial Aid," press release, July 21, 2000, https://pr.princeton.edu/reports/financial_aid/00/release_jan2000.pdf. Saleh quoted in Davidson Goldin, "Aid Packages Can Shift the Balance as the Leading Colleges Compete for the Best Students," *New York Times*, April 15, 1998, http://www.nytimes.com/1998/04/15/us/aid-packages-can-shift-balance-leading-colleges-compete-for-best-students.html. No-loan financial aid regimes are expensive to maintain. Williams College adopted no-loan policies in 2008, but reversed the decision when its endowment growth slowed (Goldin, "Aid Packages Can Shift the Balance"). For more on no-loan policies, see Hillman, *Economic Diversity among Selective Colleges*; Nicholas W. Hillman, "Economic Diversity in Elite Higher Education: Do No-Loan Programs Impact Pell Enrollments?" *Journal of Higher Education* 84, no. 6 (2013): 806–833; Anthony Abraham Jack, "What the Privileged Poor Can Teach Us," op-ed, *New York Times*, September 12, 2015, https://www.nytimes.com/2015/09/13/opinion/sunday/what-the-privileged-poor-can-teach-us.html.

7. The Pell Grant is a federal, means-tested program intended to make higher education more accessible to those from disadvantaged backgrounds. In 2016, for example, youth whose families earned less than $25,000 automatically qualified for a Pell Grant and for no-loan policies at most colleges. The Cooke Prize is awarded by the Jack Kent Cooke Foundation; see https://www.jkcf.org/our-grants/cooke-prize-for-equity-in-educational-excellence/. For an overview of demographic changes at colleges, see "The Most Economically Diverse Top Colleges," The Upshot, *New York Times*, September 8, 2014, https://www.nytimes.com/interactive/2014/09/09/upshot/09up-college-access-index.html. Colleges also changed how they communicated with families, especially

lower-income families, about financial aid. As Bridget Terry Long, an economist at the Harvard Graduate School of Education, noted in a personal communication (November 2017), "Instead of talking about the FAFSA and EFC cut-offs, they started to frame financial aid in terms of family income. Given low-income families struggle with aid forms and getting good information, this move towards a more simplified message also made a big difference in attracting low-income applicants." For a discussion of how information shapes college decisions, see Eric P. Bettinger et al., "The Role of Simplification and Information in College Decisions: Results from the H&R Block FAFSA Experiment" (working paper, National Bureau of Economic Research, September 2009), http://www.nber.org/papers/w15361.

8. We must not forget that there remains a large racial income gap. Some black college graduates earn less than their white counterparts with less education. Nevertheless, a poor black kid who goes to an elite college is far better off than a poor black kid who goes to his local community college. For a discussion of the economic payoff of a college degree, see Jennie E. Brand and Yu Xie, "Who Benefits Most from College? Evidence for Negative Selection in Heterogeneous Economic Returns to Higher Education," *American Sociological Review* 75, no. 2 (2010): 294; Dominic J. Brewer, Eric R. Eide, and Ronald G. Ehrenberg, "Does It Pay to Attend an Elite Private College? Cross-Cohort Evidence on the Effects of College Type on Earnings," *Journal of Human Resources* 34, no. 1 (1999): 104–123; Eric Eide, Dominic J. Brewer, and Ronald G. Ehrenberg, "Does It Pay to Attend an Elite Private College? Evidence on the Effects of Undergraduate College Quality on Graduate School Attendance," *Economics of Education Review* 17, no. 4 (1998): 371–376; Thomas J. Espenshade and Alexandria Walton Radford, *No Longer Separate, Not Yet Equal: Race and Class in Elite College Admission and Campus Life* (Princeton, NJ: Princeton University Press, 2009); Jerome Karabel, *The Chosen: The Hidden History of*

Admission and Exclusion at Harvard, Yale, and Princeton (Boston: Houghton Mifflin, 2005); Shamus Rahman Khan, "The Sociology of Elites," *Annual Review of Sociology* 38 (2012): 361–377; Lauren A. Rivera, *Pedigree: How Elite Students Get Elite Jobs* (Princeton, NJ: Princeton University Press, 2015).

9. Jenny Anderson, "For Minority Students at Elite New York Private Schools, Admittance Doesn't Bring Acceptance," *New York Times*, October 19, 2012, http://www.nytimes.com/2012/10/21/nyregion/for-minority-students-at-elite-new-york-private-schools-admittance-doesnt-bring-acceptance.html; Matthew Chingos and Daniel Kuehn, *The Effects of Statewide Private School Choice on College Enrollment and Graduation: Evidence from the Florida Tax Credit Scholarship Program* (Washington, D.C.: Urban Institute, September 2017, updated December 2017), https://sites.hks.harvard.edu/pepg/conferences/learning-from-longterm-effects-2018/papers/panel-i-chingos-kuehn.pdf; Anthony Abraham Jack, "Crisscrossing Boundaries: Variation in Experiences with Class Marginality among Lower-Income, Black Undergraduates at an Elite College," in *College Students' Experiences of Power and Marginality: Sharing Spaces and Negotiating Differences*, ed. Elizabeth Lee and Chaise LaDousa (New York: Routledge, 2015), 83–101.

10. Jonathan Kozol, *Savage Inequalities: Children in America's Schools* (New York: HarperPerennial, 1991); Jonathan Kozol, *The Shame of the Nation: The Restoration of Apartheid Schooling in America* (New York: Three Rivers Press, 2005); Bowen Paulle, *Toxic Schools: High-Poverty Education in New York and Amsterdam* (Chicago: University of Chicago Press, 2013).

11. Jack, "Crisscrossing Boundaries"; Anthony Abraham Jack and Veronique Irwin, "Seeking Out Support: Variation in Academic Engagement Strategies among Black Undergraduates at an Elite College," in *Clearing the Path for First-Generation College Students: Qualitative and Intersectional Studies of Educational Mobility*, ed. Ashley C. Rondini, Bedelia Richards-

Dowden, and Nicolas P. Simon (Lanham, MD: Lexington Books, 2018), 384.

12. For a theoretically informed basis for "studying up," or examining inequality beyond focusing on poverty, see Khan, "The Sociology of Elites"; Michèle Lamont, *Money, Morals, and Manners: The Culture of the French and American Upper-Middle Class* (Chicago: University of Chicago Press, 1992); Rivera, *Pedigree*. Similarly, sociologist Michael Rodríguez-Muñiz argues for moving beyond what he calls "ontological myopias," analytical blinders that restrict how we study the social world and limit the types of questions we ask; see Michael Rodríguez-Muñiz, "Intellectual Inheritances: Cultural Diagnostics and the State of Poverty Knowledge," *American Journal of Cultural Sociology* 3, no. 1 (2015): 89–122. On elite colleges as mobility springboards for members of underrepresented groups, see Bowen and Bok, *Shape of the River*; Stacy Berg Dale and Alan B. Krueger, "Estimating the Payoff to Attending a More Selective College: An Application of Selection on Observables and Unobservables," *Quarterly Journal of Economics* 117, no. 4 (2002): 1491–1527; Eide, Brewer, and Ehrenberg, "Does It Pay to Attend an Elite Private College?"

13. For a discussion of how inequality disadvantages youth in urban public schools, see Prudence Carter, *Keepin' It Real: School Success beyond Black and White* (New York: Oxford University Press, 2005); Kozol, *Savage Inequalities*; Patricia McDonough, *Choosing Colleges: How Social Class and Schools Structure Opportunity* (Albany: State University of New York Press, 1997); Kathryn Neckerman, *Schools Betrayed: Roots of Failure in Inner-City Education* (Chicago: University of Chicago Press, 2007); James Ryan, *Five Miles Away, A World Apart: One City, Two Schools, and the Story of Educational Opportunity in Modern America* (New York: Oxford University Press, 2010). For an overview of Prep for Prep, see https://www.prepforprep.org/page.

14. On the 2014 caseload for counselors, see Elizabeth A. Harris, "Little College Guidance: 500 High School Students per Counselor," *New York Times*, December 25, 2014, http://www.nytimes.com/2014/12/26/nyregion/little-college-guidance-500-high-school-students-per-counselor.html. For a discussion of pipeline programs that place lower-income and / or minority students into private high schools, see Amanda Barrett Cox, "Cohorts, 'Siblings,' and Mentors: Organizational Structures and the Creation of Social Capital," *Sociology of Education* 90, no. 1 (2017): 47–63; Rory Kramer, "Diversifiers at Elite Schools," *Du Bois Review: Social Science Research on Race* 5, no. 2 (2008): 287–307; Deval Patrick, *A Reason to Believe: Lessons from an Improbable Life* (New York: Broadway Books, 2011); Richard L. Zweigenhaft and G. William Domhoff, *Blacks in the White Establishment?: A Study of Race and Class in America* (New Haven, CT: Yale University Press, 1991). See also Simone Ispa-Landa, "Gender, Race, and Justifications for Group Exclusion: Urban Black Students Bussed to Affluent Suburban Schools," *Sociology of Education* 86, no. 3 (2013): 218–233; Megan M. Holland, "Only Here for the Day: The Social Integration of Minority Students at a Majority White High School," *Sociology of Education* 85, no. 2 (2012): 101–120.

15. Elizabeth A. Armstrong and Laura T. Hamilton, *Paying for the Party: How College Maintains Inequality* (Cambridge, MA: Harvard University Press, 2013), 10. For a detailed discussion of cultural capital, see Pierre Bourdieu, "The Forms of Capital," in *Handbook for Theory and Research for the Sociology of Education*, ed. J. G. Richardson (Westport, CT: Greenwood Press, 1986), 241–258; Annette Lareau, *Unequal Childhoods: Class, Race, and Family Life* (Berkeley: University of California Press, 2003); Annette Lareau and Elliot Weininger, "Cultural Capital in Educational Research: A Critical Assessment," *Theory and Society* 32, no. 5 / 6 (2003): 567–606; Michèle Lamont and Annette Lareau, "Cultural Capital: Allusions, Gaps and Glissandos in Recent Theoretical Developments," *Sociological*

Theory 6, no. 2 (1988): 153–168. For a discussion of social class on the college campus, see Elizabeth Aries and Maynard Seider, "The Interactive Relationship between Class Identity and the College Experience: The Case of Lower Income Students," *Qualitative Sociology* 28, no. 4 (2005): 419–443; Patrick T. Terenzini et al., "First-Generation College Students: Characteristics, Experiences, and Cognitive Development," *Research in Higher Education* 37, no. 1 (1996): 1–22; Kimberly Torres, "'Culture Shock': Black Students Account for Their Distinctiveness at an Elite College," *Ethnic and Racial Studies* 32, no. 5 (2009): 883–905. For a renewed push to investigate students' experiences when thinking about the term "first-generation college student," see Thai-Huy Nguyen and Bach Mai Dolly Nguyen, "Is the 'First-Generation Student' Term Useful for Understanding Inequality? The Role of Intersectionality in Illuminating the Implications of an Accepted—Yet Unchallenged—Term," *Review of Research in Education* 42, no. 1 (2018): 146–176.

CHAPTER I   *"Come with Me to Italy!"*

1. See Elizabeth Aries and Maynard Seider, "The Interactive Relationship between Class Identity and the College Experience: The Case of Lower Income Students," *Qualitative Sociology* 28, no. 4 (2005): 419–443; Ann Mullen, "Elite Destinations: Pathways to Attending an Ivy League University," *British Journal of Sociology of Education* 30, no. 1 (2009): 15–27; Kimberly Torres, "'Culture Shock': Black Students Account for Their Distinctiveness at an Elite College," *Ethnic and Racial Studies* 32, no. 5 (2009): 883–905.

2. For a discussion of the bias toward quantitative research in education, see Mitchell L. Stevens, "Culture and Education," *Annals of the American Academy of Political and Social Science* 619, no. 1 (2008): 97–113; Mitchell L. Stevens, Elizabeth A. Armstrong, and Richard Arum, "Sieve, Incubator,

Temple, Hub: Empirical and Theoretical Advances in the Sociology of Higher Education," *Annual Review of Sociology* 34, no. 1 (2008): 127–151.

3. Camille Z. Charles et al., *Taming the River: Negotiating the Academic, Financial, and Social Currents in Selective Colleges and Universities* (Princeton, NJ: Princeton University Press, 2009); Janice M. McCabe, *Connecting in College: How Friendship Networks Matter for Academic and Social Success* (Chicago: University of Chicago Press, 2016); Ernest T. Pascarella and Patrick T. Terenzini, *How College Affects Students: Findings and Insights from Twenty Years of Research* (New York: Wiley, 1991); Lauren A. Rivera, *Pedigree: How Elite Students Get Elite Jobs* (Princeton, NJ: Princeton University Press, 2015); Nicole M. Stephens et al., "A Cultural Mismatch: Independent Cultural Norms Produce Greater Increases in Cortisol and More Negative Emotions among First-Generation College Students," *Journal of Experimental Social Psychology* 48, no. 6 (2012): 1389–1393; Stevens, "Culture and Education"; Richard L. Zweigenhaft, "Prep School and Public School Graduates of Harvard: A Longitudinal Study of the Accumulation of Social and Cultural Capital," *Journal of Higher Education* 64, no. 2 (1993): 211–225.

4. Elizabeth A. Armstrong and Laura T. Hamilton, *Paying for the Party: How College Maintains Inequality* (Cambridge, MA: Harvard University Press, 2013); Ann L. Mullen, "Elite Destinations: Pathways to Attending an Ivy League University," *British Journal of Sociology of Education* 30, no. 1 (2009):15–27; Ernest T. Pascarella and Patrick T. Terenzini, *How College Affects Students: A Third Decade of Research* (San Francisco: Jossey-Bass, 2005).

5. Torres, "'Culture Shock,'" 885. I define culture shock as a form of class marginalization: the feeling of being an outsider because of one's class background. See Anthony Abraham Jack, "Culture Shock Revisited: The Social and Cultural Contingencies to Class Marginality," *Sociological Forum* 29, no. 2 (2014): 453–475; Anthony Abraham Jack, "Crisscrossing

Boundaries: Variation in Experiences with Class Marginality among Lower-Income, Black Undergraduates at an Elite College," in *College Students' Experiences of Power and Marginality: Sharing Spaces and Negotiating Differences*, ed. Elizabeth Lee and Chaise LaDousa (New York: Routledge, 2015), 83–101. For discussion of how the larger college culture affects undergraduates' experiences, see Armstrong and Hamilton, *Paying for the Party*; Sylvia Hurtado and Deborah Faye Carter, "Effects of College Transition and Perceptions of the Campus Racial Climate on Latino College Students' Sense of Belonging," *Sociology of Education* 70, no. 4 (1997): 324–345; Aries and Seider, "The Interactive Relationship between Class Identity and the College Experience."

6. On the lasting effects of living in poverty, see Karl L. Alexander, Doris Entwisle, and Linda Olson, *The Long Shadow: Family Background, Disadvantaged Urban Youth, and the Transition to Adulthood* (New York: Russell Sage Foundation, 2014); Camille Z. Charles, Gniesha Dinwiddie, and Douglas S. Massey, "The Continuing Consequences of Segregation: Family Stress and College Academic Performance," *Social Science Quarterly* 85, no. 5 (2004): 1353–1373; Geoffrey Wodtke, David Harding, and Felix Elwert, "Neighborhood Effects in Temporal Perspective: The Impact of Long-Term Exposure to Concentrated Disadvantage on High School Graduation," *American Sociological Review* 76, no. 5 (2011): 713–736.

7. The group, now known as Rich Kids of the Internet, is at http://therkoi.com/ and uses @rkoi as its Instagram handle.

8. On the overrepresentation of black immigrants at selective colleges, see Douglas S. Massey et al., "Black Immigrants and Black Natives Attending Selective Colleges and Universities in the United States," *American Journal of Education* 113, no. 2 (2007): 243–271; Sara Rimer and Karen W. Arenson, "Top Colleges Take More Blacks, but Which Ones?" *New York Times*, June 24, 2004, http://www.nytimes.com/2004/06/24/us/top

-colleges-take-more-blacks-but-which-ones.html?pagewanted
=all&src=pm.

9. On microaggressions, see Julie Minikel-Lacocque, "Racism, College, and the Power of Words: Racial Microaggressions Reconsidered," *American Educational Research Journal* 50, no. 3 (2013): 432–465; Daniel Solórzano, Miguel Ceja, and Tara Yosso, "Critical Race Theory, Racial Microaggressions, and Campus Racial Climate: The Experiences of African American College Students," *Journal of Negro Education* 69, no. 1 / 2 (2000): 60–73.

10. Amy J. Binder, Daniel B. Davis, and Nick Bloom, "Career Funneling: How Elite Students Learn to Define and Desire 'Prestigious' Jobs," *Sociology of Education* 89, no. 1 (2015): 20–39; Rivera, *Pedigree.*

11. Scholars have found that social integration via clubs is generally beneficial to students' well-being. See Pascarella and Terenzini, *How College Affects Students;* Jenny M. Stuber, *Inside the College Gates: How Class and Culture Matter in Higher Education* (Lanham, MD: Lexington Books, 2011).

12. See Beverly Daniel Tatum, *Assimilation Blues: Black Families in a White Community* (New York: Greenwood Press, 1987).

13. For a discussion of adolescent development and education, see Eveline A. Crone and Ronald E. Dahl, "Understanding Adolescence as a Period of Social–Affective Engagement and Goal Flexibility," *Nature Reviews Neuroscience* 13, no. 9 (2012): 636–650; Erik Erikson, *Identity and the Life Cycle* (New York: Norton, 1980); Simone Ispa-Landa, "Effects of Affluent Suburban Schooling: Learning Skilled Ways of Interacting with Educational Gatekeepers," in *The Cultural Matrix: Understanding Black Youth,* ed. Orlando Patterson and Ethan Fosse (Cambridge, MA: Harvard University Press, 2015), 393–414. High schools operate more like what sociologist Erving Goffman called total institutions than colleges do, shaping adolescents' development and understanding of self in both visible and

invisible ways; see Erving Goffman, *Asylums: Essays on the Social Situation of Mental Patients and Other Inmates* (New York: Anchor Books, 1961); Shamus Rahman Khan, *Privilege: The Making of an Adolescent Elite at St. Paul's School* (Princeton, NJ: Princeton University Press, 2011).

14. For a discussion of trends in racial and socioeconomic segregation in the United States, see John R. Logan, Elisabeta Minca, and Sinem Adar, "The Geography of Inequality: Why Separate Means Unequal in American Public Schools," *Sociology of Education* 85, no. 3 (2012): 287–301; Sean F. Reardon and Ann Owens, "60 Years After Brown: Trends and Consequences of School Segregation," *Annual Review of Sociology* 40, no. 1 (2014): 199–218.

15. Stephanie (PP,B) also mentioned that "at least three building names" were the same at Renowned as at her high school. Naming rights for dorms and libraries often require million-dollar donations. The fact that the same family names appear on buildings at both elite prep schools and colleges emphasizes the cultural and historical continuities between the two.

16. Charles, Dinwiddie, and Massey, "The Continuing Consequences of Segregation."

17. Jack and Jill Club of America is a membership organization that provides social, cultural, and educational opportunities for affluent African American children.

18. This rise in popularity of Canada Goose and Moncler outerwear is not restricted to elite colleges. Employees at companies like Goldman Sachs and JP Morgan Chase favor them as well. See Alison S. Cohn, "Openings All Over Town: Coach, Moncler, Canada Goose and More," *New York Times*, November 16, 2016, https://www.nytimes.com/2016/11/17/fashion/coach-moncler-canada-goose-new-york-shopping.html; Jacob Gallagher, "The Distinctive Jacket That's Leaving Canada Goose Parkas Out in the Cold," *Wall Street Journal*, November 2, 2016, http://www.wsj.com/articles/a-fresher-coat-1478104539.

19. Prudence Carter, *Keepin' It Real: School Success beyond Black and White* (Oxford: Oxford University Press, 2005). See also Becki Elkins and Eran Hanke, "Code-Switching to Navigate Social Class in Higher Education and Student Affairs," *New Directions for Student Services* 2018, no. 162 (2018): 35–47.

20. See Armstrong and Hamilton, *Paying for the Party;* Zweigenhaft, "Prep School and Public School Graduates of Harvard." On situational cues, see Valerie Purdie-Vaughns et al., "Social Identity Contingencies: How Diversity Cues Signal Threat or Safety for African Americans in Mainstream Institutions," *Journal of Personality and Social Psychology* 94, no. 4 (2008): 615.

21. Alexander, Entwisle, and Olson, *The Long Shadow;* Charles, Dinwiddie, and Massey, "The Continuing Consequences of Segregation."

CHAPTER 2 ❧ *"Can You Sign Your Book for Me?"*

1. Authority figures in academic institutions at every level have been shown to respond more positively to middle-class interactional styles, often spending more time with or favoring students who adopt them. See Jessica McCrory Calarco, *Negotiating Opportunities: How the Middle Class Secures Advantages in School* (New York: Oxford University Press, 2018); Peter J. Collier and David L. Morgan, "'Is That Paper Really Due Today?': Differences in First-Generation and Traditional College Students' Understandings of Faculty Expectations," *Higher Education* 55, no. 4 (2008): 425–446; Rebecca D. Cox, *The College Fear Factor: How Students and Professors Misunderstand One Another* (Cambridge, MA: Harvard University Press, 2011); Megan M. Holland, "Trusting Each Other: Student-Counselor Relationships in Diverse High Schools," *Sociology of Education* 88, no. 3 (2015): 244–262; Young K. Kim and Linda J. Sax, "Student–Faculty Interaction in Research Universities: Differences by

Student Gender, Race, Social Class, and First-Generation Status," *Research in Higher Education* 50, no. 5 (2009): 437–459; Annette Lareau, *Unequal Childhoods: Class, Race, and Family Life* (Berkeley: University of California Press, 2003); Ernest T. Pascarella and Patrick T. Terenzini, *How College Affects Students: A Third Decade of Research* (San Francisco: Jossey-Bass, 2005). For a discussion of how the Privileged Poor's socialization begins even before high school, see Amanda Barrett Cox, "Cohorts, 'Siblings,' and Mentors: Organizational Structures and the Creation of Social Capital," *Sociology of Education* 90, no. 1 (2017): 47–63.

2. Collier and Morgan, "Is That Paper Really Due Today?" 439.

3. While I was doing my research at Renowned, I observed that the students who were invited to sit on committees that set college policies, to introduce famous guests at public forums, or to go on foreign-exchange spring break trips were selected because someone had recommended them for consideration. On how finding mentors helps students, see Daniel F. Chambliss and Christopher G. Takacs, *How College Works* (Cambridge, MA: Harvard University Press, 2014); Richard J. Light, *Making the Most of College* (Cambridge, MA: Harvard University Press, 2001).

4. Mario Guerrero and Alisa Beth Rod show that attending office hours boosts academic performance in "Engaging in Office Hours: A Study of Student-Faculty Interaction and Academic Performance," *Journal of Political Science Education* 9, no. 4 (2013): 403–416.

5. Email correspondence with Dawn Poirier, August and September 2016.

6. Resident counselors often nominated students who were only tangentially qualified for an award because that undergraduate was a favorite. In one nomination meeting for an award that had a strict GPA cutoff, a counselor revealed that, instead of simply identifying the student with the highest GPA, the committee reviewed materials for five students with top marks and then lobbied for students who had the

NOTES TO PAGE 86

third and fourth highest GPAs, claiming that they were more deserving. One could view this practice as a way to counter arbitrary, capricious, or even unfair criteria, or as a method for increasing diversity or inclusion. But in this instance, the benefit only went to students whom the nominators knew. Students who do not want to share their personal histories, or do not know that they can or should do so, lose out in such a system. For students who are members of vulnerable populations, like those who are undocumented, sharing their story might come at great personal cost. Scholarship on how and when undocumented youth speak about their status shows that it is a difficult choice with serious implications for both themselves and their families. See Roberto G. Gonzales, *Lives in Limbo: Undocumented and Coming of Age in America* (Berkeley: University of California Press, 2015); Ariana Mangual Figueroa, "Speech or Silence: Undocumented Students' Decisions to Disclose or Disguise Their Citizenship Status in School," *American Educational Research Journal* 54, no. 3 (2017): 485–523.

7. Jean Anyon, "Social Class and the Hidden Curriculum of Work," *Journal of Education* 162, no. 1 (1980): 67–92; Anthony Abraham Jack, "(No) Harm In Asking: Class, Acquired Cultural Capital, and Academic Engagement at an Elite University," *Sociology of Education* 89, no. 1 (2016): 1–19; Anthony Abraham Jack and Veronique Irwin, "Seeking Out Support: Variation in Academic Engagement Strategies among Black Undergraduates at an Elite College," in *Clearing the Path for First-Generation College Students: Qualitative and Intersectional Studies of Educational Mobility,* ed. Ashley C. Rondini, Bedelia Richards-Dowden, and Nicolas P. Simon (Lanham, MD: Lexington Books, 2018), 384; Nicole M. Stephens et al., "A Cultural Mismatch: Independent Cultural Norms Produce Greater Increases in Cortisol and More Negative Emotions among First-Generation College Students," *Journal of Experimental Social Psychology* 48, no. 6 (2012): 1389–1393.

8. For a discussion of the relationship between privilege and ease, see Shamus Rahman Khan, *Privilege: The Making of an Adolescent Elite at St. Paul's School* (Princeton, NJ: Princeton University Press, 2011); Nathan D. Martin, "The Privilege of Ease: Social Class and Campus Life at Highly Selective, Private Universities," *Research in Higher Education* 53, no. 4 (2012): 426–452.

9. Delayed access matters and can have long-term effects. See Pascarella and Terenzini, *How College Affects Students;* Camille Z. Charles et al., *Taming the River: Negotiating the Academic, Financial, and Social Currents in Selective Colleges and Universities* (Princeton, NJ: Princeton University Press, 2009); Light, *Making the Most of College;* Chambliss and Takacs, *How College Works.*

10. In 2014, the national average student–faculty ratio was 16.1:1 for public schools and 12:1 for private schools, according to the National Center for Education Statistics. In under-resourced urban schools, the ratio is much higher. See https://nces.ed.gov/fastfacts/display.asp?id=28.

11. Joe Paul Case, "Implications of Financial Aid: What College Counselors Should Know," *Journal of College Student Psychotherapy* 27, no. 2 (2013): 159–173.

12. On the lack of discussion about mental health among college students, see Daniel Eisenberg et al., "Stigma and Help Seeking for Mental Health among College Students," *Medical Care Research and Review* 66, no. 5 (2009): 522–541.

13. For a discussion of different paths into mental health services, see Bernice A. Pescosolido, Carol Brooks Gardner, and Keri M. Lubell, "How People Get into Mental Health Services: Stories of Choice, Coercion and 'Muddling Through' from 'First-Timers,'" *Social Science and Medicine* 46, no. 2 (1998): 275–286.

14. "Remarks by the First Lady at Martin Luther King Jr. Preparatory High School Commencement Address," Chicago, IL, June 9, 2015, available at

https://obamawhitehouse.archives.gov/the-press-office/2015/06/09
/remarks-first-lady-martin-luther-king-jr-preparatory-high-school
-commenc. Focusing solely on grades and graduation rates downplays the
interactional dimensions of academic life. Whether or not students take
advantage of the resources available to them is worthy of investigation
and can highlight the cultural underpinnings of the reproduction of inequality in college; see Chambliss and Takacs, *How College Works;* Light,
Making the Most of College; Mitchell L. Stevens, "Culture and Education,"
Annals of the American Academy of Political and Social Science 619, no. 1
(2008): 97–113; Mitchell L. Stevens, Elizabeth A. Armstrong, and Richard
Arum, "Sieve, Incubator, Temple, Hub: Empirical and Theoretical Advances in the Sociology of Higher Education," *Annual Review of Sociology*
34, no. 1 (2008): 127–151; April Yee, "The Unwritten Rules Of Engagement:
Social Class Differences in Undergraduates' Academic Strategies," *Journal
of Higher Education* 87, no. 6 (2016): 831–858.

15. Pascarella and Terenzini, *How College Affects Students;* Chambliss and
Takacs, *How College Works;* Light, *Making the Most of College.*

16. Edward Fiske, "The Carolina Covenant," in *Rewarding Strivers: Helping
Low-Income Students Succeed in College,* ed. Richard D. Kahlenberg (New
York: Century Foundation Press, 2010), 17–70; Jenny M. Stuber, *Inside the
College Gates: How Class and Culture Matter in Higher Education* (Lanham,
MD: Lexington Books, 2011); Chandra Taylor Smith and Abby Miller
with C. Adolfo Bermeo, *Bridging the Gaps to Success: Promising Practices
for Promoting Transfer among Low-Income and First-Generation Students*
(Washington, D.C.: Pell Institute for the Study of Opportunity in
Higher Education, 2009), https://eric.ed.gov/?id=ED508915; Jennifer
Engle, Adolfo Bermeo, and Colleen O'Brien, *Straight from the Source: What
Works for First-Generation College Students* (Washington, D.C.: Pell Insti-
tute for the Study of Opportunity in Higher Education, 2006), https://
eric.ed.gov/?id=ED501693.

17. Steven R. López et al., "From Documenting to Eliminating Disparities in Mental Health Care for Latinos," *American Psychologist* 67, no. 7 (2012): 511–523; Engle, Bermeo, and O'Brien, *Straight from the Source*.

18. Personal communication, fall 2017.

19. Email correspondence with Rebecca Kissane, January 2017.

CHAPTER 3   "*I, Too, Am Hungry*"

1. For scholarly and popular discussions of the kinds of racial microaggressions that formed the basis of the "I, too" campaign, see Julie Minikel-Lacocque, "Racism, College, and the Power of Words: Racial Microaggressions Reconsidered," *American Educational Research Journal* 50, no. 3 (2013): 432–465; Daniel Solórzano, Miguel Ceja, and Tara Yosso, "Critical Race Theory, Racial Microaggressions, and Campus Racial Climate: The Experiences of African American College Students," *Journal of Negro Education* 69, no. 1 / 2 (2000): 60–73; Tanzina Vega, "Students See Many Slights as Racial 'Microaggressions,'" *New York Times,* March 21, 2014, http://www.nytimes.com/2014/03/22/us/as-diversity-increases -slights-get-subtler-but-still-sting.html. See also Elijah Anderson, *The Cosmopolitan Canopy: Race and Civility in Everyday Life* (New York: Norton, 2011); Michèle Lamont et al., *Getting Respect: Responding to Stigma and Discrimination in the United States, Brazil, and Israel* (Princeton, NJ: Princeton University Press, 2016).

2. My analysis in this chapter focuses on episodic food insecurity, when students face uncertainty about where their next meal comes from during specific times of the academic year. In this case, I focus on spring break. The United States Department of Agriculture defines two levels of food insecurity, the latter of which was experienced by students at Renowned. Low food security, also known as food insecurity without hunger, is characterized by "reduced quality, variety, or desirability of diet" but with

"little or no indication of reduced food intake." Very low food security, also known as food insecurity with hunger, describes a situation in which individuals report "multiple indications of disrupted eating patterns and reduced food intake." See "Definitions of Food Security," United States Department of Agriculture Economic Research Service, https://www.ers.usda.gov/topics/food-nutrition-assistance/food-security-in-the-us/definitions-of-food-security.aspx.

3. Elizabeth Aries, *Race and Class Matters at an Elite College* (Philadelphia: Temple University Press, 2008).

4. Scholars interested in exclusion in academic contexts generally focus on how interpersonal interactions and institutional contexts marginalize nontraditional students. See Aries, *Race and Class Matters*; Elizabeth A. Armstrong and Laura T. Hamilton, *Paying for the Party: How College Maintains Inequality* (Cambridge, MA: Harvard University Press, 2013); Sylvia Hurtado and Deborah Faye Carter, "Effects of College Transition and Perceptions of the Campus Racial Climate on Latino College Students' Sense of Belonging," *Sociology of Education* 70, no. 4 (1997): 324–345; Kimberly Torres, "'Culture Shock': Black Students Account for Their Distinctiveness at an Elite College," *Ethnic and Racial Studies* 32, no. 5 (2009): 883–905.

5. Recent research has pushed for analyzing how school and university policies structure student life. Karolyn Tyson, for example, examines how academic tracking influences students' conceptions of attainment and race in *Integration Interrupted: Tracking, Black Students, and Acting White after Brown* (New York: Oxford University Press, 2011). In her comparative study of schools in South Africa and the United States, Prudence Carter shows how rules forbidding certain "ethnic" hairstyles narrowly define what is appropriate and serve to ostracize black students (*Stubborn Roots: Race, Culture, and Inequality in U.S. and South African Schools* [New York: Oxford University Press, 2012]). Elizabeth

Armstrong and Laura Hamilton, in *Paying for the Party*, examine how Greek life puts pressure on working-class students to partake in what they call the "party pathway" through college even though they lack the money and social skills to do so. These studies document the effects of backstage processes—school policies that are largely hidden from students even as their effects are felt daily. Because this connection is invisible, students see the resulting racial and class hierarchies as naturally occurring rather than institutionally sponsored. The concept of structural exclusion highlights the direct role that college and university policies play in structuring students' social interactions, sense of belonging, and pathways through college. Structural exclusion focuses on moments when specific operational features of the college marginalize underrepresented groups in highly visible ways. Focusing on social interactions while ignoring how university policies shape those interactions limits our understanding of the reproduction of inequality. See also Loïc J. D. Wacquant and William Julius Wilson, "The Cost of Racial and Class Exclusion in the Inner City," *Annals of the American Academy of Political and Social Science* 501 (1989): 8–25; Annette Lareau and Erin Horvat, "Moments of Social Inclusion and Exclusion Race, Class, and Cultural Capital in Family-School Relationships," *Sociology of Education* 72, no. 1 (1999): 37–53.

6. I want to clarify that I do not intend to demean the work of cleaning itself. As the proud grandson of a maid and brother of a janitor, I appreciate the work and respect those who do it.

7. I used the per diem amount that athletes are given for meals at Renowned during spring break as a proxy for the cost of meals.

8. Stacy exaggerated the length of time between cleanings; Community Detail comes every two weeks, not three.

9. Kimberly C. Torres and Camille Z. Charles, "Metastereotypes and the Black-White Divide: A Qualitative View of Race on an Elite College

Campus," *Du Bois Review: Social Science Research on Race* 1, no. 1 (2004): 115–149.

10. The number of tickets offered through Scholarship Plus was not always set at five. The year before I began my research at Renowned, students were allowed an unlimited number. Administrators began limiting the number of tickets to crack down on perceived ticket sharing.

11. Poor-door policies in apartment buildings and other residential dwellings are still present in Boston, London, New York, and other cities around the world. See Emily Badger, "When Separate Doors for the Poor Are More than They Seem," *Washington Post*, July 31, 2014, https://www.washingtonpost.com/news/wonk/wp/2014/07/31/when-the-poor-want-their-own-door/; Dave Hill, "What Would a Ban on 'Poor Doors' Achieve?" *Guardian*, August 3, 2015, https://www.theguardian.com/uk-news/davehillblog/2015/aug/03/london-housing-what-would-a-ban-on-poor-doors-achieve; Justin Moyer, "NYC Bans 'Poor Doors'—Separate Entrances for Low-Income Tenants," *Washington Post*, June 30, 2015, http://www.washingtonpost.com/news/morning-mix/wp/2015/06/30/nyc-bans-poor-doors-separate-entrances-for-low-income-tenants/; Alan Wirzbicki, "Allowing 'Poor Door' a Better Alternative," op-ed, *Boston Globe*, July 26, 2014https://www.bostonglobe.com/opinion/2014/07/25/wirzbicki/oU7F3Bg25j6Hai5wbQjsCJ/story.html.

12. Anthony Abraham Jack, "It's Hard to Be Hungry on Spring Break," *New York Times*, March 17, 2018, SR4.

13. From a health standpoint, the food that students mention eating the most is a cause for concern: ramen, peanut butter and jelly sandwiches, and food from vending machines. These items might be fine in moderation, but eating them for every meal, every day for a week is not. The Food and Drug Administration, for example, recommends no more than 2,300 mg of salt intake per day. One pack of ramen contains more than half this amount.

14. See the Appendix for further discussion of my practice of taking students out for meals.

15. "Opening and Closing Information," Fairfield University, Fairfield, CT, https://www.fairfield.edu/undergraduate/student-life-and-services/student-services/housing/residence-life/closing-information/, accessed August 2015. This statement no longer appears on the website.

16. M. Pia Chaparro et al., "Food Insecurity Prevalence among College Students at the University of Hawai'i at Mānoa," *Public Health Nutrition* 12, no. 11 (2009): 2097–2103; Rashisa Crutchfield, "Serving Displaced and Food Insecure Students in the CSU," January 2016, https://presspage-production-content.s3.amazonaws.com/uploads/1487/cohomelessstudy.pdf?10000; Sara Goldrick-Rab and Katharine M. Broton, "Hungry, Homeless and in College," *New York Times*, December 4, 2015, http://www.nytimes.com/2015/12/04/opinion/hungry-homeless-and-in-college.html; Sara Goldrick-Rab et al., "Still Hungry and Homeless in College" (Madison, WI: Wisconsin Hope Lab, April 2018); Jack, "It's Hard to Be Hungry on Spring Break"; Suzanna M. Martinez et al., "Food Insecurity in California's Public University System: What Are the Risk Factors?" *Journal of Hunger and Environmental Nutrition* 13, no. 1 (2018): 1–18; Aydin Nazmi et al., "A Systematic Review of Food Insecurity among US Students in Higher Education," *Journal of Hunger and Environmental Nutrition* June 22, 2018, https://doi.org/10.1080/19320248.2018.1484316.

17. Nick Anderson, "For the Poor in the Ivy League, a Full Ride Isn't Always What They Imagined," *Washington Post*, May 16, 2016, https://www.washingtonpost.com/local/education/for-the-poor-in-the-ivy-league-a-full-ride-isnt-always-what-they-imagined/2016/05/16/5f89972a-114d-11e6-81b4-581a5c4c42df_story.html; Akane Otani, "Poor Students at Columbia Take Their Angst Public, and the School Responds," *Bloomberg*, March 31, 2015, http://www.bloomberg.com/news/articles/2015-03

-31/poor-students-at-columbia-take-their-angst-public-and-the-school
-responds.

18. One assertion that students sometimes made about Community Detail and the other policies described here was that the university had
established them with the intention of singling out and shaming
lower-income students. The intentionality behind these programs is
not something I can speak to definitively. In the case of Community
Detail, especially as a preorientation program, there was some evidence in favor of the students' assessment. The program was set up as
one of several official preorientation programs in order to secure a
certain level of participation. In the case of Scholarship Plus, the evidence pointed in the opposite direction. What is clear, however, is
that these policies undermined poor students' relationships with both
the university and their peers. In addition to making them keenly
aware of their own economic disadvantage, and causing them to endure indignities because of it, the policies also emphasized the gap
between these students and their wealthier peers, who did not have to
manage scarce resources and were thus exempt from such unsavory
experiences.

19. Michael J. Sandel, *What Money Can't Buy: The Moral Limits of Markets*
(New York: Farrar, Straus and Giroux, 2012); Russell Muirhead, *Just Work*
(Cambridge, MA: Harvard University Press, 2004). For a discussion of the
Students as Learners and Teachers (SaLT) program, see https://www
.brynmawr.edu/tli/faculty-student-partnerships-analyze-classroom
-practice.

20. Mitchell L. Stevens, Elizabeth A. Armstrong, and Richard Arum,
"Sieve, Incubator, Temple, Hub: Empirical and Theoretical Advances in
the Sociology of Higher Education," *Annual Review of Sociology* 34, no. 1
(2008): 127–151.

Conclusion

1. These changes in financial aid and outreach received a lot of media attention. See Emily Jane Fox, "Stanford Offers Free Tuition for Families Making Less than $125,000," *CNNMoney*, April 1, 2015, http://money.cnn.com/2015/04/01/pf/college/stanford-financial-aid/index.html; Anthony Abraham Jack, "What the Privileged Poor Can Teach Us," op-ed, *New York Times*, September 12, 2015, https://www.nytimes.com/2015/09/13/opinion/sunday/what-the-privileged-poor-can-teach-us.html; Richard Pérez-Peña, "Elite Colleges Differ on How They Aid Poor," *New York Times*, July 30, 2013, http://www.nytimes.com/2013/07/31/education/elite-colleges-differ-on-how-they-aid-poor.html; Richard Pérez-Peña, "Elite Smaller Colleges Struggle to Cover Financial Aid," *New York Times*, November 30, 2012, http://www.nytimes.com/2012/12/01/education/elite-smaller-colleges-struggle-to-cover-financial-aid.html; Sara Rimer, "Elite Colleges Open New Door to Low-Income Youths," *New York Times*, May 27, 2007, A1. Money still matters in college. There is often a gap between financial aid and what it takes to be a student. See Amy Bergerson, "Exploring the Impact of Social Class on Adjustment to College: Anna's Story," *International Journal of Qualitative Studies in Education* 20, no. 1 (2007): 99–119; Sara Goldrick-Rab, *Paying the Price: College Costs, Financial Aid, and the Betrayal of the American Dream* (Chicago: University of Chicago Press, 2016). For a discussion of economic barriers that lower-income and first-generation college students face, see Jennifer Engle, Adolfo Bermeo, and Colleen O'Brien, "Straight from the Source: What Works for First-Generation College Students," *Pell Institute for the Study of Opportunity in Higher Education*, 2006, https://eric.ed.gov/?id=ED501693; Goldrick-Rab, *Paying the Price*; Chandra Taylor Smith and Abby Miller, "Bridging the Gaps to Success: Promising Practices for Promoting Transfer among Low-Income and First-Generation Students. An In-

Depth Study of Six Exemplary Community Colleges in Texas," *Pell Institute for the Study of Opportunity in Higher Education*, 2009, https://eric.ed.gov/?id=ED508915.

2. Patrick T. Terenzini et al., "First-Generation College Students: Characteristics, Experiences, and Cognitive Development," *Research in Higher Education* 37, no. 1 (1996): 17. For a critique on the lumping together of lower-income students, see Anthony Abraham Jack, "Culture Shock Revisited: The Social and Cultural Contingencies to Class Marginality," *Sociological Forum* 29, no. 2 (2014): 453–475. My research draws heavily on the work of cultural sociologist Alford Young Jr., who studies the social-structural forces that shape young men's cultural endowments by examining their experiences in their families, neighborhoods, and schools. See Young, "The (Non)Accumulation of Capital: Explicating the Relationship of Structure and Agency in the Lives of Poor Black Men," *Sociological Theory* 17, no. 2 (1999): 201–227. I also build on the work of urban poverty scholars William Julius Wilson and Robert Sampson, specifically their discussion of ecological dissimilarities—how contexts of socialization are structurally different from one another—and the ways in which they shape the reproduction of inequality: Robert Sampson and William Julius Wilson, "Toward a Theory of Race, Crime, and Urban Inequality," in *Crime and Inequality*, ed. John Hagan and Ruth Peterson (Stanford, CA: Stanford University Press, 1995), 37–56. For a psychological perspective, see Nicole M. Stephens, Hazel Rose Markus, and L. Taylor Phillips, "Social Class Culture Cycles: How Three Gateway Contexts Shape Selves and Fuel Inequality," *Annual Review of Psychology* 65 (2013): 611–634.

3. For a discussion of cultural capital theory, see Elizabeth Aries, *Race and Class Matters at an Elite College* (Philadelphia: Temple University Press, 2008); Pierre Bourdieu, *Distinction: A Social Critique of the Judgment of Taste* (Cambridge, MA: Harvard University Press, 1984). For scholars who adopt a similar approach to moving beyond parental socialization, see Michèle

Lamont and Annette Lareau, "Cultural Capital: Allusions, Gaps and Glissandos in Recent Theoretical Developments," *Sociological Theory* 6, no. 2 (1988): 153–168. On pipeline programs that place students in private schools, see Amanda Barrett Cox, "Cohorts, 'Siblings,' and Mentors: Organizational Structures and the Creation of Social Capital," *Sociology of Education* 90, no. 1 (2017): 47–63; Rory Kramer, "Diversifiers at Elite Schools," *Du Bois Review: Social Science Research on Race* 5, no. 2 (2008): 287–307; Richard L. Zweigenhaft and G. William Domhoff, *Blacks in the White Establishment?: A Study of Race and Class in America* (New Haven, CT: Yale University Press, 1991).

4. Anthony Abraham Jack, "Culture Shock Revisited: The Social and Cultural Contingencies to Class Marginality," *Sociological Forum* 29, no. 2 (2014): 453–475; Shamus Rahman Khan, *Privilege: The Making of an Adolescent Elite at St. Paul's School* (Princeton, NJ: Princeton University Press, 2011).

5. Elizabeth A. Armstrong and Laura T. Hamilton, *Paying for the Party: How College Maintains Inequality* (Cambridge, MA: Harvard University Press, 2013); Kimberly Torres, "'Culture Shock': Black Students Account for Their Distinctiveness at an Elite College," *Ethnic and Racial Studies* 32, no. 5 (2009): 883–905.

6. See Camille Z. Charles, Gniesha Dinwiddie, and Douglas S. Massey, "The Continuing Consequences of Segregation: Family Stress and College Academic Performance," *Social Science Quarterly* 85, no. 5 (2004): 1353–1373. It is important to be aware of the full range of resources that colleges provide students. For example, Joe Paul Case, retired dean of financial aid at Amherst College, advocates for increased coordination between financial aid offices and counseling centers so as to fully support students' mental health and medical needs. See Joe Paul Case, "Implications of Financial Aid: What College Counselors Should Know," *Journal of College Student Psychotherapy* 27, no. 2 (2013): 159–173.

7. There is still a vast gap between what black and white college graduates earn, but that gap is smaller, and arguably easier to overcome, than the one between blacks with a college degree and those without. For discussion of economic payoff to an elite college degree, see E. Eide, D. J. Brewer, and R. G. Ehrenberg, "Does It Pay to Attend an Elite Private College? Evidence on the Effects of Undergraduate College Quality on Graduate School Attendance," *Economics of Education Review* 17, no. 4 (1998): 371–376; Thomas J. Espenshade and Alexandria Walton Radford, *No Longer Separate, Not Yet Equal: Race and Class in Elite College Admission and Campus Life* (Princeton, NJ: Princeton University Press, 2009); Lauren A. Rivera, *Pedigree: How Elite Students Get Elite Jobs* (Princeton, NJ: Princeton University Press, 2015).

8. See also the research conducted by the Transparency in Learning and Teaching in Higher Education project at the University of Nevada, Las Vegas, for evidence on how making students aware of rules and expectations aids them in their college endeavors: Mary-Ann Winkelmes et al., "A Teaching Intervention That Increases Underserved College Students' Success," *Peer Review* 18, no. 1 (2016): 31–36.

9. Anandi Mani et al., "Poverty Impedes Cognitive Function," *Science* 341, no. 6149 (2013): 976–980; Suzanna M. Martinez et al., "Food Insecurity in California's Public University System: What Are the Risk Factors?" *Journal of Hunger and Environmental Nutrition* 13, no. 1 (2018): 1–18; Sendhil Mullainathan and Eldar Shafir, *Scarcity: Why Having Too Little Means So Much* (New York: Henry Holt, 2013); Aydin Nazmi et al., "A Systematic Review of Food Insecurity among US Students in Higher Education," *Journal of Hunger and Environmental Nutrition* (2018): 1–16.

10. Valerie Purdie-Vaughns et al., "Social Identity Contingencies: How Diversity Cues Signal Threat or Safety for African Americans in Mainstream Institutions," *Journal of Personality and Social Psychology* 94, no. 4 (2008): 615. See also Jonathan E. Cook et al., "Chronic Threat and

Contingent Belonging: Protective Benefits of Values Affirmation on Identity Development," *Journal of Personality and Social Psychology* 102, no. 3 (2012): 479.

11. Monica Higgins and Kathy Kram, "Reconceptualizing Mentoring at Work: A Developmental Network Perspective," *Academy of Management Review* 26, no. 2 (2001): 264; Catherine Turco, "Cultural Foundations of Tokenism: Evidence from the Leveraged Buyout Industry," *American Sociological Review* 75, no. 6 (2010): 894–913; Rivera, *Pedigree*.

12. EdChoice, "The ABCs of School Choice: The Comprehensive Guide to Every Private School Choice Program in America, 2017 Edition" (EdChoice, 2017), http://www.edchoice.org/wp-content/uploads/2017/02/The-ABCs-of-School-Choice-1.pdf; Matthew Chingos and Daniel Kuehn, "The Effects of Statewide Private School Choice on College Enrollment and Graduation: Evidence from the Florida Tax Credit Scholarship Program" (Urban Institute, September 2017), https://www.urban.org/sites/default/files/publication/93471/the_effects_of_statewide_private_school_choice_on_college_enrollment_and_graduation_0.pdf.

13. Hugh Mehan, *In the Front Door: Creating a College-Bound Culture of Learning* (Boulder: Paradigm Publishers, 2012). See also James Coleman and Thomas Hoffer, *Public and Private High Schools: The Impact of Communities* (New York: Basic Books, 1987); Peter Cookson and Caroline Persell, *Preparing for Power: America's Elite Boarding Schools* (New York: Basic Books, 1985); Jonathan Kozol, *Savage Inequalities: Children in America's Schools* (New York: HarperPerennial, 1991); Patrick Sharkey, *Stuck in Place: Urban Neighborhoods and the End of Progress toward Racial Equality* (University of Chicago Press, 2013). For a discussion of post-college trajectories, see Rivera, *Pedigree*; Richard Zweigenhaft and G. William Domhoff, *Blacks in the White Elite: Will the Progress Continue?* (Lanham, MD: Rowman and Littlefield, 2003).

14. Kristin Blagg et al., "Assessing Food Insecurity on Campus: A National Look at Food Insecurity among America's College Students" (Urban

Institute, August 2017); Goldrick-Rab, *Paying the Price*; Nazmi et al., "A Systematic Review of Food Insecurity among US Students in Higher Education."

15. James Baldwin, *Notes of a Native Son* (Boston: Beacon Press, 1984), 9.

Appendix

1. For discussion of the use of pseudonyms, see Amy J. Binder, Daniel B. Davis, and Nick Bloom, "Career Funneling: How Elite Students Learn to Define and Desire 'Prestigious' Jobs," *Sociology of Education* 89, no. 1 (2015): 20–39; Colin Jerolmack and Alexandra K. Murphy, "The Ethical Dilemmas and Social Scientific Trade-Offs of Masking in Ethnography," *Sociological Methods and Research*, March 30, 2017, http://dx.doi.org/10.1177/0049124117701483; Shamus Rahman Khan, *Privilege: The Making of an Adolescent Elite at St. Paul's School* (Princeton, NJ: Princeton University Press, 2011); Ann L. Mullen, *Degrees of Inequality: Culture, Class, and Gender in American Higher Education* (Baltimore, MD: Johns Hopkins University Press, 2010); Lauren A. Rivera, *Pedigree: How Elite Students Get Elite Jobs* (Princeton, NJ: Princeton University Press, 2015). See also Maria K. E. Lahman et al., "Undocumented Research Participants: Ethics and Protection in a Time of Fear," *Hispanic Journal of Behavioral Sciences* 33, no. 3 (2011): 304–322; Maria K. E. Lahman et al., "A Rose by Any Other Name Is Still a Rose? Problematizing Pseudonyms in Research," *Qualitative Inquiry* 21, no. 5 (2015): 445–453.

2. My choice to focus on one institution is in line with current theories of sampling in qualitative research. Renowned met a number of criteria that allowed me to engage with and extend existing theories of social reproduction. For discussions of sampling, see David Willer, *Scientific Sociology: Theory and Method* (Englewood Cliffs, NJ: Prentice-Hall, 1967); William Julius Wilson and Anmol Chaddha, "The Role of

253

Theory in Ethnographic Research," *Ethnography* 10, no. 4 (2009): 549–564.

3.   Mitchell L. Stevens, Elizabeth A. Armstrong, and Richard Arum, "Sieve, Incubator, Temple, Hub: Empirical and Theoretical Advances in the Sociology of Higher Education," *Annual Review of Sociology* 34, no. 1 (2008): 131–132.

4.   For examples of large-sample-size studies that have inspired my approach and thinking, see Michèle Lamont, *The Dignity of Working Men: Morality and the Boundaries of Race, Class, and Immigration* (Cambridge, MA: Harvard University Press, 2000); Michèle Lamont, *Money, Morals, and Manners: The Culture of the French and American Upper-Middle Class* (Chicago: University of Chicago Press, 1992); Mary C. Waters, *Black Identities: West Indian Immigrant Dreams and American Realities* (Cambridge, MA: Harvard University Press, 1999); Jocelyn Viterna, *Women in War: The Micro-Processes of Mobilization in El Salvador,* Oxford Studies in Culture and Politics (Oxford: Oxford University Press, 2013); Roberto G. Gonzales, *Lives in Limbo: Undocumented and Coming of Age in America* (Berkeley: University of California Press, 2015); Rivera, *Pedigree*. By interviewing a large number of people at the same place, I was able to gain multiple perspectives that allowed me to conduct certain validity checks; for example, I was able to assess variation between students and administrators, as well as within these groups, in how they viewed campus life and off-campus events. On how many interviews are required for an adequate sample, see Mario Luis Small, "'How Many Cases Do I Need?' On Science and the Logic of Case Selection in Field-Based Research," *Ethnography* 10, no. 1 (2009): 5–38.

5.   Latino students' voices are largely missing from the research on inequality, especially in higher education; see Mario Luis Small and Katherine Newman, "Urban Poverty after *The Truly Disadvantaged*: The Rediscovery of the Family, the Neighborhood, and Culture," *Annual Re-*

view of *Sociology* 27 (2001): 23–45; Gonzales, *Lives in Limbo*. Latino students are growing in number and receive scholarship opportunities at both private highs schools and colleges and universities. We need to understand their experience in order to fully understand the reproduction of inequality. See Gustavo López and Eileen Patten, "The Impact of Slowing Immigration: Foreign-Born Share Falls among 14 Largest U.S. Hispanic Origin Groups" (Washington, D.C.: Pew Research Center, September 15, 2015), http://www.pewhispanic.org/2013/06/19/hispanic-origin-profiles/; Douglas S. Massey et al., *The Source of the River: The Social Origins of Freshmen at America's Selective Colleges and Universities* (Princeton, NJ: Princeton University Press, 2003); Anthony Abraham Jack and Veronique Irwin, "Seeking Out Support: Variation in Academic Engagement Strategies among Black Undergraduates at an Elite College," in *Clearing the Path for First-Generation College Students: Qualitative and Intersectional Studies of Educational Mobility*, ed. Ashley C. Rondini, Bedelia Richards-Dowden, and Nicolas P. Simon (Lanham, MD: Lexington Books, 2018), 384; Jenny Anderson, "For Minority Students at Elite New York Private Schools, Admittance Doesn't Bring Acceptance," *New York Times*, October 19, 2012, http://www.nytimes.com/2012/10/21/nyregion/for-minority-students-at-elite-new-york-private-schools-admittance-doesnt-bring-acceptance.html.

6. See Karyn Lacy, *Blue-Chip Black: Race, Class, and Status in the New Black Middle Class* (Berkeley: University of California Press, 2007); Karyn Lacy and Angel L. Harris, "Breaking the Class Monolith: Understanding Class Differences in Black Adolescents' Attachment to Racial Identity," *Social Class: How Does It Work?* ed. Annette Lareau and Dalton Conley (New York: Russell Sage Foundation, 2008), 152–178, for critiques of research that flattens the diversity among the black middle class.

7. Massey et al., *Source of the River*, 40.

8. For both historical and personal reasons, and to give primacy to students' voices, I refrain from describing them physically. I do so only if that description complements something we discussed in our interviews or speaks to parts of their personality that showed through in our interactions. For example, Joshua (DD,B), whom I described as fit and muscular in Chapter 3, discussed how important weightlifting was to him in high school. My decision is based on the observation that writers almost always describe people of color and women by how they look or their attitude but describe white men in ways that highlight their intellect or character.

9. I drew inspiration for developing targeted life history interview guides from the work of sociologist Alford Young Jr. See "The (Non)Accumulation of Capital: Explicating the Relationship of Structure and Agency in the Lives of Poor Black Men," *Sociological Theory* 17, no. 2 (1999): 201–227. On techniques for inductively coding qualitative data, see Kathy Charmaz, *Constructing Grounded Theory: A Practical Guide through Qualitative Analysis* (Thousand Oaks, CA: Sage Publications, 2006); Robert Stuart Weiss, *Learning from Strangers: The Art and Method of Qualitative Interview Studies* (New York: Free Press, 1994).

10. For a similar approach, see Nicole Arlette Hirsch and Anthony Abraham Jack, "What We Face: Framing Problems in the Black Community," *Du Bois Review: Social Science Research on Race* 9, no. 1 (2012): 133–148.

11. For a discussion of the "witnessing" that interviewers do in the course of their qualitative research, see Jennifer M. Silva, *Coming Up Short: Working-Class Adulthood in an Age of Uncertainty* (New York: Oxford University Press, 2013).

12. Weiss, *Learning from Strangers*; Charmaz, *Constructing Grounded Theory*.

13. Anthony Abraham Jack, "What the Privileged Poor Can Teach Us," op-ed, *New York Times*, September 12, 2015, https://www.nytimes.com

/2015/09/13/opinion/sunday/what-the-privileged-poor-can-teach-us
.html.

14. Stephen L. Morgan and Christopher Winship, *Counterfactuals and Causal Inference: Methods and Principles for Social Research* (New York: Cambridge University Press, 2007); Robert Sampson, *Great American City: Chicago and the Enduring Neighborhood Effect* (Chicago: University of Chicago Press, 2012); Samuel A. Stouffer, "Some Observations on Study Design," *American Journal of Sociology* 55, no. 4 (1950): 355–361; Christopher Winship and Robert D. Mare, "Models for Sample Selection Bias," *Annual Review of Sociology* 18 (1992): 327–350.

15. For differences between the Privileged Poor and Doubly Disadvantaged, see Anthony Abraham Jack, "Culture Shock Revisited: The Social and Cultural Contingencies to Class Marginality," *Sociological Forum* 29, no. 2 (2014): 453–475; Anthony Abraham Jack, "Crisscrossing Boundaries: Variation in Experiences with Class Marginality among Lower-Income, Black Undergraduates at an Elite College," in *College Students' Experiences of Power and Marginality: Sharing Spaces and Negotiating Differences*, ed. Elizabeth Lee and Chaise LaDousa (New York: Routledge, 2015), 83–101; Anthony Abraham Jack, "Class, Culture, and (Un)Easy Engagement at an Elite University," *Harvard Educational Review*, forthcoming; Jack and Irwin, "Seeking Out Support." For a discussion of ideal types, see Max Weber, *Economy and Society: An Outline of Interpretive Sociology*, ed. Guenther Roth and Claus Wittich, 4th ed. (Berkeley: University of California Press, 1978). See also Elijah Anderson, *Code of the Street: Decency, Violence, and the Moral Life of the Inner City* (New York: Norton, 1999); Prudence Carter, *Keepin' It Real: School Success beyond Black and White* (New York: Oxford University Press, 2005).

16. I used a combination of different methods to triangulate on the two groups' collective experiences. See Mario Luis Small, "How to Conduct a Mixed Methods Study: Recent Trends in a Rapidly Growing Literature,"

Annual Review of Sociology 37, no. 1 (2011): 57–86, for a discussion of various approaches to mixed-methods research. For analyses of students' experiences in pipeline programs, see Amanda Barrett Cox, "Cohorts, 'Siblings,' and Mentors: Organizational Structures and the Creation of Social Capital," *Sociology of Education* 90, no. 1 (2017): 47–63; Rory Kramer, "Diversifiers at Elite Schools," *Du Bois Review: Social Science Research on Race* 5, no. 2 (2008): 287–307; Deval Patrick, *A Reason to Believe: Lessons from an Improbable Life* (New York: Broadway Books, 2011); Richard L. Zweigenhaft and G. William Domhoff, *Blacks in the White Establishment? A Study of Race and Class in America* (New Haven: Yale University Press, 1991). For a discussion of different enrichment programs, see David Leonhardt, "'A National Admissions Office' for Low-Income Strivers," *New York Times*, September 16, 2014, http://www.nytimes.com/2014/09/16/upshot/a-national-admissions-office-for-low-income-strivers.html; Alejandro Portes and Patricia Fernández-Kelly, "No Margin for Error: Educational and Occupational Achievement among Disadvantaged Children of Immigrants," *Annals of the American Academy of Political and Social Science* 620, no. 1 (2008): 12–36; Terrell Strayhorn, "Bridging the Pipeline: Increasing Underrepresented Students' Preparation for College through a Summer Bridge Program," *American Behavioral Scientist* 55, no. 2 (2011): 142–159; W. Scott Swail and Laura W. Perna, "Pre-College Outreach Programs: A National Perspective," in *Increasing Access to College: Extending Possibilities for All Students,* ed. William G. Tierney and Linda Serra Hagedorn (New York: SUNY Press, 2002), 15–34.

17. Winship and Mare, "Models for Sample Selection Bias."

18. The sociologist Mitchell Stevens reported similar results with respect to lower-income students participating in multiple enrichment programs en route to college; Stevens, *Creating a Class: College Admissions and the Education of Elites* (Cambridge, MA.: Harvard University Press, 2007).

Acknowledgments

Undreamt dreams come true. This book is a testament to that. As I write these words I can't help but think back to growing up in Miami. Books have long been my refuge, but a complicated one. At home, books were luxury items we could not often afford. So the library was my solace. But black kids from the Grove were not always welcomed across McDonald Street or in Coral Gables where the libraries were; I was followed and admonished in libraries for being too noisy or too loud or perhaps too dark. My peers picked on me for being the pudgy nerd who liked reading and watching cartoons more than playing football. So, to be a first-generation college graduate writing the acknowledgments to a book—yes, undreamt dreams come true.

How does this happen? With tears of joy rolling down my still chubby cheeks, the answer is with a lot of help, academic and social, asked for and freely given, emotional and spiritual. What does one say after such a journey of unimaginable personal and intellectual growth? Thank you. Many times to many people. And yet, even then, I know that this list will still only be a partial one.

First I need to thank William Julius Wilson, an adviser and mentor like no other. I often think back to our first meeting. It was my first visit to the Harvard sociology department. You were running to a meeting across campus, but you circled back after seeing me enter William James Hall. You introduced yourself and said that you wanted to meet with me. You gave me your cell phone number to make sure I did not leave campus without having that meeting. That stuck with me. I didn't know it then, but it perfectly foreshadowed all that was to come. You encouraged and pushed me, not to do a project that you thought I should do, but rather one that excited me. You cared, equally committed to my intellectual projects as you were to my general well-being. The world knows you as one of our greatest thinkers, an academic giant. I concur. Not a day goes by, however, that I am not thankful to know you as a mentor. Thank you.

Michèle Lamont, you took me in, trained me, and even protected me. I still can't put into words what that meant and means to me. You took me along for so many life-changing adventures, both here in the States and even across the pond. I met a queen because of you! I cannot tell you how many emails I have received that start the same way: "I just met Michèle Lamont, and she told me about your work. . . ." Thank you.

Mary Waters, thank you for your penetrating questions. They have forced me to think critically—both about those thirty-thousand-foot questions and also about what I need to thrive as a person. Whenever college friends visit, I take them by your office. *Black Identities* is as close to mandatory reading as one can get at Amherst College. They always ask, "How was it being in the same department as Mary Waters?" With a smile, I say, "She's a mentor. And she's awesome." Thank you for the help.

Robert Sampson, I had a chance to work with you in different capacities—in class, serving as your teaching fellow, and on the colloquium committee—and gained much from each interaction.

I have been especially fortunate to befriend a diverse group of people who made an imprint on this project in significant ways.

Prudence Carter: Our conversations have been academically fulfilling and soul enriching. Thank you so much for making time for me as you traversed continents. Thank you for the phone calls where we discussed everything, from sociology and education to politics and family. To call you my friend and mentor is something I treasure.

Al Young: Where do I begin? I sent you an email out of the blue, and you answered with a phone call. That conversation served as the theoretical foundation for my methodological approach. In each of our subsequent conversations, whether in Ann Arbor or at ASA, you always checked in to make sure I was on track. You encouraged me to push harder each time. I truly appreciate the support.

Shamus Khan: You are that phenomenal friend I never knew I would find. You have helped in more ways than I know, and I cannot say thank you enough. I often think back to our dinner at Daedalus, the walk to the river, and the impromptu tour of Mather House. I never thought that a short time later I would be walking through Morningside Heights to your house for a spectacular brunch and an hourslong conversation.

Brandon Terry: Your guidance inspired me to think bigger. Your help displayed the kind of trust that I did not think I would find in such a competitive environment. You are a model for scholars like me to follow, both inside and outside the classroom.

Kristin Bumiller: I cannot thank you enough for your continued, unwavering support. In addition to the lessons on inequality, citizenship, and justice, thank you for welcoming my family into yours.

Junot Díaz: Thank you for your honesty and mentorship. Our conversations were sustaining and inspiring in ways that are beyond words.

Rakesh Khurana: Thank you for your leadership and guidance, which helped me think about the relationship between sociological theory and university governance. The time you invested in me since we first met is humbling. Thank you for lighting the path.

Elijah Anderson, Annette Lareau, Bridget Terry Long, Andrew Papachristos, and Christopher Wildeman: thank you for your time and support.

Asad Asad, Monica Bell, Matthew Clair, and David Myers Hureau: Our outings have sustained me in ways that words cannot capture. You gave me pep talks when I needed them. You supplied kicks in the butt when I deserved them. Thank you for the laughs. Thank you for helping wipe away the tears.

Caitlin Daniel: You are my friend. We pushed each other the hardest. We celebrated each other the most. Your friendship—and those magical meals paired with marvelous bottles of wine—made graduate school not something one endures, but rather something one conquers. Thank you.

Christopher Muller: I know that I can never thank you enough for your support, honesty, help, and love. You are a selfless individual who always took my calls. Whether in passing on Grant Street, or during long walks through Berkeley, I always leave our conversations wanting to know more.

Scott Poulson-Bryant and Charrise Barron: Y'all two! Where would I be without our conversations, texts, meetups, games of Words with Friends, and everything else that we got into in graduate school. You two were glimpses of home in a faraway land. I owe you both so much.

Fellow Fellows: Thank you for making Monday nights something to look forward to. Special thanks to Kelly Katz and Ana Novak for all that you do. Alexander Bevilacqua, for your patience and guidance, thank you. For taking time to comment on early drafts of this book as well as amazing conversations at dinner, a special thanks to Noah Feldman, Wally Gilbert, Barry Mazur, Elaine Scarry, Amartya Sen, Maria Tatar, William Todd, and Nur Yalman. I am thankful for the 2016 cohort of Junior Fellows, especially Joshua Bennett, Simion Filip, Xin Jin, Laura Kreidberg, Naomi Levine, Priyasha Mukhopadhyay, and Molly Schumer. Thanks for the outings and the jibing!

To my friends who answered my texts, responded to my emails, and dared to answer the phone when you knew a long rant about research was coming, thank you all. Special thanks go to Stephany Cuevas, LeShae Henderson, Véronique Irwin, and Jasmin Morales for their insightful comments.

I am thankful to have received funding from the Amherst College Memorial Fellowship, the Ford Foundation Predoctoral Fellowship, the National Science Foundation Graduate Research Fellowship, and the Spencer Dissertation Fellowship of the National Academy of Education. A grant from the Center for American Political Studies at Harvard University and the NSF-IGERT Multidisciplinary Program in Inequality and Social Policy at Harvard University (Grant No. 0333403) also supported my research. Thank you, Pamela Metz, for everything, for there is no program without you. The Spencer Fellowship introduced me to an amazing community of scholars and allowed me to hire two phenomenal research assistants, Annie Li and Ana Barros. Thank you so much for helping with the building blocks.

I have been extremely fortunate to work with Andrew Kinney at Harvard University Press, who was truly gifted at and instrumental in helping me find my voice. Thank you for pushing me to craft a narrative that I would be proud of. Thank you for your patience and time, your candor and encouragement.

I also thank David Lobenstine for helping make sure my words didn't get in the way of the story I was trying to tell. Your comments, edits, and memos paved the way for rewriting my early draft to turn it into a book. That is no small task.

A special thanks goes to J. K. Rowling for penning words that helped me when graduate school proved almost too much to bear. Thank you for a very special lesson in perspective: "It does not do to dwell on dreams and forget to live." Also, thank you Adele, Beyoncé, Chance the Rapper, Sam Smith, and the cast of *Hamilton* for being the soundtrack to a first book.

Now y'all know I would not be here without my family. My rock to stand on so as not to be caught up in the fray. My anchor to steady me when times get rough.

To my mother, Marilyn, there is nothing I can say or do that matches your love and dedication. From day one, you gave us your all. You did so much for so long, often by yourself. I wish I were half as strong as you. You continue to be my inspiration to do better and work harder. Thank you for supporting my quirky ways, never pushing me to be someone I was not. You encouraged me to be me, your son.

To my brother, Greg: when I grow up I want to be like you. I want to be the father who puts his children first, first, and first, as you do. I want to be the person who makes sure that his family has everything they need, some things that they want, and even a few things they did not dare to dream of quite yet. Growing up, you stepped in when Mama couldn't make ends meet. Now, you get mad at me when I spoil Shakia and Makayla. I am simply trying to pay back an impossible debt: what I owe you for being the best brother a cartoon-watching, Little Debbie-eating kid could ask for.

To my sister, Aleshia, I am always scared to open your texts and notes in public, for laughter is sure to burst out. Your messages are often just what I need to make it through.

Last, but surely not least, I thank those brave students who opened their hearts to me. Thank you for the smiles. Thank you for the tears. Thank you for the laughs. Thank you, in equal measure, for your words of encouragement and your shady side comments that still make me smile like a Cheshire cat. Thank you for sharing your stories and allowing me to be your voice. It is my sincere hope that this book will expand our stock of knowledge in ways that push the bastions of privilege not only to be more accessible, but also to be more inclusive.

Index

Note: All single names are pseudonyms. Page numbers followed by *f* or n indicate figures or notes.

Computers, programs to assist with purchase of, 156
Connecticut College, 174, 180, 196
Constraints, social and economic, 27, 44–45, 48, 52, 76, 138–140, 154, 186, 193. *See also* Belonging, sense of
Cooke Prize for Equity in Educational Excellence, 7, 227n7
Cornell University, 6
Corinne (DD,B), engagement with faculty and administration, 92
Cultural capital, 8, 11, 19–20, 22–23, 40–41, 49–52, 59, 81–82, 183–185; defined, 19–20
Culture shock. *See* Belonging, sense of
Customs. *See* Cultural capital

Damion (PP,B): engagement with faculty and administration, 114; food insecurity during spring break, 170
Daniel (DD,L), engagement with faculty and administration, 108–110
Dante (student), Community Detail and, 144
Dartmouth College, 156
Destiny (residential adviser), 85
DeVos, Betsy, 193
Dining hall. *See* Food insecurity, during spring break
Diversity, 78, 114, 182; among low-income students, 128, 183–189; racial, 9–10, 29, 36; socioeconomic, 6–7, 29, 35, 43, 48–49
Dormitory decorations, 65
Doubly Disadvantaged (DD): Community Detail and, 141, 142–143, 144, 145–146, 150–152, 154–156; defined, 11, 218; engagement with faculty and administration, 82, 92–98, 99, 103, 107–113, 126–127; engagement with mental health support, 95–96, 119, 121–122, 124, 126, 127; food insecurity during spring break, 134–136, 164, 165, 167–169, 170, 171, 175; high school to college transition and, 38–52, 54, 62–63; modes of discovery of college programs, 220–223, 221*f*; reactions to display of wealth and social class, 68–71, 75, 76–77; Renowned University's adoption of term, 216; Renowned University study and, 20, 208, 218–224; Scholarship Plus and, 157, 159, 161–163; value of studying and understanding contrasts with Privileged Poor, 21–24, 183–189
Duke University, 6
Durable investments, 194

Ease, in social and academic situations, 22, 30, 75–76, 78, 81–82, 102–103, 114, 117, 127, 185, 192–193. *See also* Engagement, with faculty and administration
Elise (DD,W): background of, 220; Community Detail and, 150–152; food insecurity during spring break, 170; high school to college transition, 44–46; mental health support and, 119, 121–122, 124, 127
Emma (PP,B): engagement with faculty and administration, 101; high school to college transition, 56

Employment opportunities, of selective college and university graduates, 47–48, 189, 192–193, 251n7
Engagement, use of term, 214
Engagement, with faculty and administration: and cultural capital generally, 79–87; Doubly Disadvantaged and academic support, 82, 92–98, 99, 103, 107–113, 126–127; Doubly Disadvantaged and mental health support, 95–96, 119, 121–122, 124, 126, 127; hidden curriculum and, 86, 125–126, 129, 190–192; importance of, 82–86, 238n3, 238–239n6; policy recommendations for administration and faculty, 79–84, 128–131, 196; Privileged Poor and academic support, 82, 98–103, 113–119, 126; Privileged Poor and mental health support, 119, 122–124, 126; upper income students and academic support, 88–92, 103–107, 126; upper income students and mental health support, 119–121, 122, 124, 126
Enrichment programs, for high school students, 117–118, 177, 219–220, 222–223, 257–258n16
Eviction experiences, 13, 44, 121, 122–123, 134, 171–172, 185
"Experiential core of college life," 202

Faculty. See Engagement, with faculty and administration
Fairfield University, 174
Family environment: mental health support for problems with, 119–125; social capital and, 82, 183–189, 223

Food insecurity, 174, 191, 196; defined, 242–243n2. See also Food insecurity, during spring break
Food insecurity, during spring break, 132–135, 164–175, 178–180, 191, 216; Doubly Disadvantaged and, 134–136, 164, 165, 167–169, 170, 171, 175; health effects of, 169–171, 245n13; as national problem, 174–175; policy recommendations for administration and faculty, 178, 196–197; Privileged Poor and, 135–136, 164, 165–167, 169–172, 175; upper income students and, 164–165

Gates Scholarship, 195
Georgetown University, 128
George Washington University, 174
Goffman, Erving, 235n13
Guadalupe, Community Detail and, 149–150
Guerrero, Mario, 238n4
Guilt feelings, 93–95, 113–114
Gulliver Preparatory, 2–4, 12, 185

Hamilton, Laura, 20, 243–244n5
Haverford College, 177
Hidden curriculum, 86, 125–126, 129, 190–192
Higher education: financial aid packages, 6–8, 182; stratification in, 4–6, 136, 189. See also Selective colleges and universities
High school to college transition: Doubly Disadvantaged and, 38–52, 54, 62–63; policy solutions, 184–196; Privileged Poor and, 29–30, 52–64,

Madeline (UI,B), Community Detail and, 139

Maid service. *See* Community Detail

Manuel (DD,L): high school to college transition, 40–41; Scholarship Plus and, 161–163

Marcia (DD,L): Community Detail and, 144, 154–155; engagement with faculty and administration, 92; food insecurity during spring break, 167–168

Marcus (administrator), 147

Marie (UI,B): engagement with faculty and administration, 79–83; reaction to display of wealth and social class, 65–67

Marina (PP,L): engagement with faculty and administration, 100; high school to college transition, 57–58

Marisol (student), Community Detail and, 149–150

Marshall (administrator), Scholarship Plus and, 163–164

Martha (cafeteria worker), 171

Massachusetts Institute of Technology (MIT), 6

Massey, Douglass, 208

Maxine (dorm director), 161

Maya (student), 188

Mazur, Barry, 130

Mehan, Hugh, 195

Melanie (DD,L): engagement with faculty and administration, 96–97; reaction to display of wealth and social class, 70–71, 75

Mental health support, student engagement with, 187; Doubly Disadvantaged and, 95–96, 119,

121–122, 124, 126, 127; Privileged Poor and, 119, 122–124, 126, 127; upper income students and, 119–121, 122, 124, 126, 127

Meyerhoff Scholars Program, at University of Maryland, Baltimore County, 129

Michelle (PP,L): Community Detail and, 147; engagement with faculty and administration, 117–119, 190; food insecurity during spring break, 171–172, 173, 191, 216; high school to college transition, 53–54; mental health support and, 123–124

Microaggressions, 42–43

Midtown College (pseudonym), study of Privileged Poor and Doubly Disadvantaged at, 218–219, 224

Miguel (DD), high school to college transition, 163, 190

Miranda (DD,L): food insecurity during spring break, 168–169; reaction to display of wealth and social class, 68–69

Miriam (PP,L), Community Detail and, 141

Misha (UI,B), engagement with faculty and administration, 91

Mobility springboard, college as, 7–8, 23, 39, 189, 192–193, 230n12. *See also* Employment opportunities

Molly (administrator), 85–86

Nancy (administrator), 138

Natalie (academic adviser), 84

New Colossus (Lazarus), 181

New York Times, 215

Tracey (PP,L), food insecurity during spring break, 169–170, 173, 216
Travel and vacations, displays of wealth and, 64–65, 67, 70–71, 74–75
Tyson, Karolyn, 243n5

University of California at Davis, 156
University of Connecticut, 178
University of Maryland, Baltimore County, 129
University of Michigan, 6
University of North Carolina at Chapel Hill, 6, 7
University of Virginia, 6
Upper income students: Community Detail and, 139, 145; engagement with faculty and administration, 79–84, 88–92, 103–107, 126; engagement with mental health support, 119–121, 122, 124, 126, 127; high school to college transition and, 31–38, 41, 64; spring break and, 164–165; wealth, displays of, 65–67

Valeria (DD,L): engagement with faculty and administration, 107–108, 190; food insecurity during spring break, 165, 175; high school to college transition, 48–50

Vamonos Van Gogh program, 138–140
Vassar College, 7
Virginia (PP,B), reaction to display of wealth and social class, 72–74
Virginia Commonwealth University, 196
Vivian (DD,L), Scholarship Plus and, 161
Vocabulary, hidden curriculum and, 190–191

Washington University in St. Louis, 5
Wealth, displays of, 64–67; Doubly Disadvantaged and reactions to, 68–71, 75, 76–77; Privileged Poor and reactions to, 71–75, 77
"What the Privileged Poor Can Teach Us" (Jack), 215
White, Timothy, 174
Wight Foundation, 188, 219
William (DD,W), high school to college transition, 46–48, 192
Williams College, 128, 227n6
Wilson, William Julius, 249n2
Winter coat funds, 156
Work (academic), Doubly Disadvantaged and emphasis on, 82, 92–98, 99, 103, 107–113, 126–127

Young, Alford Jr., 249n2

CHEROKEE SUMMER
ᏣᎳᎩ ᎠᏯ

LIBRARY OF CONGRESS CATALOGING-IN-PUBLICATION DATA

Hoyt-Goldsmith, Diane.
    Cherokee summer / Diane Hoyt-Goldsmith ; photographs by Lawrence
Migdale.
      p.   cm.
    ISBN 0-8234-0995-3
    1. Cherokee Indians—Juvenile literature.   I. Title.
E99.C5H79   1993
973'/04975—dc20   92-54416
                                                             CIP
                                                             AC

ACKNOWLEDGMENTS

In creating this book, we enjoyed the cooperation and enthusiasm of many people. We would like to thank the Russell family, Steve and Nancy, Dustin, Danielle, and especially Bridget for sharing part of this special summer with us. We enjoyed meeting Bridget's grandparents, Scotty and Anna Rackliff, and learning about their special heritage. Time spent with Bridget's great-grandmother, Mary Belle Russell, brought us back to another era—of kerosene lamps, oil cloth on the kitchen table, and hymns sung under the moonlight.

     We would like to thank Charlie Soap for his advice and leadership. He has been a special friend, and has opened doors for us and introduced us to many people who have made this project so successful and rewarding.

     We would also like to thank the people at the Cherokee Nation Headquarters, Pat Lewis, Don Greenfeather, and Lynn Howard, for their great cooperation and assistance. We especially appreciate the participation of Chief Wilma Mankiller. She managed to find a way to include us in spite of her busy schedule and we are very grateful.

     We give a special thanks to the family of Sam and Hattie Proctor for participating in the stomp dance. Long conversations over Hattie's Indian tacos gave us the background to understand the special nature of the stomp dance tradition. Thanks also to Tom Wildcat, his large family, and the other members of the Kee-too-wah clan who shared their dance traditions with us. We will never forget all the people who cooked the Hog Fry and worked so hard to make everything turn out just right.

     The people at the TSA-LA-GI Library were especially helpful: Durbin Feeling for discussions of Sequoyah, the Cherokee language, and for providing a modern version of the syllabary; Sequoyah Guess for sharing old Cherokee legends and new computer software for learning the native language, and to Sandy Long, who allowed it all to go on.

     Thanks also to the Grayson family, Marilyn Ragan, and Nita Cochrane for their help in the early stages of our research; to Jay Stamps and Steve Ross of Unarco in Wagoner, Oklahoma; and to Linda Hernandez.

The new version of the Cherokee syllabary is used courtesy of Durbin Feeling of the TSA-LA-GI Library, Tahlequah, OK 74465.

Special Cherokee typesetting was provided by Al Webster of Project Studio, 12545 E. 41st Street, Tulsa, OK 74146.

CHEROKEE SUMMER
ᏣᎳᎩ ᎠᏱ

by Diane Hoyt-Goldsmith

photographs by Lawrence Migdale

Holiday House · New York

This book is dedicated to
Charlie Soap

ᎠᏏᏐ

The Last One Walking

My name is Bridget. I live in a small town called Okay, Oklahoma in the northeastern part of the state. In summer, the countryside is a patchwork of green pastures and golden fields. Farmers raise cotton, grain, soybeans, and corn while ranchers fatten cattle and hogs. There are dense forests of oak and hickory that shade the valleys, and rolling fields of hay that ripen in the summer heat.

Before Oklahoma became a state in 1907, the place where I live was part of Indian Territory. I am a Cherokee Indian and a member of the Cherokee Nation. My people have a long history and a great heritage. Our strong traditions have given us an identity to be proud of.

The Trail of Tears

About a hundred and fifty years ago, my ancestors lived in the wooded valleys of the Appalachian Mountains. Their homeland covered many thousands of square miles in what are now the states of Tennessee, Kentucky, North Carolina, South Carolina, Alabama, and Georgia. The Cherokee people lived on this land for more than ten centuries before the Europeans arrived in North America.

Hernando de Soto and his soldiers were the first Europeans to meet the Cherokees. In 1540, they traveled north from Florida in search of gold. On their journey, they came across many different Indian tribes, including the Cherokees.

Our ancestors began to trade with the Europeans as early as 1673. They adopted many of the white man's customs. They dressed in coats and hats and fine dresses. When English traders brought them metal farming tools, the Cherokees began to experiment with European farming methods.

Cherokee law changed too. Before the white men came, each Cherokee family or clan had the responsibility of punishing a person who committed a crime against one of the clan's members. Gradually, this method was replaced by a court system of justice, with judges and a jury.

The Cherokees tried hard to get along with the European settlers, but problems developed. More and more white people moved into the hills and valleys where the Cherokees lived. The new settlers from Europe wanted Cherokee land for farming. Then, in 1828, gold was discovered in Georgia. Soon the situation got worse for our people.

Throughout the Southeast, settlers put pressure on the state and federal governments to open up more land for farming and gold mining. The government decided to make the Cherokees move to a new home. It gave them land that had

The Trail of Tears

KANSAS

MISSOURI

ILLINOIS

KENTUCKY

Jonesboro

Springfield

Black River

Present day
Tahlequah

TENNESSEE

Nashville

NORTH
CAROLINA

Fort
Gibson

Mississippi River

Tennessee River

Arkansas

White River

Memphis

Fort Coffee

Ross' Landing

New Echota

OKLAHOMA

Little Rock

River

GEORGIA

ALABAMA

N

LEGEND

ARKANSAS

SCALE

W — E

Land Route   Water Route

MISSISSIPPI

0   50   100   150
Miles

S

At the beginning of the removal, several thousand Cherokees traveled to Indian Territory by boat. The majority, however, went in caravans on overland routes.

been set aside west of the Mississippi River. It was called Indian Territory and no white people lived there.

Our ancestors did not want to move. They wanted to stay in their homeland. In 1838, soldiers of the U.S. government came with guns. They rounded up the Cherokees and placed them in stockades. Over 17,000 people were forced to leave their homes with only the possessions they could carry on their backs. Indians who resisted were arrested or shot. Cherokee men, women, and children traveled from Georgia and North Carolina, through Tennessee, Kentucky, Missouri, and Arkansas — more than 800 miles — to Oklahoma. The journey took many months. Conditions on the trail were harsh. The people were often hungry and cold and sick. Over 4,000 Cherokees died along the way.

We call the road on which my people traveled the "Trail of Tears." Tahlequah, Oklahoma is the town the Cherokees built at the end of the trail. It is a special place because it is where our ancestors made a new beginning.

Some Cherokees still live in North Carolina. These people are the descendants of a few brave families who escaped the soldiers and fled into the mountains. They are called the Eastern Band of Cherokees.

Tahlequah

The countryside surrounding Tahlequah has rolling hills and forests of oak and hickory.

A street sign in Tahlequah carries a phrase in Cherokee which means "The main road, Tahlequah." The Kee-too-wah are a Cherokee clan. In 1859, one of their members, Red Bird Smith, led a movement to bring back Cherokee language and culture.

The town of Tahlequah is at the heart of Cherokee County and Cherokee life. It is the capital of the Cherokee Nation. Some streets in Tahlequah have been named for the many tribes that came to settle in the Indian Territory. There is Cherokee Avenue, Chickasaw and Choctaw Streets, Muskogee Avenue, Delaware Street, and Shawnee Street.

When Cherokees first arrived here, they shared their land just as they had in the East. For more than fifty years, they farmed the rolling hills and hunted deer and wild turkeys in the forests. They built towns like Tahlequah. Some said that the new country even looked a little like the gentle mountains of Appalachia that they had left behind.

Then in 1893, the U.S. government sent representatives to make a roll or a list of all Cherokees. Because of new pressures from white settlers, the government decided to divide up the land, giving each Cherokee a small parcel or allotment as his personal property. The Indian land that was left over was sold to white people.

The Cherokees did not like having their land divided and sold. Again the government forced unwanted changes in their way of life. Because the Cherokees of Oklahoma still own their land, they do not live on a reservation like many Native Americans.

The leader of our Cherokee Nation is called a chief and is elected by the people. Her name is Wilma Mankiller. With more than 120,000 members, the Cherokee Nation is the second largest group of Native Americans in the United States. Only the Navajo Nation is larger.

The chief governs with the help of an elected deputy chief and a council of fifteen members. Together they plan and administer social programs for the Cherokee people. The

8

The Cherokee Nation has a modern headquarters in Tahlequah, Oklahoma.

chief's main goals are to provide our people with health care and the opportunity for higher education. She and the council work together to help families build decent housing and to learn about their tribal language and culture.

Although Wilma Mankiller is the first woman to be chief, our history tells of many women in important and powerful positions in the tribe. In the early days, there was a women's council that nominated the chief. Long ago women went to war along with men and were in charge of the prisoners. Even in ancient Cherokee law, women could own, manage, and sell property. In Cherokee life, women have equality with men.

The Cherokee people have a long tradition of self-government. In 1839, when our ancestors arrived in Indian Territory, they signed a new constitution in Tahlequah. Our people have never lost the sense of being an independent nation. Even today, our tribal leaders decide how to spend the funds that come from the federal government.

The Cherokees built their own courts and libraries, churches and schools. In 1851, they opened the first Native American high schools for young men and women. A newspaper called *The Cherokee Advocate* was published in 1844, one of the first in Indian Territory. The paper is still in print with bilingual articles in both Cherokee and English.

The principal chief of the Cherokee Nation is Wilma Mankiller. She was elected to a second term by popular vote of the Cherokee people in 1991.

9

Although her family's trailer is small, Bridget has her own room. She paints a picture of the Garden of Eden from a Bible story her father told her at bedtime.

My Family

I live in a small house trailer near Tahlequah with my mother and father, younger brother Dusty, and sister Danielle. My parents both grew up on farms in the countryside nearby and went to the same high school. Most of my relatives live in Cherokee County.

I go to school in Okay. Like many of my friends, I ride on a school bus. My favorite subject is art. I like to read but sometimes it is hard for me. I always have trouble with spelling. My mother helps me study. She tells me to write down all the words I don't know so I can get a mental picture of each one. My mother was a good student so I try to follow her advice.

Bridget's mother helps her sew a button on her traditional Cherokee tear (TAHR) dress. The handmade dress is worn on special occasions.

My mother works at home raising my brother, sister, and me. My father works all night in a factory where he makes shopping carts for supermarkets. He welds pieces of metal wire together. Starting at ten o'clock each night, he works until six o'clock in the morning. He goes to bed when he gets home and sleeps until two o'clock in the afternoon. Then he wakes up and spends the rest of the day and evening with us.

My mother is called a "full-blood" because both her parents are Cherokee. My dad is part Cherokee and part white. He is a "mixed-blood" and so am I. Because there has been inter-marriage with people outside the tribe, including people from other Native American groups, many Cherokees have mixed ethnic roots. There are sixty-five Indian tribes in Oklahoma—more than in any other state. Oklahoma also has the largest population of Native Americans.

Sparks fly as Bridget's father welds pieces of wire together in the factory where he works.

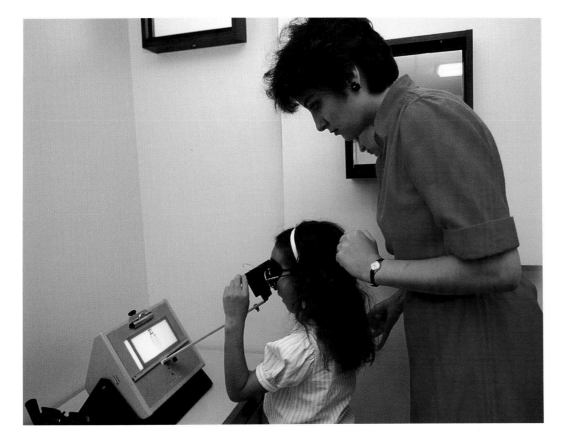

Bridget goes to an eye clinic once a week. A student studying to be an ophthalmologist helps her do eye exercises. Because Bridget's eyes do not work well together, her doctor has recommended these exercises and a special pair of glasses.

11

Bridget rides on a lawn mower with her grandfather as he cuts the grass in front of his house.

Cherokee Traditions

My Cherokee name is ᎤᏪᏄᎩ *(ooh-wah-NUH-gee)* which means "always in a hurry." I earned this name on the day I was born. While my parents were visiting my grandparents, my mother went into labor. I arrived so quickly that she didn't have time to go to the hospital. My grandmother coached my mother while my father read instructions on delivering a baby from a book they had with them. My grandfather was the one who delivered me.

Since that day, I have been close to my grandparents. In the summer, we spend a lot of time at their place out in the country. They live in what we call an "Indian House," a home built with a loan from the Cherokee Nation. The Nation loans money to Indian families for the materials and some of the labor and gives technical advice. The family then builds most of the new, modern home themselves.

When my grandparents were younger, they used their land for farming. My grandfather raised cattle, horses, and hogs. They still have some chickens, but that is all that is left of their livestock.

In the summer, my grandparents work at the Cherokee Heritage Center in Tahlequah. People go there to learn about our Nation's history and culture. The Heritage Center includes an Ancient Village where modern Cherokees demonstrate crafts and skills from centuries past.

My grandfather dresses in a leather outfit and shows visitors how to make arrowheads, blowguns, and darts. My grandmother works in the gift shop. She is known for the beautiful baskets she makes. The skills my grandparents demonstrate are traditional to our people and a precious heritage.

12

Bridget's grandmother works on a quilt outdoors under a large oak tree. Each white square is embroidered with the picture of a state bird. There is a map of the United States at the top done in stitchery.

13

Bridget's grandmother weaves a dark brown length of honeysuckle vine into the basket she is making. The Cherokee baskets have double walls which make them strong as well as attractive.

These baskets made by Bridget's grandmother have traditional Cherokee colors and patterns.

Sometimes when we visit my grandparents' farm, Grandmother lets me help her make baskets. Some are woven from honeysuckle vines that have been dried. Grandmother peels away the outside layer and then dyes them with colors made from plants that grow nearby. Deep red comes from bloodroot, and dark brown is made by boiling walnut husks in water.

The baskets we make today have the same patterns and colors and are made from the same materials as those of our ancestors hundreds of years ago. In the early days, baskets were used for gathering, storing, carrying, and even cooking food. To cook in a basket, rocks were heated in the fire. Then the hot rocks were buried in a mixture of cornmeal inside the basket. The heat from the rocks warmed the food. Grandmother tells me that tightly woven baskets were sometimes used to hold water.

My grandfather lets me help him make arrowheads. He collects flint rocks and obsidian along the riverbanks. With the point of a deer antler, he chips away at the edges until he gets the right shape and the arrowhead is sharp. Then he ties the arrowhead to a wooden shaft with a strand of sinew. He adds feathers to the end for balance so that the arrow will fly straight.

My brother likes shooting darts through the blowgun. My grandfather shows him how to put the dart into the end of a piece of hollow river cane. Then he helps Dusty aim it. Grandfather makes the darts out of thin pieces of wood and the soft petals of a thistle blossom. Our ancestors used the blowgun to hunt small animals and birds.

Using the sharp point of a deer antler, Bridget's grandfather chips away at a piece of flint rock from a nearby riverbed to make an arrowhead.

Bridget's brother, Dusty, shoots a dart through the blowgun that his grandfather has made.

15

Summer Fun

Summer is a special time for my family. The weather is hot and humid so we go outdoors as much as possible. One of our favorite pastimes is hunting for crawdads. My father and his twin brother used to catch them when they were little boys. Now my dad is an expert.

First we drive out to Grandfather's house and fix up some gigs—poles with a fork on the end for catching crawdads. Grandfather helps us make them out of a piece of wire and river cane. He cuts the wire from a clothes hanger and with a pliers, shapes it into a fork with two prongs. Then we tie it to the cane with a piece of string.

We go hunting at Spring Creek. It flows behind the house where my father grew up. My great-grandmother, Mary Belle Russell, raised him and she still lives there.

(Right) Bridget and Dusty tie the fork onto the end of the cane pole with a piece of strong twine.

(Left) Bridget's grandfather splits a piece of river cane and puts the double-prong fork into the end to make a gig for catching crawdads.

16

Ready with their gigs, Bridget, Dusty, and their father wait for a crawdad to dart out from under a rock in the bottom of the creek.

After spearing a crawdad, Bridget puts her catch into a coffee can.

The best place to look for crawdads is under the rocks near the banks of the creek. If we creep along quietly, we might find one lying out in clear view. Then, a quick jab with the gig and we have caught one. Sometimes we can turn a rock over slowly and find one hiding underneath.

My father is fast and catches three or four crawdads before I can even get to the water. Then he stands back and watches my brother, sister, and me. It doesn't take us long to catch enough to fill a coffee can. I usually catch the most.

17

Soon it's time to cook the crawdads. We build a twig fire on the shore with some dry leaves, tiny pieces of wood, and bits of wild grapevine.

After we get the fire going, we fill the can that holds the crawdads with water from the creek. We heat the can on some stones over the fire. Soon the water starts to boil. When the crawdads turn a bright red, they are cooked and ready to eat. Nothing is more delicious than a fresh crawdad cooked over a twig fire on a hot summer day.

Bridget's mother has gone hunting for crawdads every summer since she was a child. Breaking the sticks into small pieces, she helps her husband start a fire on the shore to cook the crawdads.

The Cherokee Language

My mother's parents can both speak our native language. Although my grandmother reads and writes in Cherokee, many of the younger people have stopped learning and using the language altogether.

Grandmother teaches the Cherokee language in an adult class during the school year. She has taught me a few words in Cherokee, and I like having a Cherokee name. Grandmother says that there are things she can say in Cherokee that are hard to translate into English. Our language is part of our history and our identity as a tribe. That is why we don't want to lose it.

The Cherokee language is spoken by combining eighty-five different sounds. The written language has a separate character for each sound, so Cherokee is written by using this syllabary, rather than by using an alphabet.

The Cherokees have had a written language since 1821. The syllabary was the invention of a man named Sequoyah. The English alphabet took four thousand years to develop, but Sequoyah invented our syllabary in just nine years.

When Sequoyah created our written language, he could neither read nor write in English. He watched the Europeans write and receive letters, and decided to come up with the same system for his own people.

Sequoyah was very artistic and the characters he drew for the Cherokee syllabary were done with a calligrapher's grace and beauty. Later on, as people began to use the syllabary to print books and newspapers, many original characters were changed to look more like English letter forms. However, in Cherokee the letters stand for different sounds. For example, a "D" in Cherokee stands for the sound "ah" and an "R" stands for "eh."

Bridget's great-grandmother has lived in the same house for over fifty years. She belongs to a generation that can still speak, write, and read in the Cherokee language. Only about ten percent of the Cherokee people can speak and understand the language today.

19

ᎣᏍᏫᏯ

kah-MAH-mah
BUTTERFLY

ᏲᎾ

YO-nah
BEAR

ᏔᎾᏗ

ee-NAH-dah
SNAKE

The Cherokee Syllabary

		1 (a)	2 (e)	3 (i)	4 (o)	5 (u)	6 (v)
1		D	R	T	Ꮿ	Ꮎ	i
2	(d/t)	Ꮑ	W	Ꮝ	Ꮠ	Ꮺ	V	S	Ꮸ
3	(dl/tl)	Ꮧ	Ꮮ	L	C	Ꮙ	Ꮚ	P
4	(g/k)	Ꮝ	Ꮴ	Ꮊ	Y	A	J	E
5	(gw/kw)	Ꮏ	Ꮻ	Ꮒ	Ꮴ	Ꮗ	Ꮛ
6	(h)	Ꭶ	Ꭾ	Ꭿ	Ꮅ	Ꮆ	Ꮨ
7	(j/ch)	G	Ꮳ	Ꭲ	K	Ꮷ	Ꮳ
8	(l)	W	Ꮸ	Ꮅ	Ꮆ	M	Ꮑ
9	(m)	Ꮄ	Ꮝ	H	Ꮷ	Ꮛ	
10	(n/hn)	Ꮎ Ꮏ	Ꮍ	Ꭽ	Z	Ꮕ	Ꮵ
11	(s)	Ꮝ Ꮀ	Ꮷ	Ꮿ	Ꮈ	Ꮝ	R
12	(w/hw)	G	Ꮺ	Ꮻ	Ꮼ	Ꮽ	Ꮾ
13	(y/hy)	Ꮿ	Ꮹ	Ꭷ	Ꮖ	Ꮇ	B

Durbin Feeling

PRONUNCIATION GUIDE

The following is a list of the roman alphabet used in Cherokee speech: a, ch, d, e, g, h, i, j, k, l, m, n, o, s, t, u, v, w, y. The consonant sounds are the same as in English. The vowel sounds used in Cherokee speech have only one sound for each:

a, as in ah	o, as in note
e, as in they	u, as in true
i, as in ski	v, as uh in huh

By combining the consonants and vowels listed by lines and columns in the chart, the correct pronunciation for each Cherokee syllable can be produced.

Example: The pronunciation for G is "ja". W is "la"; and Y is pronounced "gi" as in "buggy."

Exceptions to the rule that Cherokee syllables are produced by combining consonants and vowels are the syllables D R T Ꮿ Ꮎ i, and Ꮝ. The characters in the first line are produced by the single vowel sounds; and the character Ꮝ is simply an "s" sound.

Bridget works on the computer in the TSA-LA-GI (TSA-lah-gee) Library, inside the old Cherokee prison. There are still bars on all the windows. A new program for the computer helps kids learn the Cherokee language.

The Nation's TSA-LA-GI *(TSA-lah-gee)* Library is located in the old prison building. The people who work there try new ways of teaching children to become literate in the Cherokee language. For example, the Nation has a program in which Cherokee is taught in the schools. There is even a new computer program for students learning our language. When you type the sound of a Cherokee word on the computer, a mechanical voice pronounces it. Then the proper letter comes up on the screen. It is fun to use.

Another way to teach the language is by telling stories. The library puts on puppet shows in the schools, and the actors use Cherokee stories, characters, and words.

For our people, legends have been a good way for the elders to teach children about Cherokee life and the proper way to behave. Sometimes the stories explain something about the natural world. The stories almost always have a moral, and they are entertaining too.

Some Cherokee words to learn:

ᏣᎳᎩ
TSA-lah-gee
CHEROKEE

ᎪᎩ
goh-GEE
SUMMER

ᎣᏏᏲ
OH-see-yoh
HELLO

ᏩᏙ
wah-DOH
THANK YOU

ᎰᏩ
HOH-wah
YOU'RE WELCOME

21

Possum Learns a Lesson

A CHEROKEE LEGEND
retold by Sequoyah Guess

Long, long ago in the days when animals could talk, Possum had a big, bushy tail. It was even more beautiful than Fox's, and Possum was proud of it. He loved to show it off to his friends. Every day he combed it a hundred times to keep it looking shiny.

The rest of the animals grew tired of Possum's showing off. They got together and discussed what they could do to teach him a lesson. Then they came up with a plan.

Rabbit went over and talked to Possum.

"We're going to have a dance tonight," he said, "and it's in honor of your tail."

"Great! Great!" Possum replied. "But you know I'll need a special chair to sit on so I can show it off."

"Of course," Rabbit answered. "We'll get a nice chair for you. But in the meantime, I'll help you get ready. You won't have to do a thing. Just sit back and relax."

Possum was really thrilled to have so much attention paid to his tail. He lay back while Rabbit carefully washed and combed it. Possum was so relaxed and happy that he soon fell asleep.

While Possum snored peacefully, Rabbit whistled for his friend Cricket. It was time to put the rest of the plan into action. Cricket came and shaved off all the hairs on Possum's tail. Then he helped Rabbit wrap some cloth around it.

When Possum woke up, Rabbit told him, "I've got this cloth over your tail to keep it nice for tonight." Possum didn't give it a thought. He was full of excitement and couldn't wait for the dance to begin.

When night came, all the birds and the animals gathered for the dance. Chanting their ancient songs, they moved around the fire in a perfect circle, singing and dancing.

Rabbit said to Possum, "You should go out there and dance. We are all waiting to see your most wonderful tail." As he spoke, he started to unwrap Possum's tail.

Possum was in such a hurry to dance that he didn't look back. He did not notice that anything was wrong. He danced and sang, circling the fire with a huge grin on his face.

"Look at my tail," he sang. "I've got a beautiful tail. There's no tail like mine."

The animals started to giggle. They said "Oooooh!" and "Aaaaah!" Then they started to laugh out loud.

At first, Possum thought they were admiring his tail. He kept on singing. Each time he passed the animals, he sang "Look at my beautiful tail!" But the more the animals laughed, the more Possum wondered, What's wrong? Why are they making fun of me?

Then he turned and looked behind him. His beautiful tail was pink and bare! Instead of being big and bushy, it was skinny and ugly.

Possum was so embarrassed that he fell backward, his big smile frozen on his lips.

Possum never got his bushy tail back. And to this day, all opossums have a hairless tail. If you startle an opossum when you are walking in the woods, he'll play dead and grin just like Possum did. Possum learned it is not smart to brag about anything too much.

A Summer Stomp Dance

(Left) Small pieces of pork are added to hot lard in a cast-iron kettle to cook. The stove was made out of a fifty-gallon oil drum. A hole for adding wood has been cut into the sides near the bottom.

(Right) Bridget helps to sort pinto beans for the meal. Tiny pebbles and broken beans are picked out before the beans are cooked.

For the Cherokees, dancing around a fire is not something that only happens in legends and stories. Special stomp dances are still held every weekend all year round by the traditional people in the tribe. Our people keep the spirit of ancient teachings alive by singing the songs that we have learned from past generations. Because these have never been written down, the elders teach the words and melodies to their children. Attending a stomp dance has become a very special part of my summer.

Before the dances begin, the Cherokees often prepare a special feast called a "Hog Fry." Everything is cooked outdoors over an open fire. It takes all afternoon to make an evening meal for the crowd.

Everyone who comes to the stomp dance can try the dishes prepared in the afternoon: fried pork or "hog," pinto beans, roasted potato wedges, coleslaw, homemade pickled beets, iced tea, and lemonade.

Bridget and her family enjoy the Hog Fry dinner. Sitting on the trunk of their car, they taste all the dishes.

Recipe for a Hog Fry

1 hog, approximately 40 pounds, cut into 1 inch squares
1 stand of lard, approximately 10 pounds
20 pounds of pinto beans
25 pounds of flour
30 pounds of potatoes
5 pounds of sugar
1 can baking powder
1 jar mayonnaise
1 pound coffee
10 quarts of lemonade and tea

25

The Cherokees are known for their hospitality. It is a tradition that anyone who comes to a stomp dance will be fed. The meal is a time for sharing. It creates an atmosphere of friendship for the dances that follow.

Stomp dances have been performed for centuries. They are still danced by the tribes of the Southeast— the Cherokees, Creeks, Seminoles, and Shawnees. The dancers believe that the rhythmic songs and movements of the dance help put them back in balance with the world. Dancing gives them peace of mind.

Men, women, and children are free to participate in the dances. Children begin to dance when they are very young, following the movements of their parents and grandparents.

At a stomp dance, dancers from many tribes gather to visit, feast, and worship. The dances begin after dinner and usually last all night long.

The stomp dance is held on a sacred dance site or stompground. It is performed in a circle around a fire built with logs that point in each of the four directions—north, south, east, and west. The Cherokees believe that this fire is eternal. For each stomp dance, the fire is kindled by an ember from a sacred fire that is kept burning at all times.

For traditional Cherokees, the stompground is like church, and a stomp dance is like a prayer. We believe that the smoke from the sacred fire carries our songs to heaven.

Although some men wear ribbon shirts and some women wear traditional tear dresses, a special costume isn't required. Many people dance wearing jeans and a T-shirt or everyday clothes. Stomp dancers believe that what you have in your heart is more important than the clothes that you wear.

Every stompground has a leader or chief. The leader chooses a song and begins the dance. Following after the chanting leader, the dancers move in a winding line, twisting into a spiral as they circle around the fire. Only the men and boys sing.

26

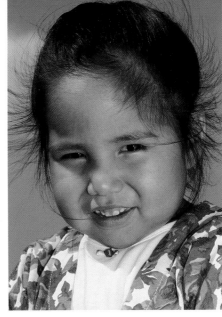

Bridget watches while the young dancers put on their shackles. The shackles can weigh a lot, so it helps for someone to hold them. The turtle shells are tied onto the leather of an old pair of cowboy boots that have been split down the side. The dancers use small pieces of towel under the shackles to protect their legs from bruises.

Some of the girls wear a modern version of shackles, made with tin cans rather than turtle shells. The cans make a nice sound when filled with tiny pebbles.

The women and girls participate by providing the rhythm for the dances. They wear shackles made from empty turtle shells tied together and filled with tiny pebbles. Often there are ten or twelve shells on each leg. Each shackle can weigh as much as thirty pounds.

When a dancer stamps her foot, she shakes the shackles, creating a rhythm. Dancing with shackles is hard work, but the women and girls are honored to become "shell shakers."

In addition to dancing, people listen to words of advice and stories about how one should live. These homilies are delivered by a spokesman for the stompground chief. The stompground chief is a religious leader, but it is traditional that he doesn't speak directly to the people. On the stompground, even the tribal chief follows his leadership. The Cherokees believe that their spiritual life is more important than anything else.

At the stomp dance, I spoke with the chief of the Cherokee Nation, Wilma Mankiller. She is a great lady and has done so much for our people. She looked me in the eye and asked me about myself and my family. She made me feel special. Although I am the smallest person in my fourth-grade class, I felt strong when I stood next to her. I'm glad to be a Cherokee like our chief, sharing our traditions on a hot summer night.

Bridget, dressed in her traditional tear dress, talks with the chief of the Cherokees, Wilma Mankiller.

Dancing around the fire, the Cherokees and their friends participate in an ancient ritual.

29

The summer hay crop near Tahlequah is harvested and collected into bales for drying. The giant hay rolls are a good place to be alone to think and dream.

On long summer afternoons, when I have the chance to be alone, I like to draw pictures and let my mind wander. I dream about what I will do when I grow up and how I will live. Perhaps I'll be an artist or a dancer. I might be a doctor or a teacher. I might even be the chief of my tribe.

For now, I feel lucky to have a loving family and to live in a beautiful place. I am proud of my Cherokee heritage, and I will work hard to keep it strong. Soon it will be time to go back to school. The weather will turn cold and the leaves will fall. But I will have the memories of this Cherokee summer—a special time in my life.

Allotment: A parcel of land given to each Cherokee as his private property. (The Allotment Act of 1887 allowed the president of the United States to divide any Indian land into individual allotments, and the right to sell the remaining land to settlers.)

Bloodroot: A plant related to the poppy that grows in Oklahoma.

Blowgun: A weapon made from a piece of long, straight hollow cane. The Cherokees blow a sharp dart through this "pipe" to hunt small game and birds.

Cherokee: A tribe of the Iroquoian Indians, now split into two groups: the Eastern Band numbers over 8,000 people who live in North Carolina; the Cherokee Nation, located in Oklahoma, is the largest group, with a population of over 120,000.

Cherokee Nation: The group of Cherokees living in Oklahoma and their tribal government.

Chief: The principal leader of the Cherokee people. The current chief is Wilma Mankiller.

Clan: Family or group of people who claim descent from a common ancestor.

Crawdad: A small freshwater shellfish, also called crawfish, similar to a lobster.

Eastern Band: Cherokees whose ancestors escaped removal to Oklahoma in 1838 and now live on a reservation in North Carolina near the Great Smoky Mountains.

Ethnic: Relating to people of the same race, nation, or tribe, or people with a common culture or language.

Fry bread: A flat, round bread made with a wheat flour and cooked in hot lard; a traditional Indian food.

Full-blood: An Indian whose parents are both members of the same tribe.

Hog Fry: A meal featuring fried pork meat cooked outdoors on a campfire as well as other traditional Indian foods such as baked pinto beans and fry bread.

Indian House: A local term for a modern home with indoor plumbing built with the financial and technical assistance of the Cherokee Nation.

Indian Territory: Originally part of the Louisiana Purchase of 1803 and set aside by the U.S. government in 1829 as a place to resettle the Indian tribes of the populated East. It became a part of the state of Oklahoma in 1907.

Intermarriage: Marriage between two persons from different ethnic groups or races.

Lard: The rendered fat of the hog used by the Cherokees for cooking and frying.

Reservation: An area of land set aside by the U.S. government as a place for Indian people to live.

Ribbon shirt: A cotton shirt with long sleeves decorated with bright colored ribbon borders and streamers. Worn by Cherokee men and boys and other tribes of the Southeast on special occasions.

Sequoyah: A Cherokee born about 1770 who completed a syllabary for the Cherokee language in 1821, making it possible for the Cherokees to read and write in their own language.

Shackles: Turtle shells filled with tiny pebbles and tied together to make cuffs. Worn on each leg, foot-stamping women and girls use the shackles to create rhythms for the stomp dance.

Shell shakers: The term given to women and girls who wear shackles in the stomp dance.

Sinew: A strong fiber that connects the muscles to the bone. The Cherokees use deer sinew to tie or sew things together.

Stockade: An enclosure made from tall posts used to keep prisoners from escaping.

Stomp dance: Performed to ancient chants and songs around a sacred fire, the stomp dance is a traditional spiritual event for the Cherokee people.

Stompground: A sacred place outdoors where stomp dances are held on weekends throughout the year. In 1907, there were over a hundred stompgrounds in use. Today there are only seventeen.

Syllabary: A system of writing in which each sound or syllable of a spoken language is expressed by a different character or letter.

Tahlequah: A town in northeastern Oklahoma that is the capital of the Cherokee Nation, the site of the tribal offices, and a commercial center for the region.

Tear *(TAYR)* **Dress:** A traditional, floor-length dress that was created on the "Trail of Tears." During the removal, the Cherokees were not allowed to bring anything sharp with them. When a woman needed a new dress, she had to "tear" the fabric into the shapes needed for sleeves, bodice, and skirt. Tear dresses are still worn by Cherokee women and girls on special occasions.

Trail of Tears: The journey made by the Cherokees in 1838 when they were forced to leave their homeland in the Southeast for the Indian Territory in Oklahoma.

Index

Numbers *in italics* refer to pages with photos.

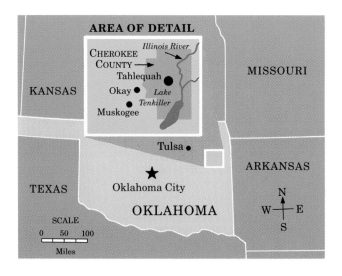